PIMLIC

392

FICTION AND THE READING PUBLIC

Q.D. LEAVIS

With an Introduction
by John Sutherland

PIMLICO

Published by Pimlico 2000

2 4 6 8 10 9 7 5 3 1

Copyright © Q.D. Leavis 1932
Introduction copyright © John Sutherland 2000

First published in Great Britain by
Chatto & Windus 1932
Reissued 1965
Reprinted 1968 and 1978
Pimlico edition 2000

Pimlico
Random House, 20 Vauxhall Bridge Road,
London SW1V 2SA

Random House Australia (Pty) Limited
20 Alfred Street, Milsons Point, Sydney,
New South Wales 2061, Australia

Random House New Zealand Limited
18 Poland Road, Glenfield,
Auckland 10, New Zealand

Random House (Pty) Limited
Endulini, 5A Jubilee Road, Parktown 2193, South Africa

The Random House Group Limited Reg. No. 954009
www.randomhouse.co.uk

A CIP catalogue record for this book
is available from the British Library

ISBN 0–7126–6504–8

Papers used by Random House are natural,
recyclable products made from wood grown in sustainable forests;
the manufacturing processes conform to the environmental
regulations of the country of origin

Printed and bound in Great Britain by
Biddles Ltd, Guildford

INTRODUCTION BY
JOHN SUTHERLAND

There's enough energy in my wife to blow Europe to pieces.
F.R. Leavis, 1961[1]

THINK up a list of the ten most influential works of British twentieth-century literary criticism. Titles crowd into mind – the problem is thinning them out (my top ten will be found at the end of this introduction). How many of those books are by women? In my round-up, just two (Virginia Woolf's *The Common Reader* is the other). Many lists, I suspect, will be unapologetically unisex. And yet, at the undergraduate and postgraduate level in our English departments, women have been a forceful presence over the century and in its later decades a majority. They just don't seem to make it to the level where the cutting edge of the discipline is ground.

The explanation is clearer if one does a parallel exercise. Compile a list of the century's ten greatest film actresses. Then compile – without access to reference books – a list of the century's ten greatest women directors. While most film-goers of a certain age could come up with a hundred actresses, none but experts could come up with more than a couple of *directresses* (we have no word for them in English – no need for it). Forget 'great'.

The structures of film production have innumerable tiers and recesses which were closed to women – and perhaps still are. Likewise the world of literary criticism, dominated in the twentieth century by the universities with their deep monastic roots and common-room culture. Women could consume (as students); they might assist (as teachers, typists and room-cleaners); but they could not, except in exceptional circumstances, produce.

In appreciating the achievement of *Fiction and the Reading Public* – a book obsessed with the machineries of production – one must take on board the struggle involved in a woman's making it (in both senses). In this author's case the struggle was so bitter as to deform and, arguably, to stifle her subsequent career. The unwritten works of Q.D. Leavis, after her first, are a lost treasury of English literary criticism.

Queenie Dorothy Roth was born in Edmonton, outer London, on 7 December 1906, the daughter of a moderately prosperous hosier and draper. The Roths were first-generation immigrants, Jewish, strictly orthodox and upwardly mobile. Their three children were abnormally gifted. Queenie's elder brother, Leonard, won a scholarship to Cambridge and went on to become a distinguished mathematician. She won a scholarship to Girton, where she went up to read English and anthropology in 1924.

As a student Miss Roth was formidably fluent and
quick thinking (*Fiction and the Reading Public* is,
above all, a readable book). As Ian MacKillop puts
it, 'From one angle she was the *writer* of the two
Leavises, lucid as Orwell or Mary McCarthy'[2]
(comparisons which would have elicited a volley of
eloquent vituperation from Q.D.L.).

At Girton, Miss Roth was taught intermittently by
a young don, Frank Raymond Leavis. He was ten
years older than she, had served in the Friends'
Ambulance Unit in the First World War, and had
written a doctoral thesis (with great labour) on
eighteenth-century journalism and society. He had
been a probationary lecturer at Emmanuel College
since 1925.

In one respect, Frank Leavis's background was
similar to Queenie Roth's. The son of a Cambridge
piano-dealer he was the first member of his family to
attend university. His non-conformist background
(with its Huguenot origins, of which he was proud)
imbued him, as orthodox Jewishness did her, with an
invincible sense of moral responsibility – something
which both of them brought to their practice of
literary criticism and their teaching.

F.R.L. was a charismatic teacher and a declared
disciple of T.S. Eliot. At this period in his life he was
reading *The Sacred Wood*, pencil in hand, several
times a year. Like Eliot, his literary touchstone was
metaphysical poetry (later D.H. Lawrence would be
another touchstone). The *Grundrisse* were laid of

what later would become the 'Leavisite School', whose doctrines would be propagated in the seditious pages of the magazine *Scrutiny*. Leavis already required of his pupils intensely 'engaged' attention to a discriminatingly selected corpus of classic texts – texts which were validated by the scrutiny which the critic brought to bear. His closest students became disciples and paladins (although from the beginning it was clear that staying close to Leavis was tricky – he was quick to scent heresy and to punish it with irrevocable exile).

As a critic F.R.L. was formidably equipped but he lacked two things. One was the ability to express himself fluently (he hated writing to the end of his career and 'journalistic' was a prime term of contempt in his lexicon). He was also disabled by a lack of confidence. He needed a comrade by his side. Ominously F.R.L. had already displayed a propensity to raise the hackles of senior colleagues. Prickly at best, he could easily turn paranoid. He had made a particular enemy of a powerful Fellow of King's – F.L. Lucas – against whose philistine prejudice he dared advocate the greatness of T.S. Eliot.

Miss Roth knew Dr Leavis from his classes at Girton but he did not, apparently, know her until they conversed at a tea party in the autumn of 1927. She was now a finalist in her third year. They apparently fell in love almost immediately. As MacKillop records, 'Leavis was slow to show his feelings. But by the end of [her last] term they came to an understanding.' It was slightly awkward, if less so then than it would be now. She was his junior by a decade, she was a student and he a teacher.

Queenie Roth took a starred first in summer 1928. A scholarship was automatic and she enrolled to do a Ph.D. (then a fairly new degree) on the topic which became *Fiction and the Reading Public*. It was, from one angle, a continuation into the nineteenth and twentieth centuries of F.R.L.'s dissertion – the first of their collaborative ventures.

The couple became engaged in February 1929. 'Marrying out' entailed an irreparable break with her orthodox family. (It is sometimes said that they sat *shiva* for her, as for a relative who had died; MacKillop thinks this 'not likely'.) When Queenie Roth came up to Cambridge, four years earlier, she had been strictly devout – keeping the Sabbath and observing a kosher diet with self-punitive severity. She now embraced secularism. All consciousness of Jewish heritage was extinguished. As her daughter Kate reminisced in later life, 'I had no idea I was half Jewish until my first year at Oxford, when I was informed accordingly by a contemporary.'[3]

The early married life of the Leavises (the years in which *Fiction and the Reading Public* was completed) were fraught with practical difficulties. F.R.L. had no permanent appointment and no powerful patrons. She was a postgraduate student with a grant designed to support a single, frugal student not a professional married couple. His prospects were uncertain. Both of them were on the brink of nervous breakdown over this precarious period.

They married on 16 September 1929 at the Cambridge Registry Office. After a honeymoon in Norfolk they took up married residence in a small terrace house in Leys Road. In January 1931, at a period of great tension for F.R.L., who understood that he was not to be continued in his lectureship after October, they moved into his family house, at 6 Chesterton Hall Crescent (both F.R.L.'s parents were now dead).

Despite the upheaval of house removals, running feuds, chronic professional uncertainty, and fraught personal relations with her supervisor, I.A. Richards (who is studiously *not* thanked in the acknowledgements to the book), Q.D.L. finished her dissertation in autumn 1931. Its full title was 'Fiction and the Reading Public: A Study in Social Anthropology'. She was examined by Richards as her 'internal' and E.M. Forster as her 'external' on 8 November. She was awarded the degree but – symptomatically, perhaps – quarrelled violently with her examiners.

The following day she wrote to Ian Parsons, a former pupil of F.R.L.'s and now an editor at Chatto (the publisher whom the Leavises regarded as the 'least unintelligent' in London, and to whom they stayed loyal throughout their careers). Chatto had, in 1930, published William Empson's *Seven Types of Ambiguity*. Empson was another brilliant doctoral student of I.A. Richards. Chatto accepted Q.D.L.'s typescript almost immediately. It was published in April 1932, pretty much in its thesis form (although without the illustrative material which Q.D.L. had compiled for the dissertation).

Fiction and the Reading Public is the first serious work of literary sociology to be published in English. It opens, typically, with a smart epigram: 'In twentieth-century England not only everyone can read, but it is safe to add that everyone does read' (p. 19).[4] In its opening section, the author looks, dispassionately but stylishly, at what 'everyone' was reading in 1930. The bestsellers which glowed luridly 70 years ago are now the dustiest cinders on literature's ash-heap: Ethel M. Dell (author of *The Way of an Eagle*), Edith M. Hull (author of *The Sheik*), A.S.M. Tomlinson (author of *If Winter Comes*, 1921, for which the term 'bestseller' was invented), Edgar Rice Burroughs, (*Tarzan of the Apes*), Marie Corelli, Rose Barclay, Michael Arlen (*The Green Hat*), P.C. Wren (*Beau Geste*), Edgar Wallace.

Having scrutinised the shop-window, Q.D.L. goes on to look at the machineries by which popular taste is stimulated, standardized, exploited, degraded and the literary product marketed. She anatomises the circulating and 'twopenny' libraries, the corrupted reviewing establishment of the metropolis, film and radio tie-in gimmicks, 'shriek advertising', and the high-powered – increasingly Americanised – publishing industry behind it all.

The twentieth-century bestseller, she concludes, is a work which enables its consumers 'to live at the novelist's expense' – a 'dream factory' in the idiom of the time. 'Escapist' is inadequate to describe the effect of contemporary popular fiction. 'The reading habit,' she declares, 'is now often a form of the drug habit' (p. 22). As the book industry has grown so massive so culture – the noble English culture represented by Shakespeare, Bunyan, Jane Austen, Henry James, and D.H. Lawrence – has been shrunk to the point of extinction. Writers like these, with their reverence for 'felt life', engage, disturb and enlarge their readers' sensibilities. Great novels (such as *Emma*, *Portrait of a Lady* or *The Rainbow*) 'do not lend themselves to fantasying [*sic*] but cause disturbing repercussions in the reader's emotional make-up' (p. 60).

For all its originality, *Fiction and the Reading Public* owes a number of debts. Her adviser, I.A. Richards (then a fellow at Magdalene College), had published the influential *Principles of Literary Criticism* in 1924 and Q.D.L.'s investigations take off from a passage in the section entitled 'Art, Play, and Civilisation':

No one who has repeatedly lived through experiences at the level of discrimination and co-ordination

presupposed by the greater writers, can ever, when
fully 'vigilant', be contented with ordinary crudities . . . And conversely, keen and vigilant enjoyment of Miss Dell, Mr Burroughs, Mrs Wilcox or
Mr Hutchinson, when untouched by doubts or the
onus of ironic contemplation, is likely to have as a
consequence not only an acceptance of the mediocre
in ordinary life, but a blurring and confusion of
impulses and a very widespread loss of value.[5]

This pessimism as to trends in popular reading
(especially the gloomy prophecy about 'widespread
loss of value') was immensely influential on Q.D.L.
It was associated with a certain kind of moralistic-
nostalgic yearning for an earlier culture (a 'golden
age' – although both Richards and Q.D.L. would
have despised the term) in which the 'greater writers'
were paramount.

Q.D.L. was also strongly affected by Richards's
'scientism' ('pseudo-scientism', as it now looks). On
one level, this took the form of a brutal reductivism,
as in the opening statement of *Principles*: 'A book is a
machine to think with'. More constructively, in
Practical Criticism (1929), Richards had undertaken
a strikingly successful piece of socio-literary fieldwork. He gave a sample selection of Cambridge
students a set of unidentified poems (some good,
some awful, all unrecognisable) together with a
questionnaire. From the responses to these 'proto-
cols', as he called them, Richards developed a theory

of how poetry worked, and how it might best be taught.

'Practical Criticism', as a pedagogic technique, went on to become the British equivalent of the American 'New Criticism'. Both dominated university classrooms until the 1960s (and sixth-form classrooms for somewhat longer). Like a scientist, Richards had gathered his data, analysed it, and developed 'valid' conclusions. As with his other prize pupil, William Empson (who had read mathematics before taking up English), the 'scientism' was a reaction against Cambridge's prevailing 'belletrism', or 'appreciative' style of literary criticism in which 'sensibility' was all.

Q.D.L. was impressed with Richards's fieldwork and the hard data it yielded. For *Fiction and the Reading Public* she devised her own questionnaires and sent them off to 60 bestselling authors. Her ten questions were blunt (e.g. '1. To what do you attribute your success as a novelist?'). Some of the replies she received could not have been invented by P.G. Wodehouse (who did not, apparently, respond to the young bluestocking from Cambridge). P.C. Wren, for example:

The bulk of my readers are the cleanly-minded virile outdoor sort of people of both sexes, and the books are widely read in the Army, the Navy, the Universities, the Public Schools and the Clubs . . . Although I now make a good many thousands per annum, I still am not a 'professional novelist', nor, as I have said, a long-haired literary cove. (p. 54)

Other responses, such as that from Edgar Rice Burroughs, were thoughtful (Q.D.L. goes out of her way to thank him in her preface).

From her partner, Q.D.L. took, *inter alia*, a presiding sense of the solidity of eighteenth-century literature, in contrast to its ephemeral and market-driven successors. Like F.R.L. she subscribed to the model of an 'organic' pre-industrial culture fragmented in the nineteenth and atomised in the twentieth centuries (it has clear affinities with T.S. Eliot's notion of what had happened to 'Literary Tradition' in the twentieth century). For both Leavises, cultural history is a catastrophic process of 'disintegration'. The utopian past is nostalgically celebrated in George Sturt's *The Wheelwright's Shop* (1923), a work for which F.R.L. had a Morrisian reverence.

Beneath the surface of *Fiction and the Reading Public* one can see a confluence of other intellectual currents. Like her husband, Q.D.L. had considerable respect for Leslie Stephen's *English Literature and Society in the Eighteenth Century* (1903), a bestseller of its day. Stephen based his treatise on the simple but radically unusual proposition that 'we must begin by asking impartially what pleased men, and then inquire why it pleased them'.[6] This, in a nutshell, is Q.D.L.'s project in *Fiction and the*

Reading Public. What pleased men in 1930 were Wren, Burroughs, Wallace. What pleased women were Dell, Barclay, Corelli, Hull. Why?

Q.D.L. calls her method 'anthropological', a nod towards H.M. Chadwick, with whom she had studied as an undergraduate. Subsequent generations have preferred to see *Fiction and the Reading Public* as a pioneering work of literary sociology. She did not like the term, associating it with the lumberingly 'Germanic' approach of L.L. Schucking (author of *The Sociology of Literary Taste*, 1924) for which neither she nor F.R.L. had much time.

The work of sociology which influenced her most was Robert S. and Helen M. Lynd's *Middletown* (1929), a social-survey based on Muncie, Indiana. This urban study discerned the growth to hegemonic power of an upwardly mobile American middle class. From this work Q.D.L. seems to have taken her model of literary culture with its stratifications 'lowbrow', 'middlebrow', and 'highbrow' (terms inherited, distantly, from nineteenth-century phrenology). Where literature was concerned, the greatest danger, as Q.D.L. saw it, was from the middle-class and their aggressive middlebrow appetite for what she called the *faux bon*.

Scientific as the procedure of *Fiction and the Reading Public* is, the argument is controlled by D.H. Lawrence's stern caveat that 'criticism can never be a science'. (Lawrence, who died in March 1930, was already a god in F.R.L.'s eyes; Q.D.L.

seems never to have entirely shared her husband's passion). Both Leavises, but particularly Q.D.L. in *Fiction and the Reading Public*, commit themselves to a delicate balancing act. They do not 'analyse', 'dissect', or 'dismantle' texts: they 'scrutinise', 'evaluate' and 'revalue'.

In his review of the English translation of Schucking's *The Sociology of Literary Taste* (the translation appeared the year before *Fiction and the Reading Public*) F.R.L. roundly declares that 'no "sociology of literature" and no attempt to relate its studies with sociological analysis will yield much profit unless informed and controlled by a real and intelligent interest − a first-hand critical interest − in literature . . . literature isn't so much material lying there to be turned over from the outside.'[7]

It is typically pontifical − *Leavis locuta, causa finita*. But it clearly raises problems for Q.D.L.'s socio-critical project. Is *The Sheik* 'literature' in the same way that *The Golden Bowl* is? And if not, what is it? Just as the totalitarian states of the 1930s created 'non-persons', so Q.D.L. creates literature that is not literature, 'that which must not be read'.

One of the paradoxes of *Fiction and the Reading Public* is that it closely examines texts with the aim of showing that they are unworthy of close examination. This is a cul-de-sac from which the Leavisite programme never found a successful way forward. It expressed itself in F.R.L.'s reiterated proclamation that once *Fiction and the Reading Public* had been done, it did not need to be done again. A work which, at the subterranean level, has been formative in the establishment of what we now recognise as 'Media Studies' and 'Cultural Studies' was, perversely, devised to make such disciplines unnecessary.

The driving energy of *Fiction and the Reading Public*, even at its most controlled, is alarmed pessimism. This urgency finds its origin in the fear inspired in the cultured classes of late Victorian and Edwardian England by the Forster Education Act of 1870. If Demos could read, what reading-matter would the monster demand? The cultivated mind recoiled at the prospect. Henry James expresses the nervousness of his class in an essay written in 1899, 'The Future of the Novel':

The published statistics are extraordinary, and of a sort to engender many kinds of uneasiness. The sort of taste that used to be called 'good' has nothing to do with the matter: we are demonstrably in presence of millions for whom taste is but an obscure, confused, immediate instinct. In the flare of railway bookstalls, in the shop-fronts of most booksellers, especially the provincial, in the advertisements of the weekly newspapers, and in fifty places besides, this testimony to the general preference triumphs.[8]

If it was so in 1899, how much worse in 1932? There is breathing through Q.D.L.'s *Fiction and*

the Reading Public (as through her European contemporary, Ortega y Gasset) a Spenglerian terror that
high culture might be doomed. Doomed in the same
way that democracy seemed to be doomed before the
onward march of totalitarianism of the Right and
Left. The great question mark hanging over *Fiction
and the Reading Public* is whether the cultured few –
the 'admirable minority of intelligent persons', as
James called it – are sufficient to save civilization.

Q.D.L. raises the stakes very high in *Fiction and
the Reading Public*. And her alarmism breaks out into
something like a cry of critical fear in the book's last,
peroratorical pages:

> I have here isolated and shown the workings of a
> number of tendencies which, having assumed the
> form of commercial and economic machinery, are
> now so firmly established that they run on their own
> and whither they choose; they have assumed such a
> monstrous impersonality that individual effort
> towards controlling or checking them seems ridicu-
> lously futile. This is probably the most terrifying
> feature of our civilization. If there is to be any hope,
> it must lie in conscious and directed effort. All that
> can be done, it must be realized, must take the form
> of resistance by an armed and conscious minority.
> (p. 213)

Cynics might object that the Nazi victory in the
November 1932 German elections was more 'terrifying' than the British reading public's incorrigible

appetite for Ethel M. Dell. And the notion of armed resistance mounted against a sinister global machinery from the plats of Cambridge is quaint. But the fear was real and Q.D.L.'s arguments still vibrate seventy years later. It was her pessimism which seems to have led to the rupture with I.A. Richards. It became obvious to her, as she scornfully put it, that 'he is an optimist'.[9]

Q.D.L. rushed her book into print because she (and her husband) needed the publication to win her a research fellowship – to put bread on their table, as she bluntly put it. F.R.L. was facing the prospect of unemployment and labouring on the last stages of *his* first book, *New Bearings in English Poetry*, as it was to be. She duly got the fellowship.

The book was, from every point of view, a remarkable achievement. More so at a period when scholarship was normally seen as a slow-ripening fruit. As MacKillop points out, in April 1932, Q.D.L. was only 26 years old, in the third year of her marriage, and technically still a graduate student. The book sold well for an academic monograph (around 2,000 in its first year), was well received (T.S. Eliot's praise in the *Criterion* must have been especially gratifying) and received the compliment of a slashing review from F.R.L.'s implacable antagonist, F.L. Lucas.

Fiction and the Reading Public was influential over the following three decades, especially in the schools and provincial universities in which F.R.L.'s students placed themselves. (A lonely and embattled figure at Cambridge, he had no patronage to dispense in the ancient universities.) It was instrumental in propagating the depressive Leavisite axiom that the present age was one of 'Mass Civilization and Minority Culture'.

More importantly, perhaps, *Fiction and the Reading Public* was the rock on which F.R.L.'s journal *Scrutiny* was founded in May 1932. The magazine took over Q.D.L.'s 'anthropologico-literary' method and she published a number of powerful articles in its pages (famously her uncollected essays on Jane Austen's fiction). Less gloriously, she also undertook much of the editorial business, inducing a health crisis and – surely – impeding any prospect of a follow-up volume to capitalise on the success of *Fiction and the Reading Public*. There were other impediments. She had her first child (of three) in 1933. In mid-life she had a bout with cancer which was overcome only at the cost of chronic debility. Denied a permanent teaching post, she was obliged to cobble together what she could and without the sabbatical leave allowed to tenured academics.

In the 'struggle' (their preferred word) over the next five decades, the Leavises always felt themselves not just embattled, but at war on many fronts. The barbarians were ever more numerous. The best-sellers were ever bigger, more vulgar, and more horribly efficient. The London 'literary racket' was on a par with Al Capone's Chicago. Even T.S. Eliot was tainted by the metropolitan corruption. And, behind their own ramparts, there was the privileged hierarchy of Cambridge. F.R.L., after much difficulty, finally got a position at Downing College. Q.D.L. never had an official post. None the less, the Leavises prided themselves that 'We were Cambridge . . . the essential Cambridge in spite of Cambridge.[10]

Q.D.L.'s bitterness in later years is legendary. It should perhaps be taken alongside the striking neglect which her book received over the next half-century – at least at the level of citation. Any number of studies take off directly from *Fiction and the Reading Public*, but scarcely offer so much as a nod of acknowledgement. L.C. Knights' *Drama and Society in the Age of Jonson* (1937), for example, can manage only one glancing footnote (accompanying a sizeable borrowed quotation). Yet, it is fair to say, Knights's sociological investigation into the material bases of the Elizabethan-Jacobean stage could never have come into being without Q.D.L.'s groundwork. Other examples come to mind. One which stands out is Richard Hoggart's *The Uses of Literacy*, a book whose approach clearly derives, and in many places (notably its attention to popular fiction) directly parallels that of Q.D.L. Hoggart's book has no reference to Q.D.L. by name. Here, as elsewhere, she is felt but not seen.

Q.D.L. herself – as a number of passing references

make clear — felt strongly that she had been slighted
and even plundered. But, equally clearly, she held
herself back. As MacKillop shrewdly suggests, her
self-suppression may have originated in her desire to
be 'a full helper to a husband (including the
avoidance of competition)'.[11] F.R.L. made gracious
acknowledgement to 'My Wife' in his dedications
and he formally acknowledged the primacy of *Fiction
and the Reading Public* in the *Scrutiny* project. But
there is some question as to how much he used
Q.D.L. as an 'invisible collaborator' — particularly in
what was his own greatest contribution to criticism
of the novel, *The Great Tradition* (1948).

F.R.L. predeceased his wife. After his death,
Q.D.L. wrote to one of his disciples, Boris Ford, that
she had 'been pushed out of the *The Great Tradition*,
which was my undertaking, and great parts of which,
besides all the first chapter and all the footnotes, I
wrote personally . . . The whole subject of our
careers and work is too painful for me to review at
present.'[12] There is no acknowledgement in F.R.L.'s
book of his wife's authorial participation. Nor did
she ever, publicly, review 'the subject of her careers'.
She herself died, three years after her husband, on 17
March 1981. She left behind her no other complete
book.

In reading *Fiction and the Reading Public*, seventy
years on, one confronts a familiar problem in literary

criticism. How can a book be so wrong, and yet so important? That it is wrong in a number of crucial ways is self-evident. In the same year that Q.D.L.'s book was published J.M.S. Tompkins brought out a published version of her postgraduate dissertation, entitled *The Popular Novel in England, 1700–1800* (1932). As Tompkins establishes, by a scrupulous survey, popular fiction has always been a debased commodity – schlock, as we would say. There was no great 'Fall', such as Mrs Leavis saw, in which a cultivated audience for fiction was deluged in the early nineteenth century. Ethel M. Dell has always been with us.

Social historians have poured scorn on the notion of a pre-industrial 'organic' community with a vibrant healthy culture, now lost. Above all, the cosmic pessimism of Q.D. Leavis has proved wrong. Her book, for example, begins with a panoramic survey of the extermination of the retail trade. 'Shops existing solely to sell books,' she observes, 'are rare outside the university towns of Oxford, Cambridge, and Edinburgh, certain parts of London and a few big cities'. (p. 19) Looking back, we can see that the destruction of retail bookselling in Britain and America was a temporary effect of the post-1929 slump. British bookshops are, as the century turns, bigger and better than they have ever been (consider those two flagship London outlets, the new Waterstone's in Piccadilly and Borders in Oxford Street.)

The booming book-chains and specialist stores which serve the present-day trade sell popular fiction by the ton (much of it more 'depraved', as Q.D.L. would have thought, than anything to be found above the counter in 1932). And yet they sell good books as well (this book, for example). What, one wonders, would Q.D.L. and F.R.L. have made of the explosion of classic reprints in the two decades following their deaths? Is the fact that Dickens, for example, sells millions more in 2000 than he did in 1900 a sign of cultural health, or simply an indication that the 'commercial and economic machinery' has become more subtle in its machinations? I would argue the former case.

Why, then, read *Fiction and the Reading Public* if its critical optic is skewed, its mood unfashionably apocalyptic, its opprobriated bestsellers wholly forgotten, and its conclusions downright wrong? It should be read for its critical energy, its lambent intelligence and, above all, because it applied those qualities to new and important topics. English criticism was, and still is, deficient in work that examines the material circumstances of literary production and consumption. *Fiction and the Reading Public*, for all that one disagrees with it, looks in the right direction and blazes a trail which has still, in my view, to be properly followed up. It remains – in my reckoning – one of the ten most important critical texts of its century.

Notes

1. Quoted by Ian MacKillop, *F.R. Leavis: A Life in Criticism* (London, 1995), p. 6. The biographical accounts of F.R.L. and Q.D.L. which follow are dependent on Mr MacKillop's authoritative biography.
2. MacKillop, p. 86.
3. MacKillop, p. 87.
4. References are to *Fiction and the Reading Public* (1932, reprinted London, 1979).
5. I.A. Richards, *Principles of Literary Criticism* (1924, reprinted London, 1960), p. 230.
6. Leslie Stephen, *English Literature and Society in the Eighteenth Century* (1903, reprinted London, 1963), p. 3.
7. F.R. Leavis, *The Common Pursuit* (London, 1952), p. 198.
8. Henry James, 'The Future of the Novel', 1899, reprinted in *The House of Fiction*, ed. Leon Edel (London, 1957), p. 49.
9. MacKillop, p. 131.
10. MacKillop, p. 142.
11. MacKillop, p. 133.
12. MacKillop, p. 255.

John Sutherland's Top Ten

T.S. Eliot, *The Sacred Wood* (1920)
Virginia Woolf, *The Common Reader* (1925)
I.A. Richards, *Practical Criticism* (1929)
William Empson, *Seven Types of Ambiguity* (1930)

Q.D. Leavis, *Fiction and the Reading Public* (1932)
F.R. Leavis, *The Great Tradition* (1948)
Christopher Ricks, *Milton's Grand Style* (1963)
Frank Kermode, *The Sense of an Ending* (1967)
Raymond Williams, *Keywords* (1976)
Terry Eagleton, *Literary Theory: An Introduction* (1983)

For

F. R. L.

Acknowledgments

FIRST I have to acknowledge my debt to the generosity of Girton College in electing me to the Ottilie Hancock research fellowship, without which I should not have been able to carry out this piece of work. And especially to the Vice-Mistress, Miss H. M. R. Murray, who from the outset has encouraged me to persist in the line of research I have chosen.

I must also record with gratitude my indebtedness to a number of junior members of Cambridge University who enthusiastically joined in the work of finding data that bore on the state of contemporary culture. My thanks in this connection are especially due to Mr. A. D. H. Thompson and Mr. W. C. Hunter, then at St. John's College.

The kindness of the novelists who replied to my questionnaire I have mentioned in the body of this book, but I should like to express my recognition of the forbearance and generosity of two of my correspondents in particular: Mrs. Maud Diver and Mr. Edgar Rice Burroughs.

CONTENTS

APPEAL
TO THE READER

THE notes to this book have unavoidably been placed at the back, but I hope they will be not less consulted than if they had appeared at the foot of the page. The material they contain has been austerely excluded from the text in order to save the reader, as far as possible, from the labour of disentangling the argument from the illustrative data. But I must urge the reader not to be deterred from sandwiching the notes parenthetically into the text, and I think it will be found that the bother of keeping the book open at two places at once (which I saw no way of obviating) will be repaid.

INTRODUCTION

THE system of working adopted in this study demands some explanation. There are two accepted methods of dealing with the Novel, and neither has scope for a kind of interest in fiction that I feel to be of great urgency. Henry James in *Notes on Novelists*, and to a much lesser degree Mr. Lubbock in *The Craft of Fiction*, have made serious attempts to grapple with the criticism of the novel, but both books, the former in part and the latter wholly, are approaches from the academic angle. I mean by this that they imply the same restrictions as the phrase used by Mr. Eliot when he refers to ' the few who can talk intelligently of Stendhal, Proust, and Henry James.' Now this method, which is that of literary criticism, can necessarily take no heed of the majority of novels— nearly everything indeed that comes under the head of ' fiction '—which have been very extensively read for the last three centuries. Yet this body of writing has exerted an enormous influence upon the minds and lives of the English people; till recently it has superseded for the majority every other form of art and amusement; and it forms the only printed matter beside newspapers and advertisements which that majority reads; from the cultural point of view its importance cannot be exaggerated. A tangle of pregnant issues is involved, questions of standards and values are raised which bear on the whole history of taste. And for this purpose it is at least as important to take account of the fiction that does not happen to be, or to have become, literature as of the novels which ultimately get into the text-books. But the text-book is the only method that has so far appeared for dealing with fiction as distinct from literature. Even as I write the bulky and authoritative volumes of what looks like being a final *History of the English Novel* are being ground out of the press. Here are recorded the plots and histories of all the well-known and many of the less well-known English novels; but there is no indication that they ever had readers, much less that they played any part in shaping the human spirit and were shaped by it; and this method precludes any serious discussion of values.

Clearly both methods, the critic's and the scholar's, need to be supplemented by a third. A novel pulled up as a unit for inspection clings with its tentacles round so many non-technical matters that it cannot always be safely severed from them. I became interested in the general question: What has happened to fiction and the reading public since the eighteenth century? I found encouragement to pursue this kind of interest in certain hints thrown out by Mr. I. A. Richards in *Principles of Literary Criticism*—*e.g.* ' there is some evidence, uncertain and slight, no doubt, that such things as " best-sellers " (compare *Tarzan* with *She*), magazine verse, mantelpiece pottery, Academy pictures, Music Hall songs, County Council buildings,

War Memorials . . . are decreasing in merit ' (p. 36);
and ' Best-sellers in all the arts, exemplifying as they
do the most general levels of attitude development, are
worthy of very close study. No theory of criticism is
satisfactory which is not able to explain their wide
appeal and to give clear reasons why those who disdain
them are not necessarily snobs ' (p. 203).

I soon found myself committed to a method of investigation which I prefer to describe as ' anthropological.' It consisted in examining all the material that
seemed to bear on this question in an unbiassed but
inquisitive frame of mind and concentrating on regis-
tering shifts of taste and changes in the cultural background, allowing such conclusions as I arrived at to
emerge simply by comparison and contrast and analysis.
The actual frame on which this study is constructed
was decided on only after rejecting several other and
more obvious structures. In studying at large any
branch of the history of taste it is essential to recollect
that the past can only be estimated through the present,
and that its significance is given for us by its relation
to the present. To be interested in cultural questions
is necessarily to set out from the contemporary situation, and I have organised the results of my research
in accordance with this principle. It will be seen that
discussion of values has as far as possible been sus-
pended till the last section of the book was reached,
since it could not conveniently be carried on until a
body of evidence was placed before the reader to which
reference could be made.

The writer is well aware how inadequately the state and history of the periodical and the Press are treated, but the whole question early showed itself to be parallel rather than subordinate to the present undertaking. The proper documentation of the assertions made in Part II. concerning the background of humble life in the eighteenth and nineteenth centuries was also rendered impossible through lack of space and fear of overloading the pages with a quite unmanageable mass of footnotes; this needs separate treatment, and will take the form of a pendent study in which conflicting culture streams that could only be referred to here will be traced to their sources.

I have throughout adopted the plan of producing evidence rather than asserting, in order that generalisations should be so fully documented as to make themselves and the reader find himself led to the conclusions as they presented themselves to me. If these conclusions are found disquieting it is not because they result from a preconceived theory. I have not set out to state a case, though I believe a very sound case might be made out on the strength of this study.

PART I
THE CONTEMPORARY SITUATION

So complete was my father's reliance on the influence of reason over the mind of mankind, whenever it is allowed to reach them, that he felt as if all would be gained if the whole population were taught to read, if all sorts of opinions were allowed to be addressed to them by word and in writing, and if, by means of the suffrage, they could nominate a legislation to give effect to the opinions they adopted.

Autobiography, JOHN STUART MILL.

It is perhaps hardly too much to say that the future of English fiction may rest with this Unknown Public—a reading public of three millions which lies right out of the pale of true literary civilisation—which is now waiting to be taught the difference between a good book and a bad. It is probably a question of time only. The largest audience for periodical literature, in this age of periodicals, must obey the universal law of progress, and must, sooner or later, learn to discriminate. When that period comes, the readers who rank by millions will be the readers who give the widest reputations, who return the richest rewards, and will therefore command the services of the best writers of their time. A great, an unparalleled prospect awaits, perhaps, the coming generation of English novelists. To the penny journals of the present time belongs the credit of having discovered a new public !

WILKIE COLLINS.

THE CONTEMPORARY
SITUATION

I

THE BOOK MARKET

IN twentieth-century England not only every one can read, but it is safe to add that every one does read. Though the Report on Public Libraries (1927) states that not more than 11 per cent. of the population make use of the public library books, yet the number of Sunday newspapers sold will correct any false impression these figures may give. On the day of leisure even the poorest households take a newspaper, though it may be of a different type from that favoured by the educated. A Sunday morning walk through any residential district will reveal the head of the family ' reading the paper ' in each front window; in the poorest quarters the *News of the World* is read on the doorstep or in bed; the weekly perusal of the *Observer* or the *Sunday Times*, which give a large proportion of their contents to book-reviews and publishers' advertisements, is in many cases the only time that even the best-intentioned business man or schoolmaster can spare for his literary education.

The *Advertiser's A B C* for 1929 gives the total net sales of eight of the chief Sunday papers alone as nearly ten millions, and there exist others nearly as popular for which figures are not available. If one remembers that a newspaper is usually assumed to be read by five people, and that the entire population of Great Britain is forty-three millions, it seems reasonable to conclude the existence of an inveterate general reading habit. The more interesting question, What do they read? cannot be answered without first indicating where and how the reading matter is obtained.

The striking peculiarity of the situation is that while, as demonstrated above, the entire population above the school age has acquired reading habits, shops existing solely to sell books are rare outside the university towns of Oxford, Cambridge, and Edinburgh, certain parts of London and a few big cities. Serious book-buying has not increased in proportion to literacy [1]; the bulk of the public does not buy many books [2] but borrows or hires them, in the former case from the not very satisfactory municipal or endowed libraries, in the latter from subscription libraries of various kinds. The investigation made in 1924 into the stocks and issues of urban libraries revealed that while they had 63 per cent. of non-fiction works on an average to 37 per cent. of fiction, only 22 per cent. of non-fiction was issued in comparison with 78 per cent. of fiction, while the county libraries, which stocked 38 per cent. of non-fiction to 62 per cent. of fiction, issued only 25 per cent. non-fiction.[3] This, considering that the 11 per cent. minority which takes advantage of its right to borrow books from the public libraries is probably the more enterprising section of the poorer reading public, shows convincingly enough the supremacy of fiction and the neglect of serious reading which characterise the age.

The fiction shelves of a public library commonly
contain the classics and hardy popular novels of the
past, representative works of all the most popular
contemporary novelists, and (more rarely) the
'literary' novels of the age (*a*), but seldom what is
considered by the critical minority to be the significant work in fiction—the novels of D. H. Lawrence,
Virginia Woolf, James Joyce, T. F. Powys, and E. M.
Forster. Apart from the fact that three out of the
five are held by the majority to be indecent,[4] a fact
suggestive in itself, four out of the five would convey
very little, if anything, to the merely literate. A
librarian who has made the experiment of putting
'good' fiction into his library will report that no
one would take out *South Wind* or *The Garden
Party*, whereas, if he were to put two hundred
more copies of Edgar Wallace's detective stories on
the shelves, they would all be gone the same day.
Attached to the public library is a reading-room,
where a number of people can always be seen looking
through the newspapers, periodicals, and magazines
provided.

The public library, then, is the chief source for the
poorer class of reading-matter in book form. For those
who can afford an annual subscription the Times Book
Club and Mudie's Library exist in London (and send
out boxes of books to their country clients), Messrs.
W. H. Smith's bookstalls provide handy circulating
libraries at railway termini and junctions, while in

(*a*) By 'literary novels' is meant those contemporary novels which the
general public accepts as 'literature.' It will be discussed at length in
Chapter III. of this part, but I will anticipate for the reader's convenience
by stating here that it includes the works of Willa Cather, Thornton Wilder,
John Galsworthy, and David Garnett, among others.

every town of any size Messrs. Boots, the multiple chemists, run similar libraries at very low rates. At these libraries, for the lowest payment (it need not be more than half a guinea a year), the subscriber may borrow such novels and works of history, biography, travel, essays, etc., as the library chooses to provide for him, while for a larger payment he may order what he wishes (except that by three of these firms a strict moral censorship is enforced). No figures are available,[5] and no information forthcoming from these libraries on application, but as a result of spending many hours at different branches of each and at different times of the day, the writer was able to conclude that the proportion of ' guaranteed ' or ' on demand ' subscriptions is not very great; that is, that in general those who are enterprising and affluent enough to subscribe to a circulating library are prepared to have their reading determined for them. And ' reading ' in this case means fiction.[6] It is not an exaggeration to say that for most people ' a book ' means a novel. This becomes apparent if one watches the process of selection, in which the assistant is generally consulted in some such formula as ' Another book like this one, please,' or ' Can you recommend me a nice book? ' The assistant glances at the novel held out and produces another novel which is accepted without question. She may ask ' Have you read this? ' and the answer will be ' I can't remember, but I'll take it.' Where criticism is offered, it almost invariably betrays a complete ignorance of values, *e.g.* a common complaint: ' I can't read Conrad, sea-stories bore me,' or alternatively: ' I like Conrad because I'm so fond of stories about the sea.' In the better districts the subscribers bring lists of novels they have copied out from the newspaper advertisements or reviews.

Undoubtedly there are subscribers who use the circulating libraries to supplement and direct their book-buying. But no one who has made a point of frequenting London and provincial branches of the book-clubs for the past few years can avoid concluding that the book-borrowing public has acquired the reading habit while somehow failing to exercise any critical intelligence about its reading. It is significant that the proportion of fiction to non-fiction borrowed is overwhelmingly great, that women rather than men change the books (that is, determine the family reading), and that many subscribers call daily to change their novels. This, along with the information volunteered by a public librarian that many take out two or three novels by Edgar Wallace a week, and the only other books they borrow are 'Sapper's' or other 'thrillers,' suggests that the reading habit is now often a form of the drug habit. In suburban side-streets and even village shops it is common to find a stock of worn and greasy novels let out at 2d. or 3d. a volume; and it is surprising that a clientèle drawn from the poorest class can afford to change the books several times a week, or even daily; but so strong is the reading habit that they do.

An article in the *Publishers' Circular* (a) called 'Pushing a Lending Library' shows the kind of fiction in demand at such places. It was apparently a small suburban circulating library, which charged 3d. a week. Its regular advertisement was—

(a) August 6th, 1927.

BOOKS!

Good Selection by

' Sapper '	Edgar Wallace
Sax Rohmer	William Le Queux
Zane Grey	Margaret Pedler
E. M. Dell	Margaret Peterson
May Christie	Kathlyn Rhodes

Olive Wadsley

These were the regular authors advertised, with the addition of Rider Haggard, Ruby M. Ayres, and Oppenheim, and the advertisement is reported as being highly successful. [It will be noticed that by the heading ' Books ' is meant novels.]

In the case of such tuppenny dram-shops the choice of reading is determined in effect by the supply, which is the shopkeeper's attempt to provide attractive reading, but even in the great subscription libraries the client is as passive. The writer of ' a *bona-fide* experience ' relates in the *Manchester Evening News* (a) how when he went into Mudie's to change a novel for his wife the assistant produced ' a detective story by J. S. Fletcher and a romantic adventure by W. J. Locke,' explaining that ' if a woman is taken up with a house all day, she doesn't want tales about married problems or misunderstood wives—she knows enough about these already; she can't be bothered with dialect after a day's work, and historical novels aren't alive enough. What she enjoys is something that is possible but outside her own experience—you see if I'm not right.' The writer adds ' And she was.'

(a) February 22nd, 1926.

The effect of all this upon taste will be examined later on in this study; the effects on the book market are thus described by Mr. Stanley Unwin the publisher in his important work, *The Truth About Publishing*:

> Circulating libraries are amongst the biggest buyers upon whom the town traveller calls, and here we enter upon a very thorny subject. There are some publishers who defend the circulating libraries; some who would like to see them abolished root and branch. In so far as they promptly and efficiently supply the public with the particular books for which the public asks, it is difficult to see that serious objection can be reasonably taken to them; but unfortunately the conditions here laid down are applicable only to what is known as 'guaranteed subscriptions,' and, although I have no statistics before me, I imagine that guaranteed subscribers form a tiny minority. There is no certainty that what other subscribers ask for they will be given. . . .
>
> The present system tends to assist the circulation of indifferent and bad books, and to retard the circulation of really good books, especially those by writers who have not yet established reputations. . . . There is one circulating library that makes a boast of the extent to which it can force its subscribers to take what is given them, which means, in that particular case, what the library can buy cheapest. . . . The remedy for all this is not necessarily the abolition of circulating libraries (the circulating-library habit has become far too engrained in England for that), but the educating of the public to see that they get the books they ask for and not substitutes. . . . I feel strongly that any form of subscription other than a guaranteed subscription is pernicious.

Without going here into the question of what Mr. Unwin means by the terms 'bad books' and 'really good books,' one can at least point out that the provision of novels by the commercial libraries for their subscribers means a provision for the widest common level of taste, since it pays better to buy (at a substantial discount) three hundred copies of one novel that every one will be willing to read than a few each of a hundred different books that will not circulate throughout the clientèle. Any bookseller if asked why people don't buy books will inevitably reply that the circulating libraries are responsible— ' look at France, where the only way to read a book is to buy it, and haven't book-sales increased in France three- or four-fold since the war?' But though the facts are correct, the explanation is inadequate. The English public will not pay for books as freely as it pays for clothes and entrance to the cinema, but it does buy the work of the journalist—magazines (at a shilling or more a month), and any number of news-papers to a family. The French buy books because France has an educated public,[7] the English buy journals and periodicals.

Scattered liberally throughout every district, even the poorest, are newsagents' shops whose function is to supply the neighbourhood's reading ; these explain the absence of bookshops. An analysis of the stock of typical newsagents [8] yielded the following repre-sentative list :

1. Periodicals. [(A) after a title signifies American.]

(*a*) Daily and weekly newspapers in great variety.[9]

(*b*) A few cultural weeklies of different levels, ranging from the *New Statesman* and *Nation* (neither obtainable unless ordered) to *John o' London's*, which contains literary gossip, and articles about books and authors by popular writers.[10] In between comes such a paper as *Everyman* or the *Week-End Review*, that sets out to tell its readers which books they will like, or the *Listener*, published by the B.B.C.

(*c*) Weekly humorous papers such as *Punch* (based on the middle-class prejudices) and the *Humorist* (lower class).

(*d*) Seven or eight luxurious shilling illustrated news magazines with a *Punch* orientation,[11] *e.g.* the *Tatler*, *Sphere*, *Sketch*, *Sporting and Dramatic*, *Bystander*.

(*e*) An occasional representative of the literary periodicals (see below).

(*f*) More than a score of substantial story magazines, 6d. or 1s. monthly—*e.g.* the *Strand*, *Happy*, *Hush Magazine*, *Nash's*, *Wide World* (' The Magazine for Men '), *True Story*, *World Stories of Thrills and Adventure*, and several devoted to detective stories, one at least, *Black Mask*, American.

(*g*) Women's magazines—*i.e.* magazines containing stories as in class (*f*) but specially designed for a feminine public by means of articles on home-furnishing, housekeeping, clothes, cookery, and beauty, with a heavy cargo of advertisements.

Twelve of these are stocked regularly—*e.g.* representative titles are *Modern Woman* (' It specialises in the *personal touch* '), *Good Housekeeping* (A), *Ideal Home*, *Delineator* (A), *Woman and Beauty*, the most popular of all being American. These frequently boast of supplying ' first-class fiction.'

(*h*) Nine film magazines—not technical but filled with fiction and articles of film interest, and film publicity designed to create ' film-fans.' Of these nine, seven are American, with such names as *Motion Picture Classics* (A) (' The Magazine with a Personality '), *Screen Romances* (A), *Screen Play Secrets* (A),

Screenland (A) ('America's Smartest Screen Magazine'), the *Motion Picture* (A), the *Picturegoer*.

A newsagent, asked of this section ' And do they sell? ' replied ' Vastly.' Perhaps here should be mentioned *College Humour* (A), an American magazine devoted to articles, stories, and jokes on college life.

(*i*) 2d. weekly papers in magazine form containing the crudest marketable fiction—*e.g. London Novels* (' Was He Her Husband? '), *Love Stories* (' Only a Painted Doll '), *Peg's Paper, Eve's Own*—at least a dozen.

2. A large stock of 6d., 9d., and 1s. paper novels [12] (by popular writers such as Oppenheim, Edgar Wallace, Baroness Orczy).

3. Benn's Sixpenny Library (light educational pamphlets).

4. A selection of Benn's Sixpenny *Augustan Poets*.

5. A row or two of Nelson's 1s. 6d. Classics and a few more of 2s. popular novels.

6. An assortment of children's books, dictionaries, and cookery books.

7. A number of sixpenny novels published by the Readers' Library and the Novel Library.

The proportions may vary slightly—class 5 may be absent, or it may swell in an affluent district to include more expensive popular novels and such safe 7s. 6d. or even half-guinea works as the Forsyte volumes, *The Good Companions, The Week-End Book*, the latest P. G. Wodehouse and Ethel M. Dell, or classes 3 and 4 may not be represented. But nevertheless the significant facts emerge, that books are not generally bought but magazines are, that of these there is an enormous steady sale at all levels and prices, although there is not enough demand for serious papers to make it worth the newsagents' while to stock them on chance,[13] and that what Mr. Oliver Madox Hueffer found in his recent investigation of a poor South London suburb is largely true of the book market all over the country:

> Literature was confined to chemists' or to drapers' shops and devoted chiefly to fiction and the cheaper magazines. The few free public libraries strove, not unworthily, to cater for more serious readers, but lack of funds prevented the acquisition of new works to any useful extent and their contents were too miscellaneous to be of great value to the student (a).

Moreover, certain reading habits have been formed and stabilised by the kind of matter provided by the magazine and the manner of its presentation. These will be discussed in Part II., but some indication of the general trend will be found in the popularity of women's and film magazines, especially those published in America and consequently in an idiom hitherto foreign to the English periodical.

Another point to be made here is that classes (a), (c), (d), (f), (g), and (h) contain at least as much advertisement as letterpress, and when the cost of printing and illustrating the paper and the rates of payment to writers and staff are considered, it becomes evident that the price which the retailer pays for the paper or magazine is a good deal less than the cost of production. That is to say, the periodical is virtually dependent upon the advertiser,[14] so that its policy is to consider the advertisers' interests above all, and (since it only pays to advertise where sales are greatest)

(a) *Some of the English* (1930), by Oliver Madox Hueffer, p. 291.

to sacrifice everything to a large circulation. The effects of this principle will be made plain in Part II.

There is one other agent whose influence upon the book market must not be overlooked. If the Times Book Club and Mudie's serve the upper middle-class and Boots' the lower middle-class, while the news-agent's represents the bookshop for most people, there is the bookshop of the working-class to consider. Where multiple stores have a branch there is usually to be found a bazaar of the American firm,. Messrs. Woolworth; here for 3d. or 6d. nearly everything necessary to existence may be bought, including literature. It is all fiction, and of three kinds. There is a counter for 2d., 3d., and 6d. paper novels by Gene Stratton Porter and the English equivalents. There is another labelled ' Yank Magazines : Interesting Reading,' where American magazines are re-maindered at 3d., and of these there is presumably a steady sale, as the stock changes frequently. There is, moreover, a brisk trade done in the Readers' Library and similar 6d. cheap editions, first introduced to the public by these stores. The Foreword to each volume explains the object of the series in these terms :

> The READERS' LIBRARY is intended to bring the best-known novels of the world within the reach of the millions, by presenting at the lowest possible price per copy, in convenient size, on excellent paper, with beautiful and durable binding, a long series of the stories, copyright and non-copyright, which every one has heard of and could desire to read.
>
> Nothing of the kind has ever before been possible, even in the days when book production has been least expensive.[15] To render it possible now it will be necessary that each volume should have a sale of hundreds of thousands of copies,

and that many volumes of the series should in due course find their way into nearly every home, however humble, in the British Empire.

The publishers have the utmost confidence that this end will be achieved, for already, in less than five years that these books have been on the market, upwards of fifty million copies have been sold in Great Britain alone.

The novels of the READERS' LIBRARY will be selected by one of the most distinguished of living men of letters,[16] and a short biographical and bibliographical note on the author and his works will be appended to each volume.

The editor started off by choosing the popular classics (*Uncle Tom's Cabin*, *The Last Days of Pompeii*, *Pilgrim's Progress*, *Westward Ho!*, etc.) and writing a critical introduction to each; but soon a new principle became apparent: whenever a super-film was released—*Love* (film-version of *Anna Karenina*), *Ben Hur*, *His Lady* (film of *Manon Lescaut*), *The Man Who Laughs* (film-version of *L'Homme Qui Rit*)—'the book of the film' was published too (and advertised as such on the dust-cover, with photogravures from the film inside). This sold so well that the next stage was to produce an eponymous book of the film or play, when none existed, put together by a hack. These, with thrillers and very popular novelettes, now hold the field and acknowledge the frank commercialisation of a series which was hailed warmly on its appearance in 1924 by statesmen and bishops. The distinguished man of letters descended in his introductions from critic to apologist, then to a champion of popular taste [17]; last of all he contented himself with a few facts about author and story.

The latest stage is the appearance of the Readers' Library Film Edition with this Foreword:

The Readers' Library Film Edition has been instituted to meet a real modern demand.   Interest in a film is by no means exhausted merely by seeing it.   The two arts, or forms of expression, the picture and the written word in book form, react one on the other. . . . In a word, the filmgoer wishes also to read the book of the film, and the reader to see the picture.

To meet this undeniable call for literature associated with the film, it would not be enough to produce books of inferior quality. . . . *Publication will coincide with the appearance of each new and important film (a).*

The distinguished man of letters has been dropped in favour of the American film-producer, a change all the easier since the ' talkie ' furnishes ready-made dialogue.   The introductory paragraph is now significantly directed away from literature, and the appeal to the reader is focussed on the film-star :

' The Rogue Song,' based on the popular romantic musical comedy ' Gipsy Love,' is one of the most colourful achievements of the talking screen.   The story makes a gripping novel, and Mr. Val Lewton's style has captured all the melody and romance of the film, which has for its star Lawrence Tibbett, America's greatest baritone. . . . This heart-throbbing romance of a gypsy bandit's love for a beautiful princess forms one of the most delightful film novels we have yet published.

There appears to be money in ' literature associated with the film,' for the Novel Library (' For Fiction Lovers ') has similarly gone over to the talkies.   Starting, like the Leisure Library Ltd. and the Detective Story Club Ltd. (*b*), as a close imitation of the Readers' Library, it has stopped publishing Wells and Galsworthy for the masses and now produces the book of the talkie :

(*a*) The italics are mine.
(*b*) All three are sold along with the Readers' Library.

Welcome Danger is introduced to the public in the language of the talkies—' Know Harold Lloyd? Sure.   Seen him in " College Days " and " Safety Last "?   Sure.   Well, you haven't laughed until you've seen him in " Welcome Danger "—the funniest thing he's done yet.   And you'll be tickled to death when you read the book, for in it you get right close up to Harold,' etc.

The effect of the increasing control by Big Business —in which it would hardly be unreasonable, on the strength of the evidence above, to include the film interests—is to destroy among the masses a desire to read anything which by the widest stretch could be included in the classification ' literature,' and to substitute something which is best described by the title-page of a specimen :

' The Girl from China '
novelized by Karen Brown.
Adapted from
John Cotton's
DRIFTING
Universal Picture
starring MARY NOLAN.

A selection of the Readers' Library is now sold by most newsagents, but the chief sale of these libraries is still at the bazaars.   Here, while passing from counter to counter to buy cheap crockery, strings of beads, lamp-shades, and toffee, toys, soap, and flower-bulbs, and under the stimulus of 6d. gramophone records filling the air with ' Headin' for Hollywood ' and ' Love Never Dies,' the customer is beguiled into patronising literature.   If it is a country town, the bazaar is packed on market-day with the country folk who come in once a week to do their shopping, so that Woolworth literature supplies the county with reading (*a*); if it is a city, the housewives of the district make their regular tour on Saturdays, though a constant stream passes along the counters handling the goods throughout the week. So paper-covered novels by Nat Gould, Charles Garvice and Joseph Hocking,[18] P. C. Wren, Sabatini and Phillips Oppenheim; American magazines—*Ranch Romances* (' Love Stories of the Real West '), *Far-West Stories*, *Love Romances* (' Gripping clean love stories '), *The Popular Magazine* (' America's Best and Brightest Fiction Magazine '), *Marriage Stories*, *Detective Classics*, *Black Mask* (' Detective Fiction '), *Gangster Stories* (' A Magazine of Racketeers and Gun Molls '); and sixpenny books—*Harem Love* (' by Joan Conquest, author of *Desert Love* '), *Officer* (' An Underworld Thriller by Hulbert Footner '), *The King of Kings* (the story of the super-film of Christianity); all go home in the shopping baskets.

(*a*) ' Before I conclude this letter, I cannot help observing that the sale of books in general has increased prodigiously within the last twenty years. According to the best estimate I have been able to make, I suppose that more than four times the number of books are sold now than were sold twenty years since. The poorest sort of farmers, and even the poor country people in general, who before that period spent their winter evenings in relating stories of witches, ghosts, hobgoblins, &c. now shorten the winter nights by hearing their sons and daughters read tales, romances, &c., and on entering their houses you may see Tom Jones, Roderick Random, and other entertaining books stuck up on their bacon racks, &c. If *John* goes to town with a load of hay, he is charged to be sure not to forget to bring home " Peregrine Pickle's Adventures " ; and when *Dolly* is sent to market to sell her eggs, she is commissioned to purchase " The history of Pamela Andrews." '—*Memoirs of the first forty-five years of The Life of James Lackington, Bookseller*, written by himself, 2nd ed. 1792, p. 386.

II

THE MIDDLEMEN

IT has been calculated by an enterprising journalist
that 'more than 200,000,000 words of new
fiction are published every month' (a). Though a
good deal of this appears in the form of stories in the
900 magazines, still there is a steady spate of novels.
Whereas publishers now lose money over poetry,
novels are notoriously their chief source of profit. As
shown in the last chapter, novel-reading is now largely
a drug habit, and the book market depends on a
public which buys its literature in accordance with
tastes acquired from its circulating library reading.
But one can go deeper into the question, What
determines the choice of books? People do not spend
anything from six shillings to half a guinea on a novel,
or even sixpence at Woolworth's or the local newsagent's, without some idea of what they are getting,
and naturally very few have both the time and ability
to sift the novels published every year themselves.

In the twentieth century a public of forty-three
millions has to be reached, since it is all, though un-
equally, literate, and that proportion of it which buys
or borrows books is so scattered in space and isolated
further by differences of development and education,
that it needs as vast an organisation as the modern Press
to serve as middleman between author and reader,
with its book-reviews, -advertisements, and literary

(a) Kenneth MacNichol, advertisement of *The Technique of Fiction
Writing, vide* p. 31.

articles. The purely literary periodicals alone can be divided on internal evidence into three classes, serving three different levels of reading public, and each would be of little use to the other's readers. The *Criterion* will review only those novels which have some pretensions to literary merit and can be criticised by serious standards (it is common even in literary circles to fling the epithet ' highbrow ' at it); the *Times Literary Supplement*, representing a ' safe ' academic attitude, will summarise and comment on the plot and merits of any work by a novelist of standing ; while a whole handful of cheap weeklies appear to satisfy a demand for literary gossip and information about the readableness of books. It will be convenient to call these levels ' highbrow,' ' middlebrow ' and ' lowbrow.' Typical lowbrow literary organs sell 30,000, 50,000, and in one case 100,000 copies of each number, whereas in the next class the *London Mercury* only reaches the 10,000 figure (*a*); for the *Criterion* figures are not available, but its oscillation from quarterly to monthly and back is suggestive of insufficient support [19]; and the *Adelphi*, a much less uncompromising periodical with a similar history, had an average of 4200 copies as a shilling monthly from 1923 to 1927, dropped to 1700 as a half-crown quarterly 1927-1930, and since becoming a shilling monthly again sells less than 4500; and the *Calendar*, at least as intelligent and severe as the *Criterion* and far livelier, died for lack of support in 1928 after three years' unequalled service. A novel received with unqualified enthusiasm in a lowbrow paper will be

(*a*) The *Times Literary Supplement*'s sale of 30,788 is due to its being a trade organ for booksellers, schoolmasters, etc.

coolly treated by the middlebrow and contemptuously dismissed if mentioned at all by the highbrow Press; the kind of book that the middlebrow Press will admire wholeheartedly the highbrow reviewer will diagnose as pernicious; each has a following that forms a different level of public.[20]

We now have, apparently, several publics, loosely linked together, with nearly a score of literary weeklies, monthlies, and a quarterly which serve to standardise different levels of taste. Their relative sales seem to show a rapidly decreasing minority of taste—to adopt for the moment the conventional prejudices. The sales of even the extremes, say 250,000 for the united lowbrow literary organs and 4000 at the other end, apparently represent little effective difference in a population of forty-five millions, yet it is worth noticing that the latter stands at face value only (most of those who read at the *Criterion* level are likely to be subscribers), whereas the *Listener, Everyman, John o' London's* . . . all serve the same level of reading public, pass through innumerable hands in the reading-rooms of public libraries, and even then have in addition a vast body of inert support in the public which buys the large-circulation dailies (selling a million or two each) and Sunday papers (one to three millions each).

It is this public which has made nearly all the big newspapers think it worth their while to pay for the services of very well-known literary figures, who provide a weekly article or batch of reviews once a week. In these they confidently recommend certain novels which, by the reputation of the critic (novelist or journalist) as much as by the publicity received,

become widely known and read. Responsible booksellers will volunteer that Mr. Arnold Bennett, for
instance, had only to mention a novel in his weekly
article to sell an edition,[21] and his successor, Mr.
Harold Nicolson, has recently sent *The Way of All
Flesh* out of print by referring to it in his B.B.C. talks ;
advertisements of novels now commonly quote simply
one of the offhand judgments these writers throw out,
in the nature of pontifical statements rather than criticisms,[22] and an enterprising publisher will reissue the
novel with a band or new dust-jacket exhibiting the
caption. All this tends to show that the majority has
its mind made up for it before buying or borrowing
its reading, for even those who do not glance at
the book-reviews in their daily and weekly papers
hardly escape being influenced by the advertisements.
Modern advertising will be discussed later, but it is
enough to observe here that it has reached a dangerous
level of efficiency.

An even more efficient standardisation of taste is
suggested by the activities of the Book Society and the
late Book Guild. The former was started on the model
of the American Book-of-the-Month Club in 1927,
the latter early in 1930, each with a Selection Committee of five novelists and journalists (nearly all of
whom are also reviewers for newspapers and
magazines). The method in each case is this :

> Publishers throughout the country are submitting their
> most important works in advance of publication to the selec-
> tion committee. From these the committee select their
> ' book of the month,' and in addition compile a supplement-
> ary list of others they can thoroughly recommend.
> On the morning of publication every member of the Book

Society receives a first edition of the book the committee have chosen. Enclosed in this book is a copy of the ' Book Society News,' which contains reviews by the members of the committee both of the selected books and of those on the supplementary list. If any members feel that the book chosen is not *their* book, they may return it within five days and will receive by return whatever book they select in exchange from the supplementary list. In point of fact, the majority of books selected are likely to be novels, because more new fiction is published than any other category of literature. . . .

Join the Book Society—and you need never miss a really good book (*a*).

The Book Society claims that ' With the help of the Selection Committee it will be impossible for you to miss any really worth-while book that is published ' (*b*), and generally encourages the impression recorded by one of its members (*c*) (reflecting ' the general tone of the articles that have poured into this office ') that by joining the Book Society they are ' permanently in touch with all that is finest in modern literature.' On what level the Selection Committee actually works may be best indicated by the kind of book it chooses or recommends—novels of such competent journalists as G. B. Stern, A. P. Herbert, Rebecca West, Denis Mackail . . ., sapless ' literary ' novels, or the smartly fashionable (Hemingway, Osbert Sitwell). By December 1929 the society had nearly seven thousand members (*d*), and it is still growing, from which the quite unbiassed observer might fairly deduce two important cultural changes : first, that by conferring authority on a taste for the second-rate (to the Book Society the publication of *A Modern Comedy* is

(*a*) Advertisement in the *Observer*, March 23rd, 1930.
(*b*) *The Books You Read* (published by the Book Society).
(*c*) *The Book Society News*, March 1930.   (*d*) *Ibid.*, December 1929.

'a real event in the story of modern English literature ' (*a*)) a middlebrow standard of values has been set up ; second, that middlebrow taste has thus been organised. An assured public of seven thousand claiming moreover to represent literary enlightenment is a formidable argument with publishers, and it is not only the massed seven thousand. As Mr. Walpole (one of the Book Society Committee) says (*b*), ' There is no doubt that many more copies of *The Edwardians, The Water Gypsies,* and *Bengal Lancer* have been sold in the bookshops than would have been the case had they not been Book Society choices.'

The same impartial observer would notice a certain irritation in the explanatory literature of the Book Guild. Though it admittedly sets out to help a public that wants something merely readable, its committee cannot guarantee to provide that without also arrogating righteousness and betraying hostility to any more serious standards :

> Out of the thousands of books published every year—there are between 12,000 and 14,000—how on earth is the ordinary person to sift the sheep from the goats?   Distinguished critics attempt to guide the public, but they are so often hopelessly ' highbrow ' and ' precious,' and simply add to the general confusion and bewilderment.
>
> When the aims of the Book Guild were explained to me, therefore, it seemed too good to be true—an organisation which would cater *for the ordinary intelligent reader*, not for the highbrows—an organisation which would realise that *a book can have a good story and a popular appeal and yet be good literature*—be good literature and yet be absorbingly interesting, of the kind you can't put down once you've started, an organisation which would not recommend a book

(*a*) *The Book Society News*, August 1929.
(*b*) *Week-End Review*, October 11th, 1930.

as a work of genius simply because it had been eulogised by
some pedantic critic or other. . . . The Book Guild, by
means of its Recommended List of Alternative Titles, is
able, as it were, to keep its fingers on the pulse of the best of
contemporary work, whilst at the same time providing something for everybody and that something the best of its kind.
One of its chief aims is to avoid indulging in the deplorable
affectation of recommending as a work of ' genius ' the sort
of thing which is dubbed clever simply because it is mainly
unintelligible and written in an obscure manner, or boosting
some foreign work simply because it is foreign, and the
author's name difficult to pronounce. [Miss Ethel Mannin
in *The Bookworm's Turn*, published by the Book Guild.]

The detective novel writers have their own clientèle,
though they make no appeal to the young ladies who throng
the counters of Boots' libraries, and but little to the sheep-like
crowd who follow the dictates of highbrow literary critics.
[George A. Birmingham in *The Book Guild Bulletin*, July
1930, accounting for the Book Guild's choice of a detective
novel.]

The state of inflammation noticeable here, of which
other indications will be apparent throughout this and
the next chapter, is perhaps the most significant feature
of, and indeed characterises, the contemporary cultural
situation.   In this connection the appeal to herd-
instinct made by the publications of both societies is
suggestive, just as publishers will advertise simply—

' OLD PYBUS by Warwick Deeping.
75,000 copies in six weeks.'

with the assumption that a novel is more likely to be
' good ' if it appeals to a horde of readers than to a
minority, and the winner of the Book Society's competition [' What the Book Society Has Meant to Me ']
declares : ' I have looked on the Book Society as a fold
into which I can creep for shelter, knowing that the

fleeces of the other sheep will be the same colour as my own.'

The same anxiety to conciliate and flatter the ' man in the street ' is an essential trait of the contemporary journalist; in Michael Joseph's *Journalism for Profit* there is an interesting chapter, ' How I make Journalism Pay,' contributed by successful journalists. A representative note is sounded here :

> . . . After that is accomplished the next business in hand is getting on the right side of the Great British Public. And keep your eyebrows well pinned down. It is quite likely you may know it all and in consequence feel enormously sorry for the Great B.P. for not having enjoyed all your advantages. But the Great B.P. is not always impressed. Very frequently it is bored stiff. Silly and presumptuous of it, but there it is. Amuse it. Cheer it up. Chat to it. Bully it a little. Tickle its funny bone. Giggle with it. Confide in it. Give it, now and again, a good old cry. It loves that. But don't, for your success's sake, come the superior high-brow over it.

This is peculiarly important, since the journalist's power as middleman in forming popular taste can hardly be overestimated. It has already been stated that story-magazines and periodicals containing fiction are sold freely from bookstalls and the innumerable newsagents' shops, in contrast to the limited sale of books in the scarce and poorly stocked bookshops. To put the difference more cogently, an exceptionally popular novel, *Sorrell and Son*, published in 1928 at 7s. 6d. and since reprinted in cheap editions, in two years, according to the publisher's advertisement, has sold half a million copies throughout the English-speaking world; the *Strand Magazine* sells 150,000 copies a month (without any American sale), *Good House-*

keeping 125,400, *Nash's* 100,000, to name three of the higher class of the couple of dozen or so shilling monthly magazines ; while at the other end cheap little weeklies of class (*i*) on p. 12 sell 175,000 (*Betty's Paper*) or more—200,000 and 300,000 in some cases. The kind of fiction published in this way—the briefest inspection will show that it is all of a kind—is carefully chosen by the editors in accordance with the policy of what is called ' Giving the Public what it wants.' By a process not difficult to imagine and easily demonstrable, this has come to mean providing fiction that requires the least effort to read and will set the reader up with a comfortable state of mind. The entire periodical-fiction trade has been organised on a scientific basis. To achieve as large a circulation as possible (in order to secure the advertiser) the editor sets out to satisfy the common measure of taste, and he cannot (or thinks he cannot) afford to publish any story which fails to conform to type. This is frankly acknowledged —for instance, in *Short Story Writing for Profit*. Mr. Michael Joseph (literary agent and author of *The Commercial Side of Literature*, *The Magazine Story*, *Journalism for Profit*, etc.) prints a chapter ' What Editors Want,' contributed by the editors themselves. Here, repeated with scarcely any variation, is a demand for ' dramatic and light-hearted stories with a strong love interest and a pleasant atmosphere '; ' Love? Yes. And romance. But nothing sordid '; ' Stories must have a strong feminine appeal and a happy ending is essential. Sad and sordid stories are not wanted '; ' The gruesome, ghostly or brutal are not required, while those dealing too frankly with problems of sex are equally unwelcome.' In order to appreciate the full significance of this specialisation one must be aware that when an editor writes ' Nothing heavy, morbid or neurotic,' he is condemning by implication (for the terms are accepted counters and used for the sake of delicacy) the living tradition of the novel.   To illustrate this point one must quote a manual by an American journalist, as being at once more outspoken and more innocent of critical standards :

> Writers of short stories who are ambitious to get into good magazines should remember further that certain subjects are in themselves undesirable, regardless of the merits of the story.   Very few periodicals admit anything sordid or depressing.   Writers like Thomas Hardy who have a dreary hopeless outlook on life are not welcomed in popular magazines, however deft their literary art.   [*The Contemporary Short Story*, Henry T. Baker.]

Since the magazine's function now is to provide reading fodder for odd moments, travelling and after-business hours, glanced through with a background of household chatter or ' the wireless,' it is essential too that the stories they provide should be short, ' snappy,' as crudely arresting as a poster and for the same reason, and easy enough for the jaded mind to take in without exertion.   What it really means is that the young writer who is potentially a serious novelist and is obliged to earn part or all of his living by his pen is in a far worse position than Trollope, Dickens, Thackeray (*a*) ; if he submits and trains himself to produce acceptable short stories and serials, then he is spoilt for literature.   An American editor puts it naively enough :

(*a*) True, Thackeray complained in the introduction to *Pendennis*, and Trollope in his *Autobiography*, that in writing serial fiction they were hampered by a certain *pudeur* in their public, but this did not mean spiritual degradation ; there is no sign in their work of thwarting or lowering of tone, which is in question above.

In effect, every magazine is a package, labelled and authoritatively sealed with the symbol of the editor's approval. . . . The young author is often confused by a rejection which simply says, ' This is not a *Harper* story.' That does not mean it is not a good story; it simply means that the tale does not, in the editor's trained mind, conform to the type of fiction which his magazine has established (*a*).

It is not irrelevant to quote an American editor here, for (as mentioned in Chapter I.) American magazines have large sales in England, and the American ideal is taking hold of the English periodical Press.[23] The close connection between the journalism of the two countries appears in the Anglo-American Manuscript Service which, undertaking to place stories on either side of the Atlantic, sends out to its clients—

Just a Little Friendly Advice.

If you want to be a successful writer for American publications, for which high prices are paid for really first-class matter, bear in mind that American fiction, in the main, is not *pessimistic*, nor is it *lewd* or irreverent, neither is it *red* nor *un-American*.

Avoid *morbidity*. The Americans don't want *gloom*, but something that will brighten life. The sun must always be shining. Treat *sex* reverently, and avoid its unsavoury aspects. Don't be *vulgar*. Remember that serious thought is not looked for in the majority of American magazines. Don't discuss *religious* questions in a manner that would offend national sentiment, and leave *evolution* out of your writings. *Religion* that brings out its boons and blessings to long-suffering humanity is deemed praiseworthy. Leave *social* and *political* problems to take care of themselves. Remember that America is a young and prosperous country, and there is nothing on God's earth to equal it.

We want to market your manuscripts. Help us to do so.

(*a*) C. Hanson Towne, *Adventures in Editing*. See also Herbert Quick (editor), *How to Print what the People Want*.

' English ' may equally well stand for ' American '
here, and, except for the evolution clause, the document states the conditions that every short story
seeking publication in an English magazine must
satisfy.   For ' not un-American ' may be substituted
the cis-Atlantic editorial stipulation: ' Stories with
foreign settings are welcomed, providing always that
they contain either an English hero or an English
heroine (*a*).'   How American magazine editors, when
they have once discovered a likely fiction-writer, will
scientifically train and bully him into submission and
affluence is explained in the *Dance of the Machine*.
Meanwhile, in England the same process is at work
less directly, and there are plenty of enterprising
literary agents eager to teach, like George G. Magnus,
How to Write Saleable Fiction.   The periodicals in
October 1930 were announcing—

You *Can* Learn to Write Stories that *Sell*.

Twelve Lectures on the Technique of Fiction-Writing.
Proof of value?   Students of the ' Twelve Lectures ' have
reported sales to *Windsor, Pearson's, Strand, Royal, Twenty-
Story, John o' London's*—almost every worth-while[24] magazine in England.

The Twelve Lectures are by the editor of the
Centurion, a completely successful journalist trained by
the famous American magazine editor, ' Bob ' Davis—
' " Write so a blind man can read it," ' Bob ' Davis
demanded.   " Write it for children to read.   If you
must say it with flowers, go sell your stuff to the highbrow magazines." ' [25]   The Twelve Lectures have been
published as a guinea book ; and it is worth quoting

(*a*) ' What Editors Want,' Michael Joseph, *Short Story Writing for Profit*.

the description of Lecture XII.—' Stories that Do Not Sell; Stories Editors do not Like; The Stories that do Sell; Selecting the Market,' etc.—to suggest how thoroughly commercialised the fiction market has become and how completely stereotyped its demands. The effect of applying the rules of scientific journalism to the magazine has been to close the market to genius, talent, and distinction, and to force instead a kind of anaemic ability to satisfy the reading habit. From the point of view of literature alone this is a serious matter, since it means that if a writer produces stories whose merits place them outside the journalist's idea of What the Public Wants, he cannot publish them; there is not one of the 900 worth-while magazines Mr. MacNichol refers to which would be open to him, and publishers are unwilling to issue volumes of short stories (which for some reason are said not to pay) (a). The potential artist of fiction would have to study the magazines, read up a manual or two, or, preferably, take a correspondence course at the Regent Institute or London School of Journalism, and set himself to produce stories to type. If he is lucky he will hit on a popular formula—P. G. Wodehouse is perhaps the most striking instance of this process—and achieve bestseller success. There is no magazine even like the *Yellow Book* to give a start to fresh talent, nowhere for a serious novelist to earn

(a) My publishers assure me that they don't, save for exceptional cases like Kipling, or in the case of writers already well known for their novels, like Aldous Huxley. First books of short stories are almost invariably ignored in the Press, distrusted by booksellers, and refused by the Lending Libraries, whose subscribers want ' something to keep them going for a good long time,' and ' a story that gets you somewhere.' Short stories, apparently, do neither. The truth is, I suppose, that they offer less opportunity for living at the expense of the author, and their public is restricted accordingly.

his living by writing serials (like the early and mid-Victorians) or short stories (like the late Victorians and the Edwardians), no *English Illustrated Magazine*, among others, to publish a Henry James. (It is true that *Nash's* in search of ' big names ' ran the last Forsyte epic as a serial, but this is not quite the same thing.) The modern magazine, then, while being very much more ' readable ' for the exhausted city worker than it ever was, has achieved this end by sacrificing any pretension to be literature ; nor does it merely set itself to amuse and soothe. It is quite explicitly defiant of other standards and ambitions. And by accustoming the reading public to certain limited appeals and a certain restricted outlook, it has spoilt the public for fiction in book form of a more serious nature.

AUTHOR AND READER

SOME further light on the contemporary situation one might reasonably expect to obtain from a scrutiny of the popular novels themselves. Yet since novels are in the nature of dramatic utterances one may easily be misled in drawing on them for data without the check of some more direct kind of evidence —for instance, information obtained from readers and authors. In this attempt to chart the condition of the reading public of to-day, the writer therefore found it advisable to invite the collaboration of a number of the most popular living novelists, a liberty which was nearly invariably condoned. Out of sixty authors invited to deal with a questionnaire, twenty-five returned effective replies, providing sufficient basis for generalisation, since the work of these twenty-five fortunately affords examples of every level of novel-reading taste.

But before any such classification can be assumed it must be shown to exist. It would not be true to suggest a stratification of novel writers and novel readers in 1760, for example, when any one who could read would be equally likely to read any novel, or every novel, published, and the only division of the novelists of that age that can be made is between good and indifferent (effective and ineffective); even a century later the same conditions hold, for though at that time Dickens, Reade, and Wilkie Collins were the idols of the man in the street and George Eliot and Trollope of the educated, yet each class read or perfectly well might have read the entire output of all the contemporary novelists, who all live in the same world, as it were, understand each other's language, live by the same code, and employ a common technique presenting no peculiar difficulty to the reader.

Comparison of the situations at these dates (chosen at random) with that exhibited in the previous chapters has brought out a significant fact: that it is a peculiarity of this last generation that a consistent selection by the majority of the ' worst ' novels ('worst' by consensus of the critical minority) has created a state exactly contrary to what the Martian or the innocent eighteenth-century observer might expect, so that ' best seller ' is an almost entirely derogatory epithet among the cultivated. Of this the ' best seller ' novelists are in general aware, and several in replying to the questionnaire took exception to it as applied to themselves. To illustrate the curiously inverse relation now existing between esteem and popularity, a state of affairs that has come to be considered normal, the literary column of the *Evening Standard* (July 19th, 1928) may be cited, where the writer (Mr. Arnold Bennett), explaining with some apologies that he has read a novel by Edgar Wallace out of curiosity, urges that—

> Nearly all bookish people are snobs, and especially the more enlightened among them. They are apt to assume that if a writer has immense circulation, if he is enjoyed by plain persons, and if he can fill several theatres at once, he cannot possibly be worth reading and merits only indifference and disdain.

The twentieth-century reader who would let this

pass as a commonplace could only be brought to realise that it is indeed something new in English history by considering as a norm Dr. Johnson rejoicing to concur with the common reader—a position that for the modern critic of equivalent standing would be ridiculous.

It is not perhaps surprising that, in a society of forty-three millions so decisively stratified in taste that each stratum is catered for independently by its own novelists and journalists, the lowbrow public should be ignorant of the work and even of the names of the highbrow writers,[26] while to the highbrow public 'Ethel M. Dell' or 'Tarzan' should be convenient symbols, drawn from hearsay rather than first-hand knowledge. But what close at hand is apparently trivial becomes a serious development when we realise that this means nothing less than that the general public—Dr. Johnson's common reader—has now not even a glimpse of the living interests of modern literature, is ignorant of its growth and so prevented from developing with it, and that the critical minority to whose sole charge modern literature has now fallen is isolated, disowned by the general public and threatened with extinction. Poetry and criticism are not read by the common reader; the drama, in so far as it ever overlapped literature, is dead, and the novel is the only branch of letters which is now generally supported. And the kind of interest taken in the novel has been indicated in these chapters.

To make this clearer it will be convenient to draw attention to a literary competition held by the *Sunday Dispatch* (net sales 1,200,767) from March 23rd to

April 13th, 1930. It is one of the most popular
Sunday papers. Those of its readers who entered its
literary competition may be presumed to be representative enough of the great public—favourably so,
since the competition required initiative and some
practice in self-expression. Competitors were invited
to send their choice (with reasons) of a post-war
book which they believe will be read a generation
hence, together with the names of five other such post-
war books, and some thirty replies were published (*a*).
By far the most votes went to a class of novelists of
whom Robert Louis Stevenson (*b*) may be named as
the rather innocent forerunner : Thornton Wilder
(*The Bridge of San Luis Rey*), Willa Cather (*Death
Comes for the Archbishop*), Galsworthy (*The Forsyte
Saga, A Modern Comedy*), J. B. Priestley (*The Good
Companions*), David Garnett (*Lady into Fox*, etc.),
respected middling novelists of blameless intentions
and indubitable skill, ' thoughtful,' ' cultured,' impressive, but lacking interest for the ' highbrow '
reader, who complains that their works are ' academy
art.' A representative criticism from the high-level
reader [27] would be that they bring nothing to the
novel but commonplace sentiments and an out-
worn technique ; echoes of the Best People of the
past, their productions would be dismissed by him
as ' literary.' ' Literary ' novels, the account would
continue, are all on the traditional model, and there-

(*a*) The editorial choice was no doubt representative, for the same authors
recur with monotonous regularity, and an original competitor who backed
Ulysses, Principles of Literary Criticism, and *The Poems of T. S. Eliot* was
published—but as a curiosity, not a prizewinner.

(*b*) ' I think *David Balfour* a nice little book, and very artistic and just
the thing to occupy the leisure of a busy life.'—R. L. S. in a letter.

fore easy to respond to, yet with an appearance of
originality; they deal (like the magazine fiction of the
age) in soothing and not disturbing sentiments, yet
with sufficient surface stimulus to be pleasing; their
style, in one case a careful eighteenth-century pastiche,
in another a point-to-point imitation of well-known
novelists of repute, but in most cases chosen merely
to give an impression of restraint and subtlety, is
easily recognised by the uncritical as 'literature.'
Not so obviously dead (in this view) as such literary
works as *The Testament of Beauty* or Landor's
Imaginary Conversations, but equally sapless, they are
far more readable, being novels, and their readers are
left with the agreeable sensation of having improved
themselves without incurring fatigue. These authors
and others of the same kind are now the staple reading
of the middlebrow; they will be observed on the
shelves of dons, the superior sort of schoolmaster
(the other sort has sets of Kipling, Ian Hay, P. G.
Wodehouse, and Masefield's poems), and in the
average well-to-do home; we have already noticed
that Book-of-the-Month Clubs by singling out such
writers for their recommendations tend to standardise
a taste for their work and impress on the public that
it is 'all that is finest in modern literature.' Indications of a widespread impression to this effect the
observant reader will find everywhere. An advertisement copy-writer of considerable standing writing in
Commercial Art (a) on 'Can Copy Be Worth Reading?'
cited *Jew Süss* and *The Bridge of San Luis Rey* as
examples of 'books of fine literary quality' that 'sell
by the 100,000,' in order to prove that successful

(a) August 1930, 'Can Copy Be Worth Reading?' by Gilbert Russell.

' copy ' need not lack the literary graces ; a reviewer will say in commendation of a new novelist ' She is the only author who reminds me of Conrad and Hergesheimer both at once ' (a), having formed his taste on the parasitic.

But what part do they play in the lives of the readers of the *Sunday Dispatch* ? It is suggestive that practically every competitor has one or two of them in his batch of six, and no more : a plausible explanation would be that these he has heard of as ' good,' and they are there because he knows he ought to admire them, like *The Testament of Beauty* (which he occasionally includes in his list too). But he fills up with the novels he has really enjoyed (Edgar Wallace, P. G. Wodehouse, Warwick Deeping, P. C. Wren, *The Constant Nymph*, Ian Hay, Kipling). Of the novelists who have already been accepted by the active minority as serious writers who have brought something of their own to the art of the novel, these representatives of the general public seem never to have heard. There is not a single mention of *Passage to India*, *Mr. Weston's Good Wine*, or the novels of D. H. Lawrence, and *To the Lighthouse* is once chosen (along with *Jew Süss* and *Peter Jackson* by Gilbert Frankau) ; *Ulysses* curiously enough is listed several times,[28] probably owing to the factitious fame censorship has conferred upon it. The major achievements of contemporary novelists appear to be unknown even by name to that part of the community journalists call the Great British Public. It does not mean that the mass of the public is simply a genera- tion behind the times, like the contemporaries of

(a) Taken from a publisher's advertisement in the *Observer*, June 22nd, 1930.

Hardy, Gissing, and Meredith, who clung to their Dickens, Thackeray, and Trollope; the impartial assessor of the evidence brought together here can hardly avoid concluding that for the first time in the history of our literature the living forms of the novel have been side-tracked in favour of the *faux-bon*. An interesting confirmation of this point comes to hand in another newspaper competition (*a*), in a provincial town this time, for essays on ' My-Favourite Author.' Summarising results, the editor gives as ' first favourites ' among the dead authors Carlyle, Dickens, Ruskin, Tennyson, Trollope, Hardy, among the living Gene Stratton Porter, P. G. Wodehouse, Warwick Deeping, Hugh Walpole, John Galsworthy, and adds, ' It is perhaps worthy of note that Thomas Hardy was the most widely-quoted among the dead authors and P. G. Wodehouse among the living.' The disparity between the standing of the dead authors chosen (all ' classics '), where recognition of standards has ruled the choice, and of the living, where the competitors had only their own taste and judgment to guide them, is significant. It is also significant that whereas the dead favourites are novelists, poets, and men of letters, the living ones are all novelists, the competitors in general not knowing or caring about other kinds of contemporary literature. A sense of standards in the older generation which has deserted their children may be illustrated by the complaint made to the writer by one of the novelists consulted in connection with this chapter, herself one of the most popular and whole-hearted bestsellers : ' I try to get my boys to read Dickens and Scott, but they won't read

(*a*) *Cambridge Daily News*, July 30th, 1930.

anything but magazines and Edgar.' [Edgar Wallace.]
After this digression we can return to the novelists,
satisfied that grounds for classifying them and their
readers exist.   Sixty authors were selected as each
answering one of the following requirements :

1. Having written ' The Novel of the Season.'
2. Being steady bestsellers over a long period.
3. Having proportionately large sales for a given
   public.

In consulting these authors, it was necessary first
to suggest the lines along which the major problems
should be discussed without providing questions that
could be answered by a mere ' Yes ' or ' No ' and yet
should pin possible discussion down to a point, and
next to ensure that the information so given should be
genuine.   The former difficulty was solved by a carefully worded questionnaire, while a covering letter
explaining the serious and academic nature of the
undertaking in which the novelist's co-operation was
required met, there is every reason to believe, the
latter.   Many of the authors consulted were kind
enough to suggest a further correspondence in which
they generously allowed themselves to be made use of.
An undertaking to preserve anonymity if desired was
given in the covering letter, and in some cases accepted
(and of course observed).   But more than this is
demanded by the conditions of such a correspondence,
in which good faith of a less definable kind could
hardly be requested from the contributors without
also being promised by implication on the other side.
What is meant may best be explained by quoting a
letter from Mr. Edgar Rice Burroughs ; it is quoted

also as suggesting a reason for the attitude the writer
has tried to adopt in compiling this book.

In submitting to you, in accordance with your courteous
letter, my answers to your questionnaire, I wish you to know
that I am fully aware of the attitude of many scholars and
self-imagined literati toward that particular brand of death-
less literature of which I am guilty.

From past experience it is only natural that I should
assume that you may, in some degree at least, share their
views. It would seem rather remarkable to me if you did
not.

However, you have asked my assistance and I have given
considerable time and thought to my reply to your questionnaire, in which I have outlined my sincere beliefs after
mature and serious considerations.

It is occasionally the practice of critics to treat my work
with ridicule and contempt, neither of which it deserves.
If it is your purpose to draw conclusions from the answers
you receive to the questionnaires you have circulated, may
I ask of you, in my case, a fair and considerate treatment of
the subject and of me?   I do not intend by this to convey
the idea that I expect you either to agree with my views or
praise my work, but I shall appreciate it if you will treat the
former with such seriousness as my careful and conscientious
reply to your request merits.

To be brightly ironical at the expense of bestsellers
would no doubt be easy, but to yield to such an unprofitable temptation is not part of the present writer's
undertaking. The very popular novelist, as Mr.
Burroughs implies, is now commonly considered a
figure of fun by those who cannot read his works with
enthusiasm; it has occurred to the writer that it
might be more useful to take him for what he is—
partner in a relation very important for literature,
the relation, of course, that exists between novelist
and reader.   In discussing the novel which has

come to be literature it is possible to neglect all other aspects of it but that which is contained between the covers: genius can manage to exist almost independent of its background, and Henry James or Jane Austen or Emily Brontë need not move a step out of the chosen path for the sake of the age they live in. But the merely popular novels and stories which have been read by one generation and rejected by its posterity, and whose existence and influence raise questions (as explained in the Introduction) of the first importance to the student of literature—where they are concerned the issues cannot be so simplified. The popular novelist, dependent upon a public for his living, frequently making it by regular contributions to the magazines [29] (whose editors nowadays have been shown to keep a scientific finger on the public pulse), is identical with his public in background of taste and intellectual environment; he is now in the closest touch with his readers, both directly by 'fan mail' and by way of such middlemen as have been considered in the previous chapter, in a fashion and to a degree that would have surprised Emily Brontë, amused Jane Austen, and outraged Henry James. But there are so few English novelists who are artists, and it would be easy to demonstrate that the English novels which are works of art are not much more numerous than those English dramatic works which are, strictly speaking, tragedies. And when we consider that so many authors of the novels which have achieved canonisation in the text-books were popular writers earning their bread by the pen—as Defoe, Fielding, Scott, Dickens, Thackeray, Trollope, to name a few of the more prominent—it becomes obvious that no sharp dichotomy exists or can be made between the works of fiction which cultivated persons have in the past found admirable and those which have amused the uncultured. As Henry James observed after trying to define what he meant by ' the Novel ' (a): ' I am perfectly aware that to say the object of the novel is to represent life does not bring the question to a point so fine as to be uncomfortable for any one. For, after all, may not people differ infinitely as to what constitutes life—what constitutes representation? Some people, for instance, hold that Miss Austen deals with life, Miss Austen represents. Others attribute these achievements to the accomplished Ouida.'

The relation between novelist and reader can be most successfully studied by interrogating the more conscious of the two : the question, Why do you read X's novels? asked even of many hundreds of readers, yields little (the writer has tried a good deal of mild inquiry of this sort); the fact that they read X's novels and not Y's, that X's novels are doing this and not that, is more reliable evidence ; to ask X in detail what he thinks he is doing when he writes his novels is a more fruitful undertaking.

To sixty authors, as explained above, the following questionnaire was submitted :

1. To what do you attribute your success as a novelist?
2. Why do you think it is that your books are able to rival in popularity the ordinary bestseller?
3. Have you any views about the bestseller?

(a) *Partial Portraits*, p. 228.

What in your opinion makes a great bestseller (*e.g. John Halifax, Gentleman, Comin' thro' the Rye, The Sheik*)? And how can you explain the fact that most bestsellers have so brief a period of popularity?

4. Do you think there are any generalisations to be drawn from your popularity and from that of popular novelists of the past—*e.g.* Scott and Dickens? Both of these were acutely aware of their public and studied its tastes and demands; is your experience in accord? Or do you find that the creative process in you is not influenced by such factors?

5. What are the circulations of your three most popular novels? Does this fluctuate? What factors in your opinion most influence the circulation of popular novels?

6. In the course of your career have you consciously learnt from the success or otherwise of your previous novels, and modified your work accordingly? If so, in what directions and with what results?

What kinds of people do you imagine the bulk of your readers to be?

7. What kind of effect do you think the story magazines are having on the public taste? and on the novel market? What connection do you find existing between the magazine story and popular novel?

8. Have any novels or novelists in particular influenced your work to any appreciable extent? What is your favourite reading? Your favourite novelist? What caused you

to turn your attention to fiction as a profession?

9. What form does the process of writing a novel
take in your case? Please give any information you can relating to the conception,
construction, writing, production, publishing,
and advertising of your novels.

10. What particular reasons do your readers give,
when they write to you, for admiring your
work?

The twenty-five whose replies were specific enough
to base conclusions upon may be tentatively classified
with respect to their readers as:

A. ' Highbrow ' (1).

B. ' Middlebrow ' read as ' literature ' (4).

C. ' Middlebrow ' not read as ' literature,' but not
writing for the lowbrow market (3).

D. Absolute bestsellers (17).

Of these, D1, 2, and 3 refused to reply at length on
the grounds that they had no illusions about their
work, which, they said, they knew did not merit
serious scrutiny; five of D (one a writer of detective
fiction), one of C, and one of B (this writer belongs to
an older generation than the other three in class B)
explained that they deliberately wrote fiction as a
comfortable way of getting a good living ' with the
minimum of exertion,' one of D even scornfully dis-
claiming any literary pretension (' I am not a literary
cove '). These might be described as successful
journalists in fiction, peculiarly interesting since they
have set out to do deliberately what the other novelists
(who all assume or claim the status of artist) have

effected by accident; they may be presumed to have some reliable notion of how they did it.

First, to note briefly facts supporting the classification adopted above: even those most innocent of literary standards have convictions about a difference between *kinds* of novels, they are not unaware of distinctions, and within each class taste is consistent. For instance, D mostly recognise candidly that each other's novels are ' bad '—*i.e.* pernicious or contemptible as literature, but are prepared to defend their own as ' clean entertainment '; or by such an argument as ' any fundamentally clean book that tends to form the reading habit and engender within the reader a love of books is well worth its place in literature '; and they recognise as admirable classes B and C :

' The bestseller ranges from rotten primitive stuff lik- *The Sheik* and some of Hutchinson's books, to suc.. fine, delicate work as *The Bridge of San Luis Rey* or *The Constant Nymph*, and even to writers like Galsworthy and Bennett.'

While C admire B, or would like to write like the class A type of novelist, and B1 and B2 also admire such highbrow novelists as Stendhal, Proust, Dostoievsky, Henry James, Conrad, Lawrence, and Joyce, and claim to have been influenced by them, B3 and B4 admire indiscriminately A and B novelists. As one might expect, the single representative of A passes only his own kind, but for a reason to be noticed later has a certain admiration for the great bestsellers.

Again, D and C miss the point of Q. 7 :
' I think the story magazines are having, on the whole, a good effect on public taste.   There are in

England practically no magazines that have to be excluded from decent households and their general tone is definitely good.'

Or even :

' I think that story magazines are having a very good effect on public taste. The technical level of the short story is far higher in England now than it was twenty years ago.'

And :

' Story magazines do no harm to the novel-market. They educate public taste.'

While an American bestseller declares :

' I believe that anything that tends to form the reading habit must eventually improve the public taste (since the inquiring and voracious mind of man is not for long satisfied by an unvaried diet and in searching for new sustenance will seek a superior rather than an inferior pabulum), increase the demand for reading matter and, therefore, exercise a beneficial effect upon the novel market.'

The only dissentient voice comes from a writer who won her public by historical novels of some substance (founded on research) :

' The magazine story is almost without exception a commercial article. Manufactured to a formula— those stories that show any art are seldom placed in magazines.'

Bestsellers of class D have a buying public of a quarter or half a million, and in some cases of a million ; of C, upwards of a hundred thousand ; of B, twenty to thirty thousand ; and of A a steady three thousand, with greater sales of five, ten, or even fifteen thousand.[30]

Answers to Qs. 1-6 and Q. 10 throw considerable light on why novels are read to-day. Not to go deeper than necessary, people in general read novels for one or more of the following reasons :

1. To pass time not unpleasantly.
2. To obtain vicarious satisfaction or compensation for life.
3. To obtain assistance in the business of living.
4. To enrich the quality of living by extending, deepening, refining, co-ordinating experience.

It is generally recognised that the universal need to read something when not actively employed has been created by the conditions of modern life. The notes made by Mr. George Sturt [31] of the changes he himself has witnessed since 1884 in the lives of both town and country workers go a good way towards explaining this. He writes in detail of craftsmen for whose personal skill the introduction of modern methods has substituted machine-tending. He observes how the comeliness has been taken from the peasant's life and his traditional way of living broken down, the ordinary worker everywhere losing the delight that a really interesting and varied round of duties gave. The old order made reading to prevent boredom unnecessary, whereas the narrowing down of labour that specialisation has produced has changed the working day from a sequence of interests to a repetition of mechanical movements of both body and mind. Analogous changes have been going on higher up in the social scale, so that life for all classes tends now to fall sharply into two sections : the hours (far fewer than formerly [32]) taken up by occupational activities, exhausting and yet not generally possible to take pleasure in, and the increased leisure for rest and amusement. In 1909 a critic in the *New Age* (an advanced weekly) recounted some observations he had made of Mudie's subscribers (then exclusively upper middle-class)— 'rarely capable of enthusiasm.' 'Why then,' he asked, 'does the backbone put itself to the trouble of reading current fiction? The answer is that it does so, not with any artistic, spiritual, moral, or informative purpose, but simply in order to pass time. It prefers novelists among artists because the novel gives the longest surcease from ennui at the least expenditure of time and money.' [33] This is now a fair account of the reading habits of all classes, which have called forth a new kind of literature—the magazine and the corresponding bestseller, designed to be read in the face of lassitude and nervous fatigue.

The extent to which this influences writers is shown by this extract from a bestseller's reply to the questionnaire (he gives the total sales of his books in England and America as eight millions up to the end of 1929, his works selling a million copies a year).

> At present I am reading a very interesting history of the genesis and development of motion pictures, which contains a most illuminating suggestion of the attitude of the general public toward entertainment, in which category fiction falls. It has been discovered through repeated experiments that pictures that require thought for appreciation have invariably been box-office failures. The general public does not wish to think. This fact, probably more than any other, accounts for the success of my stories, for without this specific idea in mind I have, nevertheless, endeavoured to make all my descriptions so clear that each situation could be visualised readily by any reader precisely as I saw it. . . . I have

evolved, therefore, a type of fiction that may be read with the minimum of mental effort.

He adds :

> I have learned from what is known in this country as ' fan ' mail that my readers are to be found in every walk of life. A great many professional people enjoy my books because they offer the mental relaxation which they require of fiction.

Under the head of ' mental relaxation ' may be included detective stories, the enormous popularity of which (like the passion for solving cross-word puzzles) seems to show that for the reader of to-day a not unpleasurable way of relaxing is to exercise the ratiocinative faculties on a minor non-personal problem. It is chiefly this use of fiction that has commercialised novel-writing, so that famous authors of bestsellers are run as limited companies with a factory called ' Edgar Rice Burroughs, Inc.' or ' Elinor Glyn Ltd.' The effect of an inordinate addiction to light reading was known (mainly by repute) to the nineteenth century; it came under the head of ' dissipation,' [34] and to read novels, as to drink wine, in the morning was far into the century a sign of vice, while to devote a fixed time to solid reading was a matter of conscience. So a self-denying age guarded its sobriety, but there is no such restriction now even among the professionally cultured. It is quite common to meet educated people who confess to having eight or more hours a day to spend in reading—what else can one do?—and by reading they mean novels, periodicals, and perhaps ' belles-lettres.' They will explain that they can read anything from the *Strand Magazine* to *Point Counter Point*, and if questioned

admit to reading indiscriminately and rarely if ever
re-reading. A suggestion that some novels are
intrinsically more worth reading than the rest calls
forth the reaction against an implied 'highbrow'
attitude, yet a similar assertion about poetry will not be
questioned, for though poetry is no longer read it has
a traditional sanction. The feeling that fiction is only
meant to entertain (in the sense in which the popular
novelist above uses 'entertainment') explains such a
common complaint as: 'Virginia Woolf? Why, you
can't read her unless your mind is absolutely fresh!'
It is relevant to note here that the author of detective
novels consulted receives letters chiefly from 'school-
boys, scientific men, clergymen, lawyers, and business
men generally,' and adds 'I think I am read more by
the upper classes than the lower classes and by men
more than women.' The social orders named here as
forming the backbone of the detective-story public
are those who in the last century would have been the
guardians of the public conscience in the matter of
mental self-indulgence.

The second reason accounts for the vast sales of the
great bestsellers in contrast to the moderate success
of merely popular novels. An illusion of life so vivid
that one can be persuaded of its reality is given by
fiction alone; poets, painters, and composers are not
known to receive 'fan mail' on the strength of their
work; the stage and cinema can compete, but their
attraction tends to centre on the personality of the
actor or 'star' irrespective of the plot. It is wish-
fulfilment in various forms that the modern bestseller
and magazine story provide, though it is never quite
so simple as this suggests. Take the case of the novel

which deals in romantic action : the classical instance—
The Three Musketeers—at once springs to mind.   Its
modern equivalent, *Beau Geste* and its successors,
have sold half a million each since *Beau Geste* appeared
in 1924.   But whereas Dumas has commonly served
as a stage in the normal boy's development, the works
of P. C. Wren are now the reading of adults, for whom
they are doing something more than kill time or
assuage a craving for adventure.   They serve to
stabilise a certain attitude, confirm certain prejudices,
as the following extracts from their author's reply
show :

> The bulk of my readers are the cleanly-minded virile
> outdoor sort of people of both sexes, and the books are
> widely read in the Army, the Navy, the Universities, the
> Public Schools, and the Clubs. . . . My favourite reading
> is the memoirs of people who have done things, and I admit,
> without shame, that my favourite novelists are Hergesheimer,
> A. E. W. Mason, Conrad and R. L. Stevenson. . . .
> Although I now make a good many thousands per annum, I
> still am not a ' professional novelist,' nor, as I have said, a
> long-haired literary cove.   I prefer the short-haired executive
> type.
> When the round well-varnished tale is finished, I send it
> to ' Mr. John Murray.'   The late Sir John Murray, Colonel
> John Murray, Lord Gorell and the other partners, are sports-
> men and gentlemen who have somehow strayed into the
> muddy paths of commerce, and somehow contrived to remain
> sportsmen and gentlemen and jolly good business men as well.

The novels of Scott and Dumas had a different
mentality behind them, that might perhaps not absurdly
be described as cultured ; at least it could be said of
them that their authors did not despise the profession
of letters and that what they wrote was not unrelated
to literature.   The difference between literature and

'clean entertainment' for 'the cleanly-minded virile sort of people' with 'tone definitely good' lies perhaps as much in the difference between the nineteenth-century public and the public of the twentieth century as in the novelists themselves. This is brought out in the reply to Q. 2 of another bestseller (whose books sell a million copies a year):

> The continued success of my books may lie in the fact that I write them primarily to please myself, upon the theory that I am a normal man and, therefore, that that which entertains me will entertain millions of others similar to me. My mind, being slightly impatient as I conceive the modern mind to be, tires of long descriptions, of minute character delineations, of lengthy moralising and of tiresome descriptions of scenery; therefore, in fiction, I desire action and so, in my novels, I subordinate all else to action.

> My success may be also partially attributable to the fact that I make no conscious effort to write down to one class or up to another, but to use English, whether good or bad, that is easily understandable, and to draw action pictures which permit my reader to visualise scenes without great effort.

The nature of that which entertains him and millions similar to him is significant:

> It was my custom as a child, and in fact it has been all my life, to day-dream romantic stories filled with action and adventure. Many of my written stories are based upon these. What suggested them, I do not know.

> It is this general atmosphere of plausibility about even my most highly imaginative stories that seems to arouse and hold the interest of the reader, a fact which is based upon the theory that readers enjoy those situations in which they may readily visualise themselves as taking a principal and heroic part.

The form of self-indulgence specified here [35] accounts for the immense success of novels like *The*

Way of an Eagle, The Sheik, The Blue Lagoon, a more detrimental diet than the detective story in so far as a habit of fantasying will lead to maladjustment in actual life.

Ten of the fourteen novelists advertised by the 3d. circulating library on p. 8 specialise in fantasy-spinning. The titles of the works of two of them are representative : *Sweet Life, The Desert Dreamers, The Lure of the Desert, Sands of Gold, The City of Palms, Wild Heart of Youth, The Mirage of the Dawn, The Golden Journey, East o' the Sun, The Barbarian Lover, The Vision of Desire, The Moon out of Reach, The Lamp of Fate, The Splendid Folly, The House of Dreams-Come-True.* The windows of any bookshop and newsagent are full of two-shilling novels with similar titles. The hero of *The Barbarian Lover* constantly declares ' It's the big, primitive things that count,' and demands that his aristocratic fiancée should ' live a primitive life ' with him in Rhodesia. When she refuses he asks incredulously, ' Do you mean that you're not willing to come with me—into the desert? ... I thought we should go together, man and mate, out into the wide, clean spaces of the world, and build our life there as men and women have done before, and make a big thing of it.' This is a fair specimen of the kind of fiction classed as day-dreaming. (Cf. too in this connection the romantic names on suburban gate-posts.) Since all the great names in popular fiction of this generation and many of those in the last generation (Marie Corelli, Florence Barclay, Ethel M. Dell, Edgar Rice Burroughs, Gene Stratton Porter) have been made on this kind of fiction, we have here important evidence of the way in which the leisure of the majority is being used and is likely to be used in the future.

The cinema, one notices, provides the same satisfaction, and in such a form as might cut out the best-seller if it were not for two considerations which together are likely to make the popular novelist's livelihood safe for at least a generation or two. True, the cinema has several advantages over the novel: the reader has not to make the effort of translating words into images—that is done for him even more effectively than by the author of *Tarzan* just quoted ; moreover, attending the cinema, like listening to the gramophone or wireless, is a passive and social amusement, whereas, since reading aloud in the family circle is no longer practised, fiction is a solitary pleasure, and the public to-day prefers communal to private pastimes. Indeed, it is only the exceptional character that can tolerate solitude and silence, distressing to modern nerves. The British Broadcasting Company reports that in 1930 every other home had a wireless set,[36] which in practice means not that a nation of music-lovers has sprung up, but that in any town two out of three houses one passes in the evening are reading and talking with the support of a loud speaker.[37] On the other hand, there is first of all the acquired reading habit whose strength has been previously demonstrated. The hold it has on the present generation, brought up on a diet of morning and evening newspaper, magazine and circulating library, is remarked in a speech made by a former Minister of Education in 1927 (*a*):

(*a*) Lord Eustace Percy to the Joint Session of the Associated Booksellers and National Book Council, July 16th, 1927.

Our purpose is not to create or stimulate the reading habit. Nearly every one in this country already has the habit and has it very badly. It has been discovered that the greatest ' mind opiate ' in the world is carrying the eye along a certain number of printed lines in succession. . . . The habit of reading is one of the most interesting psychological features of the present day. Discomfort and exhaustion seem only to increase the need for the printed word. A friend, in describing the advance of one of the columns in East Africa during the war, has remarked how his men, sitting drenched and almost without food round the camp fire, would pass from hand to hand a scrap of a magazine cover, in order that each man might rest his eyes for a moment on the printed word. One of the great evils of present-day reading is that it discourages thought.

Similarly it was noticed in France that men coming from the trenches who had been deprived of reading matter for some short while would, however weary, seize on any kind of book or periodical or even a piece of newspaper to satisfy the same craving. This the film—still more the ' talkie,' which does not even offer captions—is unlikely to displace for at least another generation, though the increase in the rate of change of habits that the last thirty years shows makes even this not impossible. The effect of listening-in alone might be to substitute for a strong mechanical habit a stronger passive habit, as it has done in the typical Middle Western community discussed in *Middletown*, where the investigators were told ' I use time evenings listening in that I used to spend in reading.' It is more possible that (besides the novel for highbrows) newspapers and magazines might remain to satisfy a persistent reading habit and the popular novel ultimately lapse. Mr. Compton Mackenzie, in answering Q. 4, puts forward some reasons for adopting this hypothesis :

This is a particularly difficult period for the professional novelist because the weekly succession of isolated master-pieces by brilliant amateurs is almost more than he can stand up to. Scott and Dickens never had to read the publisher's advertisements in the *Sunday Times* and the *Observer*. I have counted as many as fifteen works of genius published in one week. Allowing for the enthusiastic exaggeration of jaded reviewers who are always apt to overpraise a first novel, we may admit that a large number of really good novels are published every year; but if one studies the literary output it soon becomes evident that scarcely one of these brilliant creatures possesses any staying power. Two or three books are produced from personal experience and then he seems to fade out. I imagine that during the next fifty years or so the novel will only be kept alive by these more or less isolated efforts. I am convinced that the day of the professional novelist is dead, for as soon as he has done one or two books that neither the cinema nor wireless can do better, he will not be wanted as a mere entertainer, because there will be enough, and too much, to entertain the world, and his only chance will be to become a journalist and play his part in the ephemeral entertainment that the increasing rapidity of existence is already demanding. Even now a clever young man writes a couple of novels as a way to join the staff of the *Daily Mail* or *Daily Express*. Novel writing will soon be nothing but a literary apprenticeship.

Nevertheless the chief reason in favour of the best-seller's survival is that it does provide compensation for life more effectively than the cinema does at present or is ever likely to do.[38] The substitution for village and small town communities of cities composed of units whose main contact with each other outside the home is in the dance-hall, the cinema, the theatre, social but not co-operative amusements,[39] has left only fiction to fill the gap.   It offers ideal companionship to the reader by its uniquely compelling illusion of a life in which sympathetic characters of a convincing verisimilitude touch off the warmer emotional responses.   Quotations from readers' letters that D novelists gave in answer to Q. 10 show that fiction for very many people is a means of easing a desolating sense of isolation and compensates for the poverty of their emotional lives :

> You have the power by your exquisite sympathy of making your characters *live*.   They become one's friends.

> All the people who live in the pages of your work are so intensely real.   One knows them as friends.

> I am not at all a sentimental person, but I love novels like yours, which take one among big-hearted people who live interesting lives and make their corner of the world happier than it might otherwise be.   One reads numbers of clever novels, perhaps more than once; but on closing the pages one forgets that the people exist.   They have served their turn.   But one by no means forgets yours.   They are real, very lovable people who stay by one as friends and give one real help.

> Your characters are so human that they live with me as friends. . . . They are all *real men*, with real men's temptations and difficulties, and the way in which they face these temptations leaves a very deep impression.

and one of the most popular women writers reported simply ' Of course they all say " How real ! " ' while another, not much less popular, replied :

> I imagine the bulk of my readers to be fairly simple people (mostly women) who want to read of romance in a form not incompatible with their own opportunities.   People usually give as their kind reasons for liking my work (*a*) That I am ' human,' (*b*) Seem to ' understand.'

This readiness to respond to ' characters ' will bear some investigation. It almost entirely explains the undoubted popular appeal which Shakespeare makes, even to an uneducated public incapable of reading poetry. The fascination his plays have had for various bestsellers is notorious and genuine; for them, indeed for most people, Shakespeare is the ' creator ' of characters, and they translate his dramas into novels, so that nearly all Shakespearian criticism is a discussion of the supposititious lives of the dramatis personae. This kind of interest leads critics to compare the merits of novelists by the size of the portrait gallery each has given to the world.

Apparently all a novelist need do is to provide bold outlines, and the reader will co-operate to persuade himself that he is in contact with ' real people.' Novelists of class D, who both share their readers' tastes and exploit them (even if unconsciously), are aware of this :

> To my mind an author can have no greater compliment paid to him or to her than to be told that his or her characters appear to the reader *real people*. I have, in fact, written many stories with no plot or outline in mind, starting out with a character and following him rather than leading him through an entire story, letting him make his contacts with other characters and introducing him into situations after the manner of real life.

> I prefer to be seized by a character [rather than by a theme] or a purely character-situation that allows scope for development along several different lines. Such a book may be faulty in *form*, but its elasticity may give it a more spontaneous (if untidy) effect of life. My chief *and all-absorbing* concern is for the characters: to *see* them vividly, to *feel* them from many points of view (their own and the other characters'),

to convey them to the readers—*not* by analysis but by direct emotional contagion.

And the last-quoted writer gives the reason of her reader's appreciation as amounting to 'Power to create characters that *live* and remain with them as friends, so that they constantly write about them to me as if they're alive and ask for more news of them!'

It is not of course only the bestseller who could say, as one does, 'The creating of characters in my world remains a constant source of fascination to me'; Jane Austen is known to have taken a similar delight in her 'people.' But the highbrow novelist who 'creates' characters at all is apt to produce personalities that do not obey the literary agent's rule ('The principal characters must be likeable. They must be human'), that do not lend themselves to fantasying but cause disturbing repercussions in the reader's emotional make-up. Worse still, it is a fact that many highbrow novelists do not choose even to outline plausible characters, and this expectation of meeting recognisable people in fiction, amounting now to a conviction that the novelist's first duty is to provide them, is generally at the bottom of failure to respond to the finer novels. The confusion of fiction with life and the demand that fiction should compensate for life prevents enjoyment of Emily Brontë and Jane Austen, among others (*Jane Eyre* was admitted to be literature long before *Wuthering Heights*), and nowadays of D. H. Lawrence and T. F. Powys; it causes the resentful bewilderment one notices in the objections to such novelists as Virginia Woolf and Henry James, who do not offer anything in the nature of ' character.' The popular author in class D quoted above writes in answer to Q. 8 :

Jane Austen is antipathetic to me: but I admired Charlotte Brontë when younger. Of comparative moderns I admire Hugh Walpole and Anne Douglas Sedgwick. Virginia Woolf fascinates but irritates me, an effect I find she has on a good many readers. Her genius is of course undeniable.

This *may* be due to the demands Mrs. Woolf makes on the reader in the way of mental alertness, suppleness, and concentration, but assume for the moment on the strength of the last sentence that this is not so. The reader not prepared to readjust himself to the technique of *Mrs. Dalloway* or *To the Lighthouse* will get very little return for the energy he must lay out in wrestling with those involved periods. He is repaid by none of the obvious satisfactions he expects from a novel—no friendly characters, no reassuring conviction that life is as he wants to believe it, no glow of companionship or stirring relation of action. All he gets is an impression of sensuous beauty as his eye helplessly picks out clumps of words without clearly following the sense; it is true this is all the average reader of poetry or Shakespeare gets (the latter throwing in ' character ' and ' action ' too), still he knows this is the function of poetry and demands no more. But he refuses to allow a novel to act on him as ' poetry,' hence his annoyance. He is dimly aware of having missed the point and feels cheated, or at best impressed but irritated like the authoress just cited. The same holds for the failure to read Henry James, except that as most readers are unable to stand the strain of his abstract, tortuous idiom, they give up at once.

In fact, the ordinary reader is content with the general directions for what his literary training recognises as appropriate, and his imagination will do the rest. The bestseller who has collected for her ' Indian ' novels an enthusiastic public of a quarter of a million who write to tell her how ' real ' and ' true to life ' her Indian characters are, admits in some bewilderment : ' I don't know how or why I am so successful in getting the Indian quality of my characters so true. I have really known very few Indians : one didn't know them in my day. It is some sort of sympathetic insight that guides me—and guides me right.' The same public leaves *Passage to India* (where instead of the Kipling native and the right kind of Anglo-Indian there is evident a first-class critical mind at work on the human situation) on the shelves of the libraries ; the book is felt to be ' unpleasant.'

But there is something else to the great names of popular fiction—Marie Corelli, Florence Barclay, Ethel M. Dell, Gene Stratton Porter, Hall Caine—than sympathetic characters, a stirring tale, and absence of the disquieting. Even the most critical reader who brings only an ironical appreciation to their work cannot avoid noticing a certain power, the secret of their success with the majority. Bad writing, false sentiment, sheer silliness, and a preposterous narrative are all carried along by the magnificent vitality of the author, as they are in *Jane Eyre*. Charlotte Brontë, one cannot but feel after comparing her early work with modern bestsellers, was only unlike them in being fortunate in her circumstances, which gave her a cultured background, and in the age in which she lived, which did not get between her and her spon-

taneities.   It is this power that the representative of
class A recognises when he says that ' *The Rosary* will
probably live,[40] because its power is very uncommon—
as uncommon, on its lower plane, as the power of
Wuthering Heights,' and refers with respect to ' Mrs.
Barclay, who was undoubtedly a great writer *on her
plane*—Shakespeare of the servants' hall. Her power
is terrific—at any rate in *The Rosary*. I had infinitely
rather have written *The Rosary* than *The Forsyte Saga*,
for example.' This is the fascinated envy of an ever-
intellectual novelist for the lower organism that
exudes vital energy as richly as a manure heap.   Unfortunately the power of these writers is not harnessed
in the service of literature ; they are what their age
has made them, and though ' education ' might have
turned Marie Corelli into a Mrs. Humphry Ward
or Gene Stratton Porter into an H. G. Wells, yet no
' education ' could have given Mrs. Humphry Ward's
novels the qualities which make Maria Edgeworth's
best work interesting to the highbrow of to-day or
could have made Mr. Wells' novels as acceptable to
such a reader as Mrs. Gaskell's. Mrs. Gaskell and
Maria Edgeworth were not geniuses, they had nothing
like the natural talent and range of interests of Mr.
Wells and Mrs. Humphry Ward, they have very little
of the emotional drive and luxuriant vitality of Marie
Corelli and Gene Stratton Porter, but they had the
inestimable benefits of a culture such as no modern
writer is born to but must struggle for as best he can,
unaided, or else accept the materials the age offers.
The materials that the contemporary bestseller finds to
hand have been discussed in Chapter II., and to these
it is necessary to add the idiom and kinds of appeal

exploited by modern advertising and the cinema and
by religious organisations such as the Y.M.C.A. and
the Church Publicity Section (a), and Rotary.

What these highly popular novelists have won their
reputation by, in fact, is this terrific vitality set to
turn the machinery of morality.   In a novel by Marie
Corelli, Hall Caine, Florence Barclay, Gene Stratton
Porter, the author is genuinely preoccupied with
ethical problems, whatever side attractions there may
be in the way of unconscious pornography and
excuses for day-dreaming.   (One has only to read
their memoirs and biographies [41] to realise this, and
to realise also that they were in many ways remarkable persons.)   Unfortunately, since the author, for
reasons already explained, has been educated neither
in thinking nor in feeling, the moral passion exhibited is fatally crude; fatally only by the standards
of the sophisticated, however, for there is a large
and increasing public of suitable readers.   By a
' suitable ' reader is meant one who can read a novel
in the spirit in which it was written, because at a
corresponding stage of development to the author.
*The Rosary, The Christian, The Sorrows of Satan, The
Harvester*, have aroused such torrents of enthusiasm
because they excite in the ordinary person an emotional
activity for which there is no scope in his life.   These
novels will all be found to make play with the key
words of the emotional vocabulary which provoke the
vague warm surges of feeling associated with religion
and religion substitutes—*e.g.* life, death, love, good,
evil, sin, home, mother, noble, gallant, purity, honour.
These responses can be touched off with a dangerous

(a) Which produces the Wayside Pulpit mottoes.

ease—every self-aware person finds that he has to
train himself from adolescence in withstanding them—
and there is evidently a vast public that derives great
pleasure from reacting in this way.   This vocabulary as
used by bestsellers is not quite the everyday one; it is
analogous to a suit of Sunday clothes, carrying with it
a sense of larger issues; it gives the reader a feeling
of being helped, of being in touch with ideals.[42]
As Mr. P. C. Wren writes (not ironically): ' The
great bestseller contains a searching appeal to the
honest simple feelings and "all that is best" in the
great heart of the great public.'   In a sense this is
true.   Without playing upon those readily released
responses a novelist to-day can hardly hope to reach
the great public (unless he has discovered how to tap
the newspaper appeals—*e.g.* Nat Gould, the racing
news; Edgar Wallace, crime).   The essential features
of this success are summarised in *The Life of Florence
L. Barclay*—By One of Her Daughters :

> She was out to supply her fellow men with joy, refresh-
> ment, inspiration.   She was not out to make art for art's sake,
> or to perform a literary *tour de force*, or to rival the makers
> of fiction of the past.   The busy men and women who form
> the majority of the reading public, and who read fiction by
> way of relaxation and enjoyment, do not desire to have pro-
> ductions of literary ' art ' supplied to them, that their critical
> faculties may be exercised and their minds educated to a
> precise valuation of dramatic form, powerful realism, high
> tragedy.   They ask merely to be pleased, rested, interested,
> amused, inspired to a more living faith in the beauty of human
> affection and the goodness of God.

The age of Marie Corelli and Hall Caine, for
reasons that will be discussed in Part II., was the first
to hit on the bestseller formula.   In the second genera-

tion their post-war successors have taken over their evangelism and work the spiritual-emotional responses in a more dubious fashion. The high-level reader of Marie Corelli and Mrs. Barclay is impelled to laugh, so ridiculously inadequate to the issues raised is the equipment of the mind that resolutely tackles them, and, on the other hand, so absurdly out of proportion is the energy expended to the objects that aroused it (for instance, in Marie Corelli's novels, female smoking and low-cut gowns). But the moral passion, though it may be a nuisance, is at least a respectable one ; at worst it could be accused of promoting the complacent virtue that infuriates the ungodly. The writings of Gilbert Frankau and Warwick Deeping (to take the most striking cases of contemporary bestsellers) are not merely doing this. A few extracts will make this plain. They are representative of the tone of the novels from which they come :

'That's the new Cenotaph,' said Cranston; and he uncovered his head. . . . 'My men!' he thought, simply as a child; and again, visualising their haggard faces, 'my men ! ' (a)

All the way from Bloomsbury to Portland Place, that note, those unborn children beckoned to him: so that he understood, almost with the suddenness of revelation, his inward self; so that this subconscious need became, for the first time, conscious, a living force in his soul. ' Art ! ' ran his revelation. ' You console yourself with it, as a child consoles itself for unkindness with a toy. The woman of your first portrait ! You prick yourself with her memory—as a drug-fiend pricks himself with the morphia needle—to forget that there can be no other woman, that you are what you are, a man reft of his life-force, no man at all.' (b)

(a) Gilbert Frankau, *Gerald Cranston's Lady* (1923).
(b) Gilbert Frankau, *Life—and Erica.*

For Sorrell still kept his trousers creased, nor had he reached that state of mind when a man can contemplate with unaffected naturalness the handling of his own luggage. There were still things he did and did not do. He was a gentleman. True, Society had come near to pushing him off the shelf of his class-consciousness into the welter of the casual and the unemployed, but, though hanging by his own hands, he had refused to drop. [He has accepted a post with an antique dealer.] 'He may want us to live over-over the shop.' 'Over-over the shop.' Yes, the word had cost him an effort. 'Captain Sorrell, M.C.' ['Before the war he had sat at a desk and helped to conduct a business.'] (a)

This for the sensitive minority is no laughing matter: these novelists are read by the governing classes as well as by the masses, and they impinge directly on the world of the minority, menacing the standards by which they live. And whereas their forerunners were innocent of malice, devoting themselves to assuring their readers of 'the beauty of human affection and the goodness of God,' these writers are using the technique of Marie Corelli and Mrs. Barclay to work upon and solidify herd prejudice and to debase the emotional currency by touching grossly on fine issues. In this, as we have noticed earlier, they are at one with their background. They also exhibit a persistent hostility to the world of letters which is quite unprecedented.[43] They are uneasily aware of the existence of other standards by which their work is despised, and they are not supported by the sense of vocation that accounts for the assurance of their forerunners. They are to be observed defending their own as in some way better or more genuine than mere 'clever' work:

(a) Warwick Deeping, *Sorrell and Son* (1925).

Lance smiled; he was smiling at the Lance of yesterday, and looking with a ruthless self-knowledge at the Lance of to-morrow. ' Till he took me in hand,' he reflected, ' I was just damned clever, a precious young highbrow. I suppose he taught me to feel.' (a)

After all, what was a burnt book at five and twenty? Better a burnt book at that age than a charred cleverness at five and forty. For if Lance was destined to write the great stuff that touches the heart of the world—then he—Lance— must have the heart to do it. No use being just damned clever (b).

Well, a good novel is real, far more significant than most of the highbrow stuff—so called (c).

and this sentiment has become common—almost any copy of the more popular literary journals and story magazines will prove this. For example, Gilbert Frankau writing in the *Daily Mail* (1926) declares, ' Authorship is not so much a function of the brain as it is of the heart. And the heart is a universal organ.' Similarly, bestsellers replied indignantly to Q. 3 :

Even if many of them [bestsellers] are not works of art, they are on the whole (except the very bad ones) closer to the fundamentals of life and of romance than much of the cleverer stuff that springs mainly from the brain and so fails to reach the *heart*.

Technique is not one of the living qualities and the novel is primarily concerned with *life*. The core quality of the born novelist is *human*, not literary.

This antithesis between a novel of the heart and a novel of the brain and the exaltation of the former at the expense of the latter is a noticeable feature of the

(a) Warwick Deeping, *Old Pybus* (1928).　　　　(b) *Ibid.*
(c) Warwick Deeping, *Sorrell and Son* (1925).

contemporary bestseller; it is perhaps not surprising
that the readers should share it.

The reader of the great bestsellers goes to them
partly to be confirmed in his prejudices and ' uplifted,'
as the novelist-hero of one of Mrs. Barclay's books
explains : ' " The thing of first importance is to
uplift your readers; to raise their ideals; to leave
them with a sense of hopefulness, which shall arouse
within them a brave optimism such as inspired
Browning's oft-quoted noble lines." ' The reader
of the C class of novelists is looking for something
in effect not so very different. It has been described
earlier as desire to obtain assistance in the business
of living, formerly the function of religion. Defoe's
readers, for instance, untroubled by social problems
and with a Puritan code behind them, only asked
of the novel that it should reflect their own interests
without conflicting with the demands of their morality.
With the decline of religious authority and of the
satisfaction obtainable from first-hand living the
novel has come to mean a great deal more for all those
in any way inclined to serious-mindedness. And as a
result of the stratification of taste noticed earlier, this
demand is met at different levels : the suitable reader of
This Freedom and of *The Middle of the Road* and of
Ann Veronica are alike in very little but a genuine sense
of something wrong with the world. They expect the
novelist to answer real questions (in the form of What
should I . . . ? and How should I . . . ? and Is it
right to . . . ?)—in effect, to help them manage their
lives by dramatising their problems and so offering a
solution, by lending his support to their code of
feeling and generally by expressing their own half-

conscious or perplexed ' feelings about ' Life. The
case of *The Middle of the Road* illustrates this. First
published in November 1922, it had been reprinted
twenty-two times by February 1925; on the jacket
of the uniform edition we read, ' In days to come Sir
Philip will be remembered as a novelist of the people
whose stories are imbued with sincerity and an
optimism that the man in the street finds particularly
comforting. He writes in and of a time when the
world seems a little mad, and his sanity, his belief in
the vast possibilities of his own age, and lastly his
sympathy for and understanding of youth, make him
a writer whose books are treasured by all who would
know more intimately of the thoughts and ideals
animating the rising generation.' The novel deals
with all the problems that might be supposed to have
existed for the man in the street in the years immediately after the war, and the plot consists of a
simple linking together of them—the problems of
France, Ireland, Germany, Russia, ex-service men,
post-war morality, class-consciousness, marriage,
family life, and socialism. The title is symbolic of the
suggested solution. The work is done with a decent
honesty; so is the work of Mr. A. S. M. Hutchinson
and Mr. H. G. Wells. These writers are all ' sincere,'
that is convinced of the integrity of their intentions
and useful as far as a certain lack of awareness and
crudeness of sensibility allow. Indeed, it cannot be
doubted that in various degrees they are making for
enlightenment and, in a confused way, for more desirable (but not finer) feeling. They have a wide public
and are doing a very necessary work in a society of
dwellers on a rising series of plateaux, the work of

keeping the lower levels posted with news of what is
stirring higher up. The rate at which cultural news
penetrates from one level to another is surprisingly
slow : ideas and modes of feeling which were commonplace among the intelligentsia before the war are still
filtering through to the masses by way of the plays of
Shaw and Galsworthy and the novels of Wells and Sir
Philip Gibbs. Such work must be done in order that
some kind of communication may be kept up, and only
the novel can do it, for, as we have seen, the general
reading public touches nothing more serious than the
novel or newspaper. A pertinent objection is that the
process necessitates a simplification of the issues that
lets slip the essentials and leaves only some unmeaning
and often misleading facts. Hence this kind of novel
dies as soon as it has begun to date; the work of Shaw
and Wells and of their equivalents for the lower levels
must be done afresh twice a generation—*Robert
Elsmere* (a) and *The Heavenly Twins* (b) are long forgotten though they caused mighty reverberations in
their day, and as the A novelist observes, ' *Tono-Bungay*
was an admirable book in 1912 or whenever it came
out (c). It is now simply non-existent.' Non-existent,
that is, for the intelligentsia, but one has only to in-
spect a circulating library shelf full of D novels to see
that the bestseller public would still consider *Tono-
Bungay* and *Ann Veronica* 'advanced' and painfully
' modern.' [44] The bestsellers of the intelligentsia are
all too frequently of this class : *The Way of All Flesh* is
now seen to have been not a great novel but a useful
one, and its successor, *Death of a Hero*, is repeating

(a) Mrs. Humphry Ward (1888).
(b) Sarah Grand (1893).   (c) Actually, 1909.

Butler's services for a post-war generation very much more crudely.

These authors who act as communication officers resent the associations attached to ' bestseller,' and claim to be serious writers promoting the truth.   This is from a reply to the questionnaire by a C novelist :

> Personally I object very strongly to being called a ' bestseller ' as though my novels owed their success to some trick of pleasing the popular mind.   I am no more of a bestseller than John Galsworthy, Hugh Walpole, or the authors of such successful novels as *The Constant Nymph*, *Portrait in a Mirror*, *All Quiet on the Western Front*, *The Bridge of San Luis Rey* or *Sorrell and Son*, to name a few recent successes.   And you will see by that short list that the reading public buys or mostly borrows books that cannot come under any definite description such as ' mawkish sentiment,' ' romance,' or ' realism.' My own view is that such freak sales as those of *The Sheik* are not representative of the general reading public of average intelligence—a public which is steadily growing larger and more critical.
>
> The moderate success of my own novels, none of which has attained a freak sale, is due I believe to my interest in contemporary life and post-war problems with which I have dealt sincerely and sympathetically with a fair amount of experience among different types of humanity in England and Europe.   For instance, my most successful novel, *The Middle of the Road*, which has sold 97,000 copies, deals with the problem of the ex-officer and the conditions of life after the war in England, Ireland, France, Germany, and Russia. I suppose people read it because they wanted to know certain things I happened to be able to tell them, and because I dramatised this post-war world and tried to show the way out from hatred and conflict.   Most of my novels, indeed all of them except one (I mean those written after the war), have been a kind of social history, revealing as far as I could the thoughts and character and difficulties and problems of the younger crowd to-day and their challenge to the old traditions.   I

never think of my public when I am writing a novel, nor do I modify my views or style to please those whom I imagine to be my readers. I just try to tell my story and get as much truth into it as happens to be in my own mind and mood. As it happens, I get large numbers of letters from my readers, and they are of all classes and types, both men and women— ex-service men, miners, settlers in the Dominions, city clerks, professors, scientists, students, the mothers of the younger generation, the fathers of grown-up daughters, the daughters themselves, American university girls, German officers, British officers, and all sorts of people worrying about modern ideas and their own attitudes to life.

I am honestly convinced that there is a very great reading public at the present time eager to read any novel which reveals or seems to reveal some key to the riddle of the human mind, which draws the veil aside from some aspect of life, which unlocks secret cupboards, and which gives them a sense of getting closer to truth. The younger crowd will not shirk any kind of coarseness as in *All Quiet on the Western Front* if it seems to bring them nearer to things they want to know—this ' truth ' for which they are looking.

It has still to be shown where the literary novel (class B) and the highbrow reader come in. In reading any novel one is for the time being living at the level of the writer ; one can with justice say ' This is how life appears to him, these are his interests, this is the nature of his sensibility.' And because of the vivid reality of fiction the novel takes its place eventually in the body of one's experience (one can see this process at work in the unconscious testimonials on p. 58). It would seem desirable that an influence so highly formative should not be abused ; some evidence has been offered to show that at present in its better-known forms it is not being handled to beneficial ends. The best that the novel can do, it may be suggested, is not to offer a refuge from actual life but to help the reader to deal less inadequately with it; the novel can deepen, extend, and refine experience by allowing the reader to live at the expense of an unusually intelligent and sensitive mind, by giving him access to a finer code than his own. But this, we have seen, the popular novels of the age do not do. On the contrary, they substitute an emotional code which, as Part II. will try to show, is actually inferior to the traditional code of the illiterate and which helps to make a social atmosphere un-favourable to the aspirations of the minority. They actually get in the way of genuine feeling and responsible thinking by creating cheap mechanical responses and by throwing their weight on the side of social, national, and herd prejudices. The most popular contemporary fiction, it has been shown, unfits its readers for any novel that demands readjust-ment.[45] Take a couple of quotations in answer to Q. 10 from D novelists' readers :

> I've read on and off such a lot of morbid modern analytical stuff that your books come to me like a breath of your own heather and pines. There is a saneness, a wholesome sin-cerity about them—a tonic effect that no mere clever novel can produce.

> It is pure mental refreshment to read a book of yours: the *rightness* of everything as against the *jars* one gets in so many modern books that are supposed to be good.

These people clearly mistake the relief of meeting the expected, and being given the desired picture of life, for the exhilarating shock that a novel coming from a first-class fully-aware mind gives. But take a more subtle case. The intelligent educated reader who happens not to have given himself an explicitly literary training (and the bulk of the cultured class are now of this kind) is in the same plight. A letter received from such a reader explains—

> what the cheaper forms of literature really do achieve for those to whom they appeal. (Speaking as one of the herd to whom Priestley and Walpole have meant a good deal, these last five years, and Eliot and Lawrence practically nil, and who can quite honestly read P. G. Wodehouse with profit) I am not sure that you do not underestimate the extent to which the existence of any real channel of 'communication' between any artist and his public depends on his managing a symbolisation of something which was previously the property of that public: in this sense the crime of 'giving the public what it wants' has another and not necessarily evil meaning (though this does not justify the usual or Northcliffe idea of doing so). I think the intrinsic qualities of a work of art are impotent unless they can symbolise, reflect, and focus in a convenient form, something that is already to some extent present in the mind of the man who hears, sees, or reads the work. Thus any art that I appreciate appeals because it symbolises (not necessarily formulates explicitly) something that is already in my fund of experience. That is why a writer like Walpole, who is probably not sensitive to more than the common doings of rather common people, is to me a very great man, whose greatness is never really likely to be approached by artists whose work can only symbolise, or evoke the response of, a sensitivity that I and the vast majority have never experienced. I have been enormously impressed by Priestley's latest book because, I think, it succeeds in symbolising, and thus coheres and concentrates, some knowledge I already had in a dim and confused way, e.g. that most people, as uneducated as myself, are a curious mixture of the comic, the pathetic, and the tragic, are moved chiefly by little things of which they ought to take no notice, are preoccupied constantly and frequently inspired or terrified, by the unnecessary, the trivial and the accidental, and have no conscious sense of values about anything, and most of all dislike trying to think about anything subtle.

It is no fault of his but of his age. The literary novel, arranged not to disturb the prejudices of the educated, is providing him only with a variety of the bestseller. For the crude power of the bestseller the literary novelists substitute a more civilised tone; the temperature of their writing is slightly below instead of a good deal above normal; they deal in the right kind of humour (the *Punch* kind), and are the best fellows in the world. The arguments used by the correspondent above, that what these novelists do for him is essentially the same as what the 'artist' does for the highbrow, will not bear consideration. To think of such works as *The Forsyte Saga, Hans Frost, The Good Companions, No Love, The English Miss, Rogue Herries, Our Mr. Dormer (a)*, and then of the living achievements of contemporary novelists—*Sons and Lovers, Ulysses, To the Lighthouse, Mr. Weston's Good Wine, Passage to India, St. Mawr (b)*, is to realise this. A convincing comparison can only be made in terms of minute particulars and will be attempted in due course (in Part III.). It can only be said here that for the trained critic there can be no doubt that the first group betray either a faked sensibility or else a suggestive insensitiveness to the life round them, a lack of discrimination and the functioning of a second-rate mind. There is space here for but a few general indications: for instance, the quality of the irony exhibited in *The Forsyte Saga* compared with the free play of ironical intelligence in *Passage to India* and *To the Lighthouse*; the highly charged pulsating prose of Virginia Woolf's later manner and

(a) By John Galsworthy, Hugh Walpole, J. B. Priestley, David Garnett, R. H. Mottram, Hugh Walpole, R. H. Mottram.

(b) By D. H. Lawrence, James Joyce, Virginia Woolf, T. F. Powys, E. M. Forster, D. H. Lawrence.

the inefficient imitation of the same style in *Hans Frost*
(where the pattern is reproduced inanely); the complacent hearty knowingness of *The Good Companions*,
coarse in texture, as against the superb command of
life, serene yet compassionate, that informs T. F.
Powys's writings; the inert weight of Mr. Mottram's
stolid optimism and the refreshing sardonic vigour of
D. H. Lawrence; the persuasive setting for a display
of distinguished emotion which is after all never produced in *No Love* in contrast to the illuminating
subtlety with which E. M. Forster exposes the inner
life.

Perhaps the most apposite comment on the letter
just quoted is that in any other age it would have hardly
been possible for an educated man to be content to
shut himself off from the best work of his contemporaries. But to affirm this is to anticipate. It will at
any rate not be disputed that our correspondent after
a course of amusing himself at something below his
own habitual degree of awareness has become unable
to make the effort necessary to tackle a novel that does
not offer commonplaces of observation and reassuring
sentiment. Reassuring in the same way as the more
popular bestsellers already discussed. By this is not
meant merely the moral or thesis (though cf. *The Bridge
of San Luis Rey, Go She Must, The Good Companions . . .*)
but a more persuasively insinuating effect. Here, for
instance, is one that deals explicitly with the cultural
situation (*a*). There is behind the book the figure of
a certain Henry Galleon, a mythical novelist, who is
imposed on the reader as a great artist. The reader is
introduced to the best literary society in London,

(*a*) Hugh Walpole, *The Young Enchanted* (1921).

and a discussion takes place in which a modest middlebrow novelist overthrows the objectionable highbrows :

> Campbell was a novelist who had once been of the Galleon school and full of Galleonish subtleties, and now was popular and Trollopian. He was, perhaps, a trifle overpleased with himself and the world, a little too prosperous and jolly and optimistic, and being in addition the son of a Bishop, his voice at times rose to a pulpit ring, but he meant well, was vigorous and bland and kindly.

The highbrow critics, contemptible figures so interested in Art as to lack Humour, thoroughly despise him, we are given to understand, but he of course sees through them. He is drawn into a discussion with them, and ' something on this occasion had become too strong for him and dragged him into a public declaration of faith, regardless whether he offended or no.' He tells them they are ' " All wrong." ' ' " Arrogance, Arrogance, Arrogance—that's the matter with all of you—and the matter with Literature and Art to-day, and politics too." ' The editor of a highbrow journal puts up the author's conception of a defence of the critical attitude : ' " Why shouldn't I select the good work and praise it and leave the rest alone? " " Yes," said Campbell ; " what's good work by your over-sophisticated, over-read, over-intellectual standard. . . . About contemporary Art one can only be personal, never final. . . . Don't think there's personal feeling in this. There might have been ten years ago. I worried then a terrible deal about whether I were an artist or no ; I cared what you people said, read your reviews, and was damnably puzzled by the decisions you gave. And then suddenly I said to myself, ' Why shouldn't I have some fun? Life's short. I'm not a great artist, and never shall be. I'll write to please myself.' And I did. And I've been happy ever since. . . . I'm nearer real life than you are, any of you. . . . What do you people know about anything save literary values? There aren't any literary values until Time has spoken." ' He suggests that we should ' " take everything a little less solemnly . . . respond to beauty." ' We subsequently learn through the medium of the thoughts of the dark-horse novelist hero that ' Campbell was a happy man, and a man who was living his life at its very fullest. He was not a great artist, of course—great artists were never happy— but he had a narrative gift that it amused him to play with every morning of his life from ten to twelve, and he made money from that gift and could buy books and pictures and occasionally do a friend a good turn. Monteith and Grace Talbot and the others were more serious artists and were more seriously considered, but their gifts came to mighty little in the end—thin, thin, little streams.'

This account of a novel widely read and admired by the educated has been given because it affords a valuable glimpse of the temper of the age. The similarity of this author's outlook to that of the low-level bestsellers is obvious; the accent of ' I'm nearer real life than you are, any of you,' etc., is the note of the quotations on p. 68. It is notable, then, that the principal endeavour of the popular contemporary novelists at all levels (for no highbrow novelist can really be called popular with a market of 3000 in a reading public of 43 millions) is to persuade the ordinary prosperous citizen that life is fun, he is living it at its fullest, and there are no standards in life or art other than his own. Whether this is for the community a desirable state of affairs or not is a question which does not come within the limits of this section. Before it can be discussed we must first enquire whether the situation we have examined presents any essentially new features or whether, as those inclined to take a serious view of it will find themselves assured, ' things have always been the same.'

PART II
THE PAST

Much of the influence of fine literature must be wasted until something more is known about the public than is known at present. Who are the people who read books? Who are the people who read books of this sort and of that? Where are they to be found? It is only when these questions can be satisfactorily answered that authorship and publishing can flourish, and the finest ideas can permeate the community. Statistics of the operation of ideas are surely not of less public importance than statistics of employment, ages, births and deaths.

The Influence of the Press, R. A. SCOTT-JAMES.

If 50,000 people buy a novel whose shortcomings render it tenth-rate, we may be sure that they have not conspired to do so, and also that their strange unanimity is not due to chance. There must be another explanation of the phenomenon, and when this explanation is discovered some real progress will have been made towards that democratisation of art which it is surely the duty of the minority to undertake, and to undertake in a religious spirit. . . . I am aware that a few of the minority regard the democratisation of art as both undesirable and impossible, but even they will admit that this particular problem in the 'psychology of crowds'—the secret of popularity in art—has sufficient intrinsic interest to be attacked for its own sake, apart from any end which the solving might or might not serve.

Fame and Fiction, ARNOLD BENNETT.

Perhaps you will say I should not take my ideas of the manners of the times from such trifling authors; but it is more truly to be found among them, than from any historian: as they write merely to get money, they always fall into the notions that are most acceptable to the present taste.

Letters of Lady Mary Wortley Montagu.

THE PAST

I

THE BIRTH OF JOURNALISM

SO remote from us in every way is the first English reading public—for what can the age of cinema and mass production make of Shakespeare's and Nashe's public?—and so limited is our knowledge of it, that it is more than any one dare to speak of it with confidence. All that can be safely attempted is an examination of such of their reading matter as has survived, bearing in mind that reading did not play the same major part in the life of any class that it now does, as has been shown, in the life of all classes. In the sixteenth and even the seventeenth centuries it was music that filled the leisure of rich and poor and the working hours of the people [46] as well, and by this is meant active participation in vocal and instrumental music in which at that time England was unrivalled. Chappell (a) summarises his account of the musical interests of the Elizabethan age thus : ' Not only was music a necessary qualification for ladies and gentlemen, but even the city of London advertised the musical abilities of boys educated in Bridewell and Christ's Hospital, as a mode of recommending them as servants, apprentices, or husbandmen. Tinkers sang catches ; milkmaids sang ballads ; carters whistled ; each trade, and even the beggars, had their special

(a) Chappell, *Old English Popular Music*, Vol. I.' The Age of Elizabeth.'

83

songs; the base-viol hung in the drawing-room for the
amusement of waiting visitors; and the lute, cittern,
and virginals, for the amusement of waiting customers,
were the necessary furniture of the barber's shop. They
had music at dinner; music at supper; music at
weddings; music at funerals; music at night; music
at dawn; music at work; and music at play.' Dr.
John Case observed how 'Every troublesome and
laborious occupation useth musicke for solace and
recreation. . . . And hence it is that manual
labourers, and mechanical artificers of all sorts keepe
such a chaunting and singing in their shoppes—the
tailor on his bulk—the shoemaker at his last—the
mason at his wall—the ship-boy at his oar—the
tinker at his pan—and the tiler on the housetop,' and
even the Puritan interlude seems not to have broken
the tradition,[47] for in 1676 old Thomas Mace the
musician remarked the 'common tunes . . . which
are to be known by the boys and common people
singing them in the streets. Among them are many
very excellent and well-contrived,' of which he noticed
the characteristic 'neat and spruce ayre.' All this
implies a valuable kind of education that even the
poorest seem to have received or picked up; the
common people who sang their well-contrived and
often exquisite tunes about the streets, the 'trades-
men and foremen' who in the middle of the seventeenth century were accustomed to sing together out of
Pleyford's Catch-book, the gentlemen who could sing
complicated music at sight,[48] did not need a regular
supply of fiction to amuse them. And this implies
too a genuine social life at every level.

In London they had too the theatre, where for ?

penny one could hear Marlowe's mighty line and the
more subtle rhythms of his successors. And to object
that most of the audience could not possibly understand the play and only went to the theatre because
the alternative to *Hamlet* was the bear-pit is beside the
point for the purposes of the student of cultural
history; the importance of this for him is that the
masses were receiving their amusement from above
(instead of being specially catered for by journalists,
film-directors, and popular novelists, as they are now).
They had to take the same amusements as their
betters, and if *Hamlet* was only a glorious melodrama
to the groundlings, they were none the less living for
the time being in terms of Shakespeare's blank verse
(there seems to be a sound case, at any rate, to be made
out for the theory that the audience positively liked
the long soliloquies that are so often the high water-
mark of the Elizabethan dramatists' poetry); to argue
that they would have preferred Tom Mix or *Tarzan of
the Apes* is idle. Happily they had no choice, and
education of ear and mind is none the less valuable for
being acquired unconsciously. The importance of the
training in listening to the sustained expression of
complex modes of thought and feeling that the age of
Elizabeth and James endured has never been adequately stressed, though to take amusement in the form
of listening to choirs and ' the minstrels of the towne,'
sermons of the sixteenth and seventeenth century
divines,[49] and the Elizabethan drama, is in itself
suggestive of a standard of mental alertness and concentration that has never been reached by the London
public since.

But that public was probably no more than a quarter

of a million out of a population of nearly five millions. The life of the nation as a whole is only to be gauged as the force behind the literature of the age; its abundant vitality—for it suggests the epithet ' lusty ' rather than ' fine '—was the soil from which that amazing literature flowered. The modern reader is at once struck by the body of traditional lore the people must have possessed which served instead of the ' knowledge ' (*i.e.* acquaintance with a mass of more or less unrelated facts, derived principally from an elementary school education and the newspaper) that forms the background of the modern working-man's mind. The Elizabethan peasant or 'prentice inherited a folk-history of England (for the historical plays, so dull to us, so enthralling to them, imply a remarkable acquaintance with the kind of history that centres on personalities and factions, and the ballads confirm this), a picturesque store of classical, medieval, and biblical legends, on which the ballads embroidered endlessly, a series of traditional heroes of the people and their adventures (so that all a penurious scribbler like Deloney need do was to string them together), and the broad but not always unsubtle humour of the jest-books; and all this supported an idiom rich in proverbial wisdom, that explains in some degree the wealth of allusion in the drama and pamphlets of the age, and helps us to understand how the audience or reader could possibly have followed even the thread of the argument, so. tangled to us whose minds are furnished with mere information, a kind of knowledge not rooted in the soil but depending on print, and who have been accustomed for two centuries to have the writer smooth the way for us. For the next thing that one notices is how much less was done for the common reader by the Elizabethan popular writer or dramatist than by the modern popular author or journalist. If the novel has been getting more difficult, fiction in general has been getting easier; compared with the Elizabethan pamphlet twentieth-century journalism is pre-digested food. The journalist who could declare, like Ingenioso in *The Returne from Parnassus*, ' for the husbanding of my witt, I put it out to interest and make it returne twoo pamphlets a weeke,' had also to affirm ' Ile have my pen run like a spigot, and my invention answer it quick as a drawer.' The spirited plunging sentence of Nashe whose horses, tugging in different directions, are always running away with him, is representative. Take a sentence at random from *The Unfortunate Traveller*:

> Verie devout Asses they were, for all they were so dunstically set forth, and such as thought they knew as much of God's minde as richer men: why inspiration was their ordinarie familiar, and buzd in their eares like a Bee in a boxe everie hower what newes from heaven, hell, and the land of whipperginnie, displease them who durst, he should have his mittimus to damnation *ex tempore*, they would vaunt there was not a pease difference betwixt them and the Apostles, they were as poor as they, of as base trades as they, and no more inspired than they, and with God there is no respect of persons, onely herein may seeme some little diversitie to lurk, that *Peter* wore a sword, and they count it flat hel fire for anie man to weare a dagger: nay, so grounded and gravelled were they in this opinion, that now when they should come to Battell, theres never a one of them would bring a blade (no, not an onion blade) about hym to dye for it.

Such prose, high-spirited, breathless, and frequently inconsequential—for the Elizabethan sentence was a bag into which anything that lay by the way was swept

—requires slow reading and unusual mental activity to follow the sense, disentangle the essentials, and secure the implications. And the texture of Pierce Penilesse's writings differs only from that of Dekker's and Greene's pamphlets and the work of all the other journalists who would ' yark up a Pamphlet in a night and a day,' not to speak of the Martin Marprelate tracts on both sides,[50] in being on the whole livelier and fuller-blooded. By modern standards they show an insulting disregard of the readers' convenience : the dashing tempo, the helter-skelter progress, the unexpected changes of direction and tone so that the reader is constantly faced with a fresh front, the stream of casual allusion and shifting metaphor, leave us giddy as the Elizabethan dramas leave us stunned. The fact is, that Elizabethan popular writers were able to make use of a rich speech idiom ; they wrote for a people whose social intercourse had developed the art of conversation—their punctuation in this connection is highly suggestive, and so is the size of their vocabulary. There was here no poverty of emotional life needing fantasy to nourish it, no relief in vicarious living. The drama, the sermon, and the prose of the age are different aspects of one phenomenon.

The court was more particularly catered for by such works as ' *A Petite Palace of Pettie his pleasure : Containyng many pretie Hystories, by him set foorth in comely colours and most delightfully discoursed* ' (*a*), ' *Euphues*, The Anatomy of Wit ' (*b*), Sidney's *Arcadia* (*c*) ; of these and their imitators two things

(*a*) George Pettie (1576). By 1613 there were seven editions.

(*b*) John Lyly (1578). Esdaile records twenty-six editions by 1718.

(*c*) Published first in 1590, though handed about in manuscript for a few years before. ' Now the sixt time published,' 1622.

are to be noticed : that they are all addressed more or
less explicitly to the ladies [51] and in consequence set
out to refine manners and provide elegant amusement,
and that their authors were not journalists but dilettante
engaged in exploiting the newly discovered possibilities of style, unlike the pamphleteers whose prose
is too much in earnest to be ' quaint.' Dull as their
work is now (for its interest depended on the creation
of word patterns), it embalms one aspect of the
Elizabethan civilisation, that as a whole presents to
us—in Shakespeare, for instance—an inexplicable
mixture of the profound and the naïve, the fine and the
gross, the subtle and the crude. Forde, no courtier
or scholar but a man with a living to make, turned out
popular romances on the model of the *Arcadia* that are
by no means dreary but add to their originals a lively
charm. Forde is important as a document of the more
or less cultivated taste of the age. He was enormously
popular,[52] he dealt of course in what Nashe scornfully
described in the *Anatomie of Absurditie* as ' feyned nowhere acts,' and the substance can be dismissed as
nonsense. But Forde's claims to respect can be
perceived if one contrasts him with the twentieth-
century equivalent. The value of his work can best
be made plain by a series of negatives. It is not un-
healthy, it satisfies no morbid cravings, offers nothing
in the way of wish-fulfilment or opportunities for
emotional orgies, the story is the opposite of exciting,
the characterisation is so unpronounced and abstract
as to give no scope for day-dreaming,[53] and the style is
sweetly detached and strictly unsentimental. It will be
objected that this is only because Forde didn't know
his job, and it must be admitted that his virtues are

those of innocence, an innocence, be it added, that no novelist after Richardson could exhibit.   Again and again an Elizabethan romancer will lead up to a dramatic situation full of possibilities (the reunion of lovers after many vicissitudes, an avowal, the discovery of a long-lost child or parent), and then abandon it at the critical moment with a dismissive gesture. The history of popular taste is largely bound up with the discovery by the writing profession of the technique for exploiting emotional responses.   Now Forde and his kind can be trusted never to exploit an emotional or even a pathetic scene ; they coolly proceed with the business of getting on with the plot (the intricate meaningless web that Sidney popularised), so that the sophisticated twentieth century cannot understand what their public read them for.   There is no means of knowing, but that fresh innocence of Forde's says a good deal for both author and reader.   Childish as the romance formula was, it had a certain delicate beauty that the succeeding age replaced by a hardy cynicism.   Forde's characteristic virtues may be demonstrated by quoting the opening scene of *Ornatus and Artesia* :

> Ornatus above all things, delighted in hawking, and on a day being weary, he wandered without company with his hawk on his fist into a most pleasant valley, where by he shrowded himself under the shadow of a tuft of green trees, with purpose to rest himself, and even when his eyes were ready to yeild to slumber, he was revived from his drowsiness by the noise of a kennel of hounds that past by him in chase of a stag, after whom, Arbastus and divers of his company (though to him unknown) followed, who being passed by, whilst he was in a deep study, to think what they should be, he espied a beautiful damsel entering the same valley,

who being somewhat weary, liking the prospect of that shady tuft of trees, alighted there, which Ornatus seeing, withdrew himself from her sight, whilst she tying her steed to a bush, laid her delicate body down upon the cooling earth, to cool herself, and dry the sweat, which the sooner to accomplish, she unlaced her garments, and with a decent and comely behaviour, discovered her milk-white neck and breast beautified with two round precious teats, to receive the breath of the cool wind, which was affected with a delight to exhale the moistened vapours of her pure body. Ornatus seeing all, and unseen himself, noted with a delight each perfect lineament of her proper body, beauty, sweat, savour, and other comeliness, which filled his heart with exceeding pleasure, therewith growing into an unrestrained affection towards her, and a great study what she should be, when suddenly his hawk feeling his fist unmoveable thinking to perch herself with quiet, primed herself and with the noise of her bells made Artesia to start, who as one half agast, with a fearful behaviour rose from the ground, looking about her from whence that sound came, she espied Ornatus, who unwilling she should perceive he had seen her, lay as if he had slept, Artesia marvelling what he should be, and accordingly thinking he had slept, closed her naked breast with great haste, and unloosing her horse, thought to go away unespied. Which Ornatus perceiving, and unwilling without speaking to her to lose her sight, seemed to awake, and raising himself, steadfastly behold her, which infused such a red vermillion blush into her beautiful cheeks, and withall such a bashfull confusion spread itself in her conceits, that she stood like one half amazed or ashamed.

Which Ornatus perceiving, drew towards her, and greeted her with these speeches. Fair damsel, be not abashed with my presence, though a stranger, which shall no way (if I can choose) offend you, but rather command me, and I will be ready to do you any service. Artesia, notwithstanding his speeches, withdrew herself aside, leading her horse to a bank, where with ease she mounted, and so rode away, not giving him any answer at all.

One is reminded of the ' neat and spruce ayre ' which old Thomas Mace remarked as characteristic of the common songs.   Looking through the pages of Chappell's *English Popular Music,* one observes the same quality of unpremeditated innocence in the tunes of the sixteenth and seventeenth centuries.   Compare them with the dragging movement of the nineteenth-century drawing-room ballads and the lascivious syncopated rhythms of the twentieth-century song- and dance-records.   Forde's readers, high and low, liked their song-lyrics to have a basis of unromantic good sense, and the absence of sentimental appeal noticeable in the lyrics from the Elizabethan song-books is parallel to the quality of Forde's tales.

Lower down Deloney the ballad-journalist found a public for fiction,[54] dedicating his works to the cloth-workers and shoemakers and cordwayners, and deploying much the same transparent arts as Defoe for flattering his readers.[55]   He produced an agreeable mixture of fairy-tale and matter-of-fact observation of the life around him, drawing on the jest-book anecdotes and writing up the traditional folk-heroes like Crispine and Crispianus, Simon Eyre, and the Six Worthy Yeomen of the West ; and there is again no day-dream but a sturdy acceptance of things as they are, often disconcertingly unromantic and not even providing a happy ending or a suitably pathetic one.   Take, for instance, the tale of Richard (*a*) who was beloved by the two delightful maids, Margaret of the Spread Eagle and Gillian of the George (Margaret incidentally is the Long Meg of Westminster of jest-book fame) ; the history of their attempts upon him is told at length,

(*a*) *The Gentle Craft*, Part II.

but in the end he marries some one else (unnamed) and the story is polished off thus :

> O God (quoth Margaret) have I been so chary to keep my honesty, and so dainty of my maiden-head that I could spare it no man for the love I bore to hard-hearted Richard, and hath he served me thus? Well Gillian (quoth she) let us go, never will I be so tide in affection to one man again while I live; what a deale of time have I lost and spent to no purpose since I came to London? and how many kinde offers have I forsaken, and disdainfully refused of many brave Gentlemen, that would have bin glad of my good will? . . . Thus Margaret in a melancholy humor went her waies, and in a short time after, she forsooke Westminster, and attended on the King's army to Bullio, and while the siege lasted, became a landresse to the Camp, and never after did she set store by her selfe, but became common to the call of every man, till such time as all youthful delights was banished by old age, and in the ende she left her life in Islington, being very penitent for all her former offences.
>
> Gillian in the end was well married, and became a very good house-keeper, living in honest name and fame till her dying day.

Even when we have discounted for the ' quaintness,' the pleasure that we get from contact with an idiom to which we are unaccustomed, there is still a great deal to admire. Deloney's cheerful realism, his use of homely (and therefore vigorous) speech,[56] and of the humour of the people, his Chaucerian clarity and freshness and his innocence of any literary artifice, may well make the modern reader wonder whether, after all, the author of *The Good Companions* and *Angel Pavement* has gained more than he has lost by having the whole of English literature behind him and the novels of Dickens and Arnold Bennett at his back, by writing for an educated public and laying claim to the title of artist.   It is easy at any rate to see what he has lost.

How much could be done by using what lay at hand Nashe's solitary novel shows.   It is the product of journalism in an age when no distinction existed between journalism and literature, when journalism that set out to amuse had to compete with the stage. So Nashe's prose has all the vitality that Sidney and Lyly had sacrificed to ceremony.   Almost any passage will show the effect of writing for a public accustomed to watching the drama, and the same dramatic imagination is visible in Greene's pamphlets, as opposed to the dreary Euphuistic contortions of his *Carde of Fancie*. The general public at the end of the sixteenth century could apparently be counted on for a certain mental agility acquired from frequenting the playhouse and Paul's Cross, produced by a culture in which conversation was an art.

If in this brief sketch of the reading capacity of the Elizabethans an impression has been given of any decided differentiation in their reading, it must at once be corrected.   The public was too narrow for any specialisation of the kind described in Part I., and journalism so new that the possibilities of the printed word had not been discovered.   Though *Euphues* and later the *Arcadia* were all the wear at court and never reached the people, it was much commoner for a writer to address himself to the community at large, like Dekker on the title-page of his *Bellman of London*, which he recommends as ' profitable for Gentlemen, Lawyers, Merchants, Citizens, Farmers, Masters of Households, and all sorts of servants, and delightful for all men to read.'   The primitive character of the literary

market is depicted in *Shakespeare's England* (a); the
absence of an organised 'Trade' made it necessary
for authors to do their own advertising on their title-
pages, as Dekker quoted above, and Deloney in *The
Gentle Craft* ('Being a most mery and pleasant
Historie, not altogether unprofitable, nor any way
hurtful : verie fit to passe away the tediousnesse of the
long winter evenings'). One result of the limited
reading public was that it meant a genuine community, as yet unspoilt by the traffic in literature :
there is the same healthy emotional spontaneity in the
novels of both Deloney and Forde. Even the humblest
literary jobs reveal a pleasingly unbusiness-like zest—
the popular jest-books, for instance. ' The Pleasant
Conceits of Old Hobson, the merry Londoner, full of
humorous discourses and witty merriments, whereat
the quickest wits may laugh, and the wiser sort take
pleasure' (1607, 1634, 1640, and doubtless other
editions, being the kind of book that is worn to shreds)
is introduced thus :

> Of Master Hobson's description.
>
> In the beginning of Queene Elizabeths most happy Reigne,
> our late deceased Sovereigne, under whose peacefull govern-
> ment long flourished this our Country of England, there
> lived in the Citie of London a merry Citizen, named old
> Hobson a Haberdasher of female wares, dwelling at the lower
> end of Cheape-side, in the Poultry, as well known through
> this part of England as a Sergeant knowes the Counter gate :
> he was a homely plaine man, most commonly wearing a
> button Cap close to his eares, a short Gowne girt about his
> midle, and a paire of slippers upon his feete of an ancient
> fashion, as for his wealth it was answerable to the better sort
> of our Citizens, but of so merry a disposition that his equall

(a) Vol. II. chap. xxiii.

therein is hardly to be found: hereat let the pleasant disposed people laugh and the more grave in carriage take no exceptions, for here are merriments without hurt, and humorous jests savouring upon wisdome: read willingly but scoffe not spightfully, for old Hobson spent his dayes merrily.

So small was the community that an eccentric tradesman was a well-known figure; there was room for personalities. It was the journalist who suffered from the narrowness of the market; the typical Elizabethan journalist 'contended with the colde and conversed with scarcitie,' as Nashe wrote of himself, was imprisoned for debt and died destitute. It was in a later age that the journalist learned how to grow prosperous at the expense of culture.

THE PURITAN CONSCIENCE

THE next distinct phase to be observed in the history of English taste is represented at its purest by Bunyan; Defoe was its journalist and Milton its poet. And the influence of this phase is traceable throughout the eighteenth and nineteenth centuries, so that the sudden break at the end of the last century in the hitherto continuous tradition of more than two hundred years is of some significance.

It is not fantastic to assert that it was the Puritan culture as much as Bunyan that produced *Pilgrim's Progress*. Its instant success, its innumerable imitators, testify to its acceptability, and its religious aim made it as indispensable to every respectable home as the Bible, till the Puritan conscience itself decayed.[57] It was the greatest good luck for the English that three of their early literary masterpieces (the Authorised Version, *Pilgrim's Progress*, and *Paradise Lost*) should have been explicitly religious works, so that even the grimmest and poorest Puritan household possessed at least the first two of these; and that a journalist of genius should have been impelled by force of circumstances to make the most fascinating of all games (playing at house) a suitable Sunday book. These four works remained the inevitable if not the only books in the home of the decent working man for a couple of centuries, an invaluable educational influence with whatever purpose they may have been read, for to read Bunyan and Milton for religious instruction, as to

attend Elizabethan drama for the ' action,' is to receive
an education unconsciously.

What in sum is it that Bunyan and Defoe do for
their readers? Or, to put the same question in another
way, what kind of testimony do they bear to the nature
of the interests of their readers? The closer one looks
the more fully one is persuaded that the life of the
people at the end of the seventeenth century and of the
shopkeeper class at the beginning of the eighteenth
century was in general both finer in quality and more
satisfying in substance than that of their descendants
whose reading habits have been described in Part I.
For *Pilgrim's Progress* is among other things an
excellent advertisement for the age that reared Bunyan.
In spite of the allegorical names his characterisation is
really subtle,[58] and so is his morality. Unlike the
major eighteenth century and Victorian novelists he
has no sharp black and white, vice and virtue, and no
cheap system of rewards and punishments. His
method is that of the best novelists—to reveal men for
what they are : the gentlemanly Mr. Worldly Wiseman who always went to the town of Morality to church,
and those other gentlemen his friends—Mr. Legality
and his simpering son Civility, Mr. By-ends of the
town of Fair-speech and his highly respectable school-
fellows, are the only 'villains' of the book, and nothing
more happens to them in the way of poetic justice than
to the gross and stupid who are the villains of Jane
Austen's novels—they are merely left to themselves
for ever. And similarly, Mr. Badman who cheats
his customers, robs his creditors, drinks, swears, and
whores, and so breaks his pious wife's heart, prospers
all his days, and except for a tang of the pox in his

bowels dies as peacefully as a Christian.[59] Bunyan
had observed the life around him as closely as Defoe,
and he was free from the necessity which made Defoe
a journalist. His observation is truer and his morality
juster (that is to say, wiser) than Richardson's, his
version of the pattern of life is more satisfying than
Richardson's, proceeding from a finer mind. In
consequence he is a better novelist, and whereas
Richardson's interest for the reader of Dostoievsky
and Henry James is almost entirely historical, Bunyan's
is intrinsic.

Bunyan's vigour derives from the soil. The shrewd
percipience and the respect for ' character ' that still
distinguish the English peasant are pervasive ; it was
no mere Puritan who could appreciate the variety of
stiff-necked courage that supported Mr. Haughty and
Mr. Lustings at their trial in *The Holy War* (' "My
Lord, I am a man of high birth, and I have been used
to pleasures and pastimes of greatness. I have not been
wont to be snub'd for my doings " '). But Bunyan's
attitude—inherent in the culture which produced him
—is fundamentally antithetical to that of the twentieth
century. To explain what is meant in Bunyan's own
terms : the town of Stupidity that lieth about four
degrees beyond the City of Destruction is worse than
the City of Destruction itself, lying more off from the
sun, and so more cold and senseless ; the very brisk
lad Ignorance was decent, honest, and God-fearing, he
had done all the right things (' I knew my Lord's will,
and I have been a good liver ; I pay every man his
own ; I pray, fast, pay tithes, and give alms, and have
left my country for whither I am going '), and he gets
to the Celestial City without half that difficulty which

Christian and Hopeful met with, but at the threshold it is commanded to take Ignorance and bind him hand and foot and have him away; the book ends not with the vision of the City as Christian enters but the damning of Ignorance—' Then I saw that there was a way to hell, even from the gates of heaven, as well as from the City of Destruction.' With this attitude and its implications the public which has been investigated in Part I. would hardly sympathise. Bunyan's religious vocabulary has only to be translated into the more general language of conduct and sensibility for it to become evident that he is on the side of the highbrow.

But how is it then, one asks, that Bunyan was able to write the most popular book of his age and one of the most popular of the subsequent ages? The explanation is to be found in Bunyan's use of language. It was noticed in Chapter III. that twentieth-century best-sellers employ with great effect what were described as the keywords of the emotional vocabulary which is associated with religion, using them to touch off certain easy responses, producing vague surges of warm feeling. This use of language derives, of course, from the Authorised Version, and it is obvious at even the most cursory reading that the effect of *Pilgrim's Progress* is bound up with the effect of the Authorised Version, both the material of the allegory and a large proportion of the phrases and idioms coming from the latter. But the *success* of *Pilgrim's Progress* is more subtle than this suggests. Bunyan's mode of thinking and feeling is English and Puritan, and it is this that reminds one throughout his work that one is in contact through him with a genuine culture. He is really as much concerned with his neighbours as Thackeray, and manages to work on two planes at once by modulating from allegory to realism and correspondingly from the movement and language of the Bible to the movement and idiom of common speech. Thus the characteristic effect of reading a passage of Bunyan is a stirring of the blood—the Biblical phrases and cadences evoke overtones, and the peculiarly thrilling quality of the prose is due to this technique which enables a precise particular occasion to draw on the accumulated religious associations of a race. Bunyan's work could no more than Shakespeare's have been done in any other language.

At this point a digression is necessary to describe how Bunyan differs from the bestsellers of Part I. in his use of the emotional keywords. His use of them may be called serious : he is concerned with the good life, and his integrity of purpose justifies his handling of the most important part of our vocabulary, which is in consequence enriched with another layer of associations after passing through his works. They use it unconscionably : to make a splash, bring off an effect too easily, indulging the reader in the luxury of unfocussed emotion ; they call out the religious attitude to support an unworthy code (Kingsley for his muscular and provincial Christianity, for instance, Gilbert Frankau and James Douglas for their brand of religio-erotic stimulant), and the result is necessarily disgusting to the sensitive. It is in this way that popular novelists and journalists have debased the language of the Authorised Version. Bunyan, of course, made the process possible, just as Swinburne, starting in nearly the same place and in much the same way, made possible the verse of Kipling and Masefield—bestsellers in verse and prose have evolved along the same lines, reinforcing each other's work. As a result, no serious twentieth-century writer can touch Bunyan's vocabulary without self-consciousness, and to use it he must exert tact and ingenuity if he is to avoid the wrong kind of response.

Defoe, having spent a lifetime in every kind of literary hack-work and being finally discredited as a political writer with both parties, at the age of fifty-nine turned to, or rather, luckily drifted into, prose fiction to support himself. His readers were of ' the middle state, or what might be called the upper station of low life ' (a), and Defoe made a brilliant success by providing suitable entertainment for their leisure, a nice task since that leisure had been by custom given over to improving reading of the ' Drelincourt's Book of Consolations against the Fears of Death ' type. If fiction could be disguised so that it could be acceptable to the virtuous (for whom ' invention ' meant lying, and more particularly the immoral literature and drama of the Restoration Court), fiction could be made to pay. Defoe therefore concentrated on literary devices which actually preclude the creation of a work of art. Nevertheless, while making his living as a journalist, giving a public what it wanted, he was able—as no twentieth-century journalist — to produce literature unawares. Journalism, necessarily related to speech, is dependent on the quality of the idiom at its disposal, and since idiom is an expression of the sensibility of an age, the journalist's virtues and vices are—before the era of big-circulation papers—those of his public.

(a) *Robinson Crusoe*, p. 2.

Defoe's luck lay in having a pure contemporary idiom in use ; he wrote as he spoke, and thus was able to write so fast and so well. And he had no literary ambitions and so no literary notions of ' style '—unlike Scott and Dickens, who, while not producing at anything like the same rate, wrote in general very ill, their idea of ' style ' being something alien from speech.

How single-minded Defoe was in his aims an inspection of *Robinson Crusoe* will show. He is to be observed at the beginning cautiously feeling his way, with a passage of five hundred words devoted to praise of ' the middle station,' introduced solely to flatter the middle-class reader,[60] followed by a matter-of-fact account of young Crusoe's running away to sea, which gives plenty of opportunity for pious commentary. Once the reader is fairly entangled Defoe can go his own way. But he was of his public as well as outside it, he is himself the sober Nonconformist citizen, and in pleasing them he appears to have been also pleasing himself (he chose to follow up the success of the two parts of *Robinson Crusoe* by *Serious Reflections during the Life and Strange Surprising Adventures of Robinson Crusoe. With his Vision of the Angelick World*).

Defoe's interests, then, may be taken as identical with those of his readers, and they are almost completely opposite to the interests in which the bestsellers of Chapter III. deal. The public for which *Roxana* was written was being indulged with a day-dream carefully moulded to its heart's desire : but a day-dream in which the solid unromantic bourgeois interests ruled. Hence the stress in all the novels on ' portable property,' the lists of stolen goods, booty, and possessions generally, the tiresome balancing of pros and cons in every possible situation, and the mental stock-taking which is a substitute for both psychology and emotion. And so, too, the running moral commentary. The reader is only interested in what touches his own daily life, and with all the opportunities of providing Count of Monte-Cristo attractions one observes in *Roxana* nothing of the kind; the middle station in Defoe's day was satisfied with its own way of living, and self-respecting enough to see no reason for coveting the splendours of high life. The reader of two centuries later can hardly realise how it should be that in a popular novel the appeal is anti-sentimental and anti-romantic, yet when Moll roundly declares, 'I had been tricked once by that cheat called Love, but the game was over; I was resolved now to be married or nothing, and to be well married, or not at all,' the author clearly anticipated approval. Again, one is struck with the tolerance of the Puritan. Defoe, the notorious dissenter writing for a Protestant public, can make a minor hero of a ' French Popish priest,' [61] and represent the Spaniards, England's traditional enemies, as virtuous gentlemen in contrast to the ruffianly English seamen.[62] The age of the novels of the brothers Kingsley, for instance, shows up badly in comparison.

The Puritan bourgeois code if deficient in fineness was not wanting in either decency or good sense. Its taste in morality—as represented in Defoe's work—was crude but not cheap; it did not insist on vice being brought to book (Colonel Jack and Captain Singleton, Moll and Roxana are permitted to escape a richly deserved Nemesis), but it did demand an assurance that the conscience of the wicked is not at peace, and this Defoe provides whenever he remembers.[63] Yet in doing this he never trespasses on delicate ground—he never does anything analogous to the bestsellers quoted on pp. 66-7—because his idiom affords no scope for such appeals. And if it had, what response would they have been likely to receive from an age so hopelessly incurious where its feelings were concerned and so ready to be entertained with a description of the contents of its pockets? So he never tampers with the religious emotions; in his moralising interludes he is engaged not in exploiting 'religion' but in satisfying the moral proprieties: it is merely 'Religion joined in with this prudential' as Robinson explains when trying to find reasons for not attacking the cannibals. And there are no emotional appeals; Friday is casually killed off ('to my inexpressible grief') in half a sentence, and a couple of pages later buried as an afterthought, a neglect of opportunities that no writer after 1740 could fail to despise. Even the famous footprint episode is a flat piece of narration. Dickens, the Victorian equivalent of Defoe, was appropriately astonished at the absence of emotional appeal in *Robinson Crusoe*.[64] Yet the absence of felt sentiment, the concentration on facts of the housekeeping and property-owning kind, the decent moralising, the business-like 'placing' of character, are all characteristic of the popular writing before Richardson. In the previous chapter the virtues of the Elizabethan and Jacobean novelists were ascribed to innocence, and though Defoe is by no means prelapsarian, his lack of sophistication in those quarters where our literary experience leads us to anticipate it is equally engaging, so that contemporary critics are inclined to credit him with an artistry which he never possessed.

But he was no artist, and as a journalist all his conscious ingenuity was directed to trying to pass off fiction as fact; to us his journalistic arts seem childishly cunning, transparent, and spasmodic, not psychological and insidious like those of our own age.

Defoe and Bunyan were writers outside what Steele called ' the circumference of wit,' and their public was outside it too. But there is some reason for supposing that the writings of Defoe and Bunyan, and the Authorised Version, are no bad substitutes for a formal education; they do something more positive for the reader than amuse. And if one inspects the memoirs (a) of the many self-educated men who achieved distinction in the eighteenth and early nineteenth centuries, one finds almost invariably that their earliest contact with culture was through *Pilgrim's Progress*, the Bible, *Paradise Lost*, *Robinson Crusoe*. In any part of England, however remote, even in the eighteenth century, it was apparently possible for the poorest child to learn to read if he chose, from his parents or companions or at a dame school, and the rest he could do for himself. The typical self-made man of the 1750-1850 period was born into the respectable poor, attended a dame school

(a) For instance: *Memoirs of the first forty-five years of The Life of James Lackington* (born 1746) ; *Memoirs of Thomas Holcroft* (b. 1745) ; *The Life, Character and Literary Labours of Samuel Drew* (b. 1765) ; Francis Place, various documents (b. 1771) ; *Memoirs from Childhood*, by Wm. Hone (b. 1780) ; *Early Days*, by Samuel Bamford (b. 1788) ; *The Life and Struggles of William Lovett, in his pursuit of Bread, Knowledge and Freedom* (b. 1800) ; *Memoirs of Wm. and Robert Chambers*, by Wm. Chambers (b. 1800 and 1802) ; *The Life of Thomas Cooper, Written by Himself* (b. 1805) ; *The Autobiography of a Working Man by ' One who has whistled at the plough '* (Alexander Somerville, b. 1811).

for a short while where he picked up reading and
writing, was apprenticed to a craft or trade, and either
through religious conversion or, later on, political
sympathies was moved to self-cultivation. In every
case though material circumstances were against him,
as in our age of compulsory education and limited
working hours they could never be, yet psychologically
things were surprisingly easy for him : somehow or
other he always got hold of the best literature and that
without much seeking, had no difficulty in finding
congenial company wherever he went, and read quite
naturally because he enjoyed his reading without any
thought of ' raising ' himself by his efforts. A type-
case is James Lackington, whose autobiography,
first published in 1791, displays his likeness labelled
' J. Lackington, Who a few years since began Business
with five pounds, now sells one Hundred Thousand
Volumes Annually.' The son of a poor shoemaker, he
was apprenticed to the same trade at Taunton, and his
master's two sons having been converted by Wesley, he
was infected with religious fervour by them. The
theological disputes that the family engaged in
' created in him a desire for knowledge,' and he
persuaded his mistress and her sons to teach him to
read. So strong was his ' desire to be talking about
religious mysteries, etc.,' that in spite of working from
six in the morning till ten at night he ' could soon read
the easy parts of the Bible, Mr. Wesley's Hymns, etc.,
and every leisure minute was so employed.' Working
next as a journeyman at Bristol, he found his companions equally susceptible to ' enthusiastic notions.'
To them he ' strongly recommended the purchasing of
books,' and they spent their working hours in religious

disputations while ' all worked very hard, particularly
Mr. John Jones and I, in order to get money to
purchase books, and for some months every shilling
we could spare was laid out on old bookshops, stalls,
etc., insomuch that in a short time we had what *we*
called a very good library.'

What shoemakers' hands at about 1765 called a
good library was an enormous number of standard
theological and ' enthusiastic ' works (the Bible of
course they knew nearly by heart), Wesley's journals
and sermons, all Bunyan, *Paradise Lost*, Gay's *Fables*,
Pomfret's poems, Walker's translation of Epictetus
(' read it over and over in raptures '), and Hobbes's
Homer (' I had somehow or other heard that Homer
was a great poet, but unfortunately I had never heard
of Pope's translation of him, so we very eagerly
purchased that by Hobbes. . . . We that evening
began with Hobbes's Homer, but found it very difficult
for us to read, owing to the obscurity of the translation,
which, together with the indifferent language, and want
of poetical merit in the translator, somewhat dis-
appointed us ; however we had from time to time
many a hard puzzling hour with him '). There was
no consciousness in all this of education for a material
end ; they read first to inform themselves on the matter
of religion and finally for pure enjoyment—' so
anxious were we to read a great deal, that we allowed
ourselves but about three hours sleep in twenty-
four . . . and when all were up, my friend John and
your humble servant took it in turns to read aloud to
the rest, while they were at work.' Their reading
acquainting them that ' there had been various sects
of philosophers amongst the Greeks, Romans, etc.,' he

bought at the bookstalls 'Plato on the Immortality
of the Soul, Plutarch's Morals, Seneca's Morals,
Epicurus's Morals, the Morals of Confucius the
Chinese philosopher and a few others' which made
'a very deep and lasting impression on my mind,'
teaching him ' to bear the unavoidable evils attending
humanity and to supply my wants by contracting or
restraining my desires.' By 1774, when he opened a
second-hand bookshop with a borrowed capital of
five pounds, his private library included Young's
Night Thoughts (which he and his young wife—a milk-
maid—had sacrificed their Christmas dinner to buy),
the first twenty numbers of Hinton's *Dictionary of the
Arts and Sciences*, and odd magazines. He continued his reading with acquaintances and friends in
the same way for the rest of his life, so that summing
up his knowledge of literature at the time of writing
(*æt.* 45), he mentions how he proceeded from the
controversial divines to moral philosophy, studying
Shaftesbury, Bolingbroke, Tindal, Mandeville . . .
' Helvetius, Voltaire, and many other free-thinkers.'
He claims to have read also ' most of our English
poets, and the best translations of the Greek, Latin,
Italian, and French poets; nor did I omit to read
History, Voyages, Travels, Natural History, Biography. . . . I had like to have forgot to inform you,
that I have also read most of our best plays. . . .
Another great source of amusement as well as know-
ledge I have met with in reading almost all the best
novels; by the *best*, I mean those written by Cervantes,
Fielding, Smollett, Richardson, Miss Burney, Voltaire,
Sterne, Le Sage, Goldsmith, and some others.'

Similarly William Hone describes how his father

taught him to read from the Bible, besides which
' Our family library consisted of a mutilated copy of
Milton's *Paradise Lost, Mrs. Glasse's Cookery*, in worse
condition, an old book of Farriery, and some pamphlets
of Mr. Huntingdon. With any other book I was
wholly unacquainted, and the addition of such a book
as the *Pilgrim's Progress* to such a collection as ours was
to me an event. . . . All the cuts were rude, yet they
all pleased me; but the pleasure I derived from the
work itself is indescribable. I read in it continually,
and read it through repeatedly.' His father next
bought him *The Holy War*, and by the time he was
nine he had borrowed Foxe's *Book of Martyrs*; at
eleven he was begging for books from neighbours, and
in this way got hold of Gesner's *Death of Abel* from a
copper-plate printer (' a continual feast to me. It
impressed me deeply ') and an *Essay on the Weakness of
the Human Understanding* from a staymaker (' Huet's
Essay first led me to *reflect* '). Later on we find him
taking in ' Cook's Poets ' in weekly numbers, and
getting access somehow by way of the Parochial
Board to 'a good English library,' reading in his
leisure hours 'many books, particularly Rollin's *Ancient
History*, Plutarch's *Lives*, Pope's *Homer*, and most of
Swift's works.' In the same way Samuel Bamford
when a warehouse porter in Manchester was 'delighted with the acquisition of Homer's Iliad translated by Pope ' and Milton's poems; he speaks of
knowing Burns thoroughly, of reading Shakespeare
' with avidity ' and using his spare moments in ' reading many books of which I had only heard the names
before, such as Robertson's history of Scotland,
Goldsmith's history of England, Rollin's ancient

history, Gibbon's decline and fall of the Roman
Empire, Anachaises' travels in Greece; and many
other works on travels, geography, and antiquities. I
also enlarged my acquaintance with English literature,
read Johnson's Lives of the Poets, and, as a consequence, many of their productions also.' At the
little bookseller's in Peebles, William and Robert
Chambers towards the end of the eighteenth century
were privileged, through 'the strong intellectual
tastes' of their father (a poor weaver) to borrow books
from the circulating library recently established, 'and
thus it came about that by the time we were nine or ten
years of age, my brother and I had read a considerable number of the classics of English literature, or
heard our father read them; were familiar with the
comicalities of Gulliver, Don Quixote, and Peregrine
Pickle; had dipped into the poetry of Pope and
Goldsmith, and indulged our romantic tendencies in
books of travel and adventure.[65] When lately attending the Wells of Homburg, I had but one English
book to amuse me, Pope's translation of the *Iliad*, and
I felt it as towards myself an affecting reminiscence,
that exactly fifty years had elapsed since I perused the
copy from Elder's library, in a little room looking out
upon the High Street of Peebles.' When William was
fifteen we hear of him reading aloud Smollett's and
Fielding's novels and *Gil Blas* from five to seven-thirty
every morning to a baker's family in exchange for a hot
roll before starting his day's work, and later on rising
at dawn to read the *Spectator* thoroughly ('I carefully
scrutinised the papers of Addison and other writers,
sentence by sentence, in order to familiarise myself
with their method of construction and treatment ').

Thomas Cooper the distinguished Chartist began life as a poor Lincolnshire widow's son, of pious stock; from earliest childhood *Pilgrim's Progress* was his 'book of books,' and he was familiar with *Paradise Lost*; the travelling 'number-man' lent him *Pamela*, and from the Gainsborough circulating library he was allowed to borrow Shakespeare, Dryden's plays, Cook's Voyages, and the Waverley Novels. He was apprenticed to a lively young shoemaker who 'spoke passionately of' the poetry of Byron and lent him the poems of Burns; at fifteen he 'formed the valuable friendship of . . . a Methodist, but a reader and a thinker' who directed his mind into more solid reading (history and theology); another friend, a draper's assistant, suggested forming a Mutual Improvement Society, at which they read weekly essays and debated; and yet another, a grocer's apprentice ('of serious and pious habits' but also a Byron enthusiast), who appears to have had plenty of pocket-money, bought 'forty volumes of the English Essayists and Langhorne's Plutarch . . . and a translation of Voltaire's *Philosophical Dictionary*,' which they read and discussed together on Sundays. His next friend was a draper 'not only well read in standard English literature, more especially divinity, but he was passionately attached to metaphysics,' was 'a broad general reader, had an excellent library, and made me welcome to the loan of every book in it that I desired to read.' All these the little town of Gainsborough had provided for him before he was nineteen. He now set up as a cobbler to support his mother and himself, but finding time and energy for a scheme of self-education which besides languages and theology included committing 'the entire *Paradise Lost* and seven of the best plays of Shakespeare to memory'—an ideal nearly achieved. In addition he learnt by heart 'thousands of lines by Burns and Coleridge, and Wordsworth, and Scott, and Byron, and Keats,' and when he 'diverged into miscellaneous reading' it was Warton's *History of Early English Poetry*, Johnson's *Lives of the Poets, Rasselas,* and other works, Boswell's *Johnson, Frankenstein,* and every number of the *Quarterly* and *Edinburgh Reviews* and *Blackwood's Magazine.* When he was sent to Stafford Gaol for political offences we find him fighting successfully for the right to keep his box of books, spending his captivity in re-reading Gibbon, 'revelling in Shakespeare and Milton,' *Don Quixote,* Virgil, Byron, and a pirated Shelley.

The venerable Samuel Drew (a) spent his first earnings as a journeyman shoemaker on *Pilgrim's Progress,* which had made 'a deep and lasting impression on him.' When he set up his little shop in St. Austell it became a centre for 'persons partial to religious or literary enquiries' and debates, and in spite of extreme poverty and working anything up to eighteen hours a day, he managed to 'indulge his taste for literature and metaphysics' and read with the many young men 'of good information and enquiring minds' who frequented his house. And Thomas Holcroft, the friend of Godwin and revolutionary novelist, started his career as a stable-boy, who picked up an education by way of the Bible, old ballads, Bunyan, and odd volumes of Swift and Addison.

These few cases have been chosen as representative

(a) Variously known as 'The Locke of the 19th Century' and 'The English Plato.'

histories of a great many such men born before 1860. Their autobiographies make impressive as well as fascinating reading : born to poverty and often wretchedness, without any formal education or ever mixing with cultured people, these men acquired a feeling for literature—perfectly genuine, as the language in which they record their delight in their reading shows—which would be looked for in vain among their twentieth-century equivalents who have the advantages of compulsory free schooling, public libraries, cheap books and periodicals, and a forty-eight-hour week. One is struck almost equally by two things that emerge—the ability that these barely literate working-men display to tackle serious works, and the absence of any but material difficulties in their way. Having learnt to read they would straightway read the seventeenth and eighteenth-century classics, and even before they could read they seem to have heard of them, like Samuel Bamford ; and chance invariably threw the right books in their way. Their histories, whether they were born in Cornwall, Scotland, Somerset, Lincolnshire, London, Yorkshire, or Lancashire, are curiously alike, and form a not unreliable basis for some generalisations.

The Puritan background gave the mind a certain positive inclination which there seems every reason for supposing made more than amends for the absence of formal education ; for the child who had learnt his letters there was little in the way of children's books obtainable, only *Chevy Chase*, *Robinson Crusoe*, and *Æsop's Fables*, and from these the step to Bunyan and Milton was not so steep as at first sight appears. No doubt Bunyan and Milton were at first mastered only because they had a religious sanction and lay at hand, but a delight in them for their own sake soon followed, and the initial religious jog was reinforced by Methodistic [66] or political fervour later on. These were enough to provide further stimulus in themselves, but the absence of any distractions of the kind that beset the twentieth century left our reader single-minded in his interests. The Puritan education had taught him the value of cumulative pleasure, which enabled him to sit down undismayed to Gibbon and Locke, Johnson, Pope's Homer and Robertson's histories, solid reading that gives little immediate repayment. And the tone of the age was all in his favour. The general agreement as to what was ' good ' prevented that smothering of the best by the inferior, and of literature generally by journalism, which was noticed in Part I. as characteristic of the modern situation. The requisites of a liberal education were pretty widely known ; Hume, Gibbon, Locke, Dr. Johnson, Shakespeare, Milton, Dryden, Pope, Gray, Burns, were the beginnings of any one's reading in the period we have been surveying, and if novels were in question, then Lackington's list of ' the best ' was the accepted one ; the models of style were Swift, Addison, and Goldsmith, odd volumes of whose works were the foundation of any small second-hand bookseller's stock till Scott's day, and these and their imitators provided the periodical literature. No energy was wasted, the edge of their taste was not blunted on bad writing and cheap thinking.

When revolutionary idealism began to replace ' enthusiasm ' in the consciousness of the working-man, it was still an essentially religious interest, the same

Puritan vigour directed to a slightly different end. *The Age of Reason*, *The Rights of Man*, Godwin's *Enquiry Concerning Political Justice*, and ' Godwin on Necessity ' [67] were the bestsellers of a working class brought up on the ' polemical divines ' of Lackington's library. Chartism itself was associated with such men as William Lovett, Samuel Bamford, Thomas Cooper, and Francis Place, and meetings of Chartist organisations were quite likely to be of the nature of ' Mutual Improvement ' societies : that run by Thomas Cooper in Leicester was equally political, religious, and literary, and held on two or three nights a week, when ' Unless there was some stirring local or political topic I lectured on Milton, and repeated portions of *Paradise Lost*, or on Shakespeare, and repeated portions of *Hamlet*, or on Burns, and repeated *Tam o' Shanter* ; or I recited the history of England, and set the portraits of young Englishmen before young Chartists who listened with intense interest.' It was the next two generations that formed the Mechanics' Institutes, the Mutual Improvement Societies, the Athenæums and Philosophical Institutions which gradually allowed the Victorian passion for ' science ' or practical information to usurp the place literature had hitherto held in the esteem of the artisans, craftsmen, and labourers. So that when the Rationalist Society became in its turn the focus of the aspirations of their children seeking self-improvement, the Puritan interests, still religious in their devoted earnestness to ideas and their pathetically resolute seeking for light, were turned into a channel that left the literature of the age untouched. The sixpenny paper editions published by the R.P.A. in hundreds of thousands were wholly scientific and philosophical—Darwin and Huxley, J. S. Mill and Herbert Spencer, Comte and Lecky, are the literature of the movement, and Newman's *Apologia* was only included for its bearing on theology. And here for the moment we must leave the history of popular culture. The difference that the disappearance of the Sunday book a generation ago has made, its effect on the outlook and mental capacity of the people, would repay investigation. It was, of course, both a cause and a symptom. It was inevitable that the modern popular Press when it appeared at the end of last century should play a part in the break-up of the Puritan tradition, and that the cheaper gratification to be derived easily and immediately should be preferred by the younger generation to the finer cumulative pleasure that literature gave their fathers. We may conclude that as a training of the mind any serious reading is beneficial (by which, of course, is not meant Sunday-school fiction or parish magazines); it appears axiomatic that one cannot spend Sundays over the Bible and *Pilgrim's Progress* and read the *Windsor Magazine* happily in the week.[68] But if for the Bible and *Pilgrim's Progress* are substituted the *News of the World* and the *Sunday Express*, it will be evident that popular taste is likely to be in some danger.

THE GROWTH OF THE READING PUBLIC

BUNYAN stands for the English people at the end of the seventeenth century, but the unregenerate upper class were reading translations of Cervantes (the *Exemplary Novels* at least as much as *Don Quixote*), of the Sieur de Calprenède, of Brémond, Mlle. de Scudéry and Scarron.[69]   So when Aphra Behn turned to prose fiction to eke out her living she chose as pattern the French and Spanish novelettes she knew to be in favour.   She represents the Restoration court culture in fiction, and the interest of her work to-day is that it alone shows the exquisite poise of Restoration comedy in the form of the novel. It is the novelette of high life, but written for the ' high life ' world by one who has the freedom of it (*a*) ; Aphra's stories imply a cultured background, that is, a cultural tradition and a code of manners, wit, and polite intercourse.   In the descriptions of her heroes and heroines, for instance, the emphasis invariably falls on breeding.[70]   Her novels are the work of an amateur, as different as possible from Defoe's, as can be seen by the highly characteristic opening of *The Nun, or the Perjured Beauty* :

Don Henrique was a person of great birth, of a great estate, of a bravery equal to either, of a most generous education, but of more passion than reason.   He was besides of an opener and freer temper than generally his countrymen are

(*a*) *Vide* Note 77.

(I mean, the Spaniards) and always engaged in some love-intrigue or other.

One night as he was retreating from one of those engagements, Don Sebastian, whose sister he had abused with a promise of marriage, set upon him at a corner of a street, in Madrid, and by the help of three of his friends, designed to have despatched him on a doubtful embassy to the Almighty Monarch. But he received their first instructions with better address than they expected, and dismissed his envoy first, killing one of Don Sebastian's friends, *etc.*

One notices the ease and simplicity of the writing, the air of good breeding which presents the extraordinary as a matter of course and assumes that the reader shares the writer's code. There is no attempt to dramatise or work up an effect—in fact, the writer is innocent of such a possibility, narrating with an offhand casualness what would have been spot-light scenes in a post-Richardson novel, and though there are plenty of opportunities in her stories for a pornographic appeal, she makes no attempt to work upon the reader's feelings in this—or any other—way. Her touch is always cool and light. She is so innocent of literary devices that she never even seems to have decided whether she is writing comedy or tragedy ; there is no poetic justice. Her stories are purely a triumph of manner and tone (*a*) ; she begins the delightful topical sketch *The Court of the King of Bantam* with the easy familiarity of conversation among equals :

This money certainly is a most devilish thing ! I'm sure the want of it had like to have ruined my dear Philibella, in her love to Valentine Goodland ; who was really a pretty deserving gentleman, heir to about fifteen hundred pounds

(*a*) ' Tone,' *vide* Pt. III.

a year; which, however, did not so much recommend him, as the sweetness of his temper, the comeliness of his person, and the excellence of his parts.

and ends *The Nun*, perhaps the best example among her novels of the peculiar poise of the Restoration wit, with a touch of something too delicate to be called burlesque that throughout her fiction balances the luxuriant romance of the plot. Sebastian and Henrique were rivals for the hand of the perjured Ardelia shut up in a convent along with Henrique's jilted mistress Elvira; Elvira has betrayed to Henrique her brother Sebastian's plot to elope with her rival; Ardelia is killed in the struggle and

They fought with the greatest animosity on both sides, and with equal advantage; for they both fell together: ' Ah, my Ardelia, I come to thee now!' Sebastian groaned out. ' 'Twas this unlucky arm, which now embraces thee, that killed thee.' ' Just Heaven!' she sighed out, ' Oh, yet have mercy.' [Here they both died.] ' Amen,' cried Henrique, dying, ' I want it most—Oh, Antonio! Oh! Elvira! Ah, there's the weight that sinks me down. And yet I wish forgiveness. Once more, sweet Heaven, have mercy!' He could not outlive that last word; which was echoed by Elvira, who all this while stood weeping, and calling out for help, as she stood close to the wall in the garden.

This alarmed the rest of the sisters, who rising, caused the bells to be rung out, as upon dangerous occasions it used to be; which raised the neighbourhood, who came time enough to remove the dead bodies of the two rivals, and of the late fallen angel Ardelia. The injured and neglected Elvira, whose piety designed quite contrary effects, was immediately seized with a violent fever, which, as it was violent, did not last long: for she died within four-and-twenty hours, with all the happy symptoms of a departing saint.

It is the poise of an aristocratic society. The gulf

between Defoe the journalist of the bourgeois and Aphra Behn the journalist of the court seems impossible to be bridged, and it is the achievement of Steele and Addison that they succeeded in striking a compromise, invaluable while it lasted. The importance of their work is suggested by the letter—' very explanatory of the true Design of our Lucubrations '—in *Tatler 64*, where the writer having applauded the ' wholesome Project of making Wit useful ' continues : ' I smile when I see a solid Citizen of Threescore read the Article from *Will's Coffee-house*, and seem to be just beginning to learn his Alphabet of Wit in Spectacles ; and to hear the attentive Table sometimes stop him with pertinent Queries, which he is puzzled to answer.' As early as No. 5 the characteristic note is struck in a review of Swift's *Project for the Advancement of Religion* :

> It is written with the Spirit of one who has seen the World enough to undervalue it with good Breeding. The Author must certainly be a Man of Wisdom as well as Piety, and have spent much Time in the Exercise of both. The real Causes of the Decay of the Interest of Religion are set forth in a clear and lively manner, without unseasonable Passions; and the whole Air of the Book, as to the Language, the Sentiments, and the Reasonings, shews it was written by one whose Virtue sits easy about him, and to whom Vice is thoroughly contemptible. It was said by one of this Company, alluding to that Knowledge of the World the Author seems to have, the Man writes much like a Gentleman, and goes to Heaven with a very good Mien.

Addison's and Steele's compromise, then, is related to Aphra Behn on the one hand and Defoe on the other (using them as symbols of different cultures), but less interesting than the former and less stable than the latter. In order to include Sir Andrew Freeport in the

Club poise was sacrificed to sedateness, and this often results in a precarious complacency at which one is moved to laugh, or a sermonising dulness which gradually gained the upper hand : the *Tatler* is much livelier and subtler than the *Spectator*, and compared with it often surprisingly *risqué*, so that whereas the latter naturally suggests Goldsmith and Johnson the former looks back to Congreve ; while the *Guardian* is practically unreadable. What happened is that the balance descended heavily on the bourgeois side : Richardson's novels, Goldsmith's verse, Johnson's essays, are bourgeois art. But meanwhile, the culture of the *Tatler* was a compound. The moral aim evident throughout the two papers is not, as in Defoe, separated from the polite world, the stress falls not on morals but on *mœurs*. As Addison claimed in the dedication to the first volume of the *Spectator*, it was ' a Work which endeavours to Cultivate and Polish Human Life.' And a more explicit statement occurs in *Spectator 58* :

> As the great and only End of these my Speculations is to banish Vice and Ignorance out of the Territories of Great Britain, I shall endeavour as much as possible to establish among us a Taste of polite Writing.

He succeeded. The influence of this triumph of ' the Familiar Way of Writing ' is to be seen throughout the eighteenth century, not merely in the two hundred odd periodicals started in imitation of the *Spectator*, but in the lucid, easy, uncoloured prose of the novels, belles-lettres, journals, and correspondence for nearly a century afterwards. Like Addison's and Steele's, it was based on contemporary speech,[71] until Johnson and Burke made a fresh start on an oratorical basis. The rate of penetration can be guessed from the sales. In *Spectator 10* Addison writes : ' My Publisher tells me that there are already Three thousand of them distributed every Day : So that if I allow Twenty Readers to every Paper, which I look upon as a modest computation,[72] I may reckon about Threescore thousand Disciples in *London* and *Westminster*.' It appears to have risen steadily to 20,000 or even 30,000, which by Addison's modest computation gives half a million or more readers. In addition there are the sales in volume form to consider : ' an Edition of the former Volumes of *Spectators* of above Nine thousand each Book, is already sold off ' (*Spectator 555*). Now the population of England in 1700 was not much over six millions, and a little mental arithmetic will prove how immediately pervasive the influence was. In the history of the self-educated in the eighteenth and early nineteenth centuries, which has been traced in the previous chapter, volumes of the *Tatler* and *Spectator* were observed to turn up in the homes of the respectable poor as their early reading, so numerous were the editions. Even now it is cheaper to buy an eighteenth-century set of the two papers than a modern edition.

It is important to notice that the *Tatler* and *Spectator* and their innumerable imitators stood for serious standards, however playfully they may have supported them. They made possible the eighteenth-century novel in more ways than one. To begin with, they combined two hitherto separate reading publics (Aphra Behn's and Bunyan's), and gave it a code which may without much fear of contradiction be termed a desirable one ; they were preoccupied with life as their readers lived it, and endeavoured to be helpful in the rather naïve manner suggested here :

> I am heartily concerned when I see a virtuous man without a competent knowledge of the world; and if there can be any use in these papers, it is this: that without representing vice under any false alluring notions, they give my reader an insight into the ways of men, and represent human nature in all its changeable colours. . . . The Virtuous and the Innocent may know in speculation what they could never arrive at by practice, and by this means avoid the snares of the crafty, the corruptions of the vicious, and the reasonings of the prejudiced. Their minds may be opened without being vitiated (a).

This code is defined by such characteristic dicta as : ' What I should contend for is, the more virtuous the man is the nearer will he be to the character of genteel and agreeable,' ' to undervalue the world with good breeding,' ' a Philosopher, by which I mean a gentleman.' Now in uniting the reading public by means of this code the writers of the *Tatler* and *Spectator* were putting into currency a certain set of terms. Or to put it more precisely, they were finding an idiom for common standards of taste and conduct. It is on the general recognition and acceptance of this particular idiom that the novelists from Richardson to Scott and Jane Austen depend; by means of journalism the conventions were established which enabled the eighteenth-century novelist to use quite simply words and phrases like ' honour,' ' manly virtue,' ' the man of candour and true understanding,' and to write such an urbane shorthand as Addison's, ' I shall always make reason, truth and nature the measures of praise and dispraise,' and be sure of being understood.

(a) *Spectator* 245.

Fielding's effects, for instance, depend on the simplification he was thus able to achieve *without sacrificing precision*. In comparison, the twentieth-century novelist's vocabulary is loosely emotive, and the highbrow novelist is obliged either to employ such absolute terms ironically or else to go out of his way to avoid them.

And the give-and-take of journalism when it took the form of essays written ' in an air of common speech ' (*a*) provided the novelist with the best of all styles, combining the maximum flexibility with complete absence of pretension. The ' polite writing ' for which Addison set out to establish a taste meant merely good writing, simple, decent, and realistic. To open at random a story by a popular writer between the *Tatler* and Richardson is almost inevitably to alight on prose of this kind. [The heroine's coach has been jostled off a bridge into the river] :

> By good Luck, this Bridge was at the Entry of a little Village, so that People hastened to their Assistance; some helping the Horses, some the Coach, and some with Difficulty getting out Galesia; who, however, when she was got out, found no Hurt, only was very wet: She was much pity'd by the good People; amongst whom there was a poor Woman took her under the Arm, and told her she would conduct her to a House, where she might be accomodated with all Manner of Conveniences.
>
> All wet and dropping, she got to this House, which was a poor Village-Alehouse; and a poor one indeed it was; It being Evening, the Woman of the House was gone out a Milking, so that the good Man could come at no Sheets, that she might have got rid of her wet Cloths, by going to Bed; However, he laid on a large Country Faggot; so she

(*a*) *Tatler* 5.

sat and smoaked in her wet Cloaths, 'till the good Woman
came; who hasten'd and got the Bed Sheeted, into which
she gladly laid herself; but the poorest that her Bones ever
felt, there being a few Flocks that stank; and so thin of
the same, that she felt the Cords cut through. The Blankets
were of Thread-bare Home-spun stuff, which felt and smelt
like a Pancake fry'd in Grease; There were Four Curtains
at the Four Corners, from whence they could no more stir,
than Curtains in a Picture; for there were neither Rods nor
Ropes for them to run upon; no Testern, but the Thatch
of the House; A Chair with a Piece of a Bottom, and a
brown chamber-pot furr'd as thick as a Crown Piece (a).

The fabric of Fielding's and Smollett's work is of
this nature. And even Richardson, though he is
working on the easy responses associated with the
word 'sentimental'—his chief contribution to the
novel was the discovery of the Tears of Sensibility—
nevertheless has the virtues of this prose and this
manner. Even an apparent departure from it such as
Sterne's will be found on inspection only to be an extension of the possibilities of this manner.

The history of popular taste in fiction from Aphra
Behn to Fielding is sufficiently illustrated by the
writings of Mrs. Haywood, the female Defoe. Like
him she was obliged to earn her living by the pen, and
so followed current fashion with amazing fertility;
like him she produced her best work at the end of a long
career—its merits have never been recognised since
her own day. She started on little romances adapted
from the French, and drawing on her dramatic experience produced that stylisation of heroic romance

(a) 'A Patch-Work SCREEN for the LADIES; or LOVE and VIRTUE
Recommended: In a COLLECTION of Instructive NOVELS.' By Mrs. Jane
Barker, of Wilsthorp, near Stamford, in Lincolnshire. 1723.

which, always acceptable to the unsophisticated, petered out in Victorian melodrama. *Love in Excess* (1719) is a type-title,[73] and it reached a sixth edition in 1725. She continued with the popular ' Secret Histories ' and about 1729 abandoned these for the realistic ' Memoirs ' and ' Lives of ' ; and finally, after the publication of *Pamela*, she turned to domestic fiction and wrote among other things two little masterpieces— *The History of Miss Betsy Thoughtless* (1751—4th ed. 1768) and *The History of Jemmy and Jenny Jessamy* (1753—2nd ed. same year, etc.). They are usually dismissed as imitations of Fielding and Richardson, but this is to simplify unduly. The eighteenth-century ethos had undergone a considerable simplification since the *Tatler*—the settling-down process is evident in the tone of the *Spectator* and its imitators—and the same environment in fact equally produced Richardson, Fielding, Smollett, Mrs. Haywood, and ultimately Goldsmith and Jane Austen. Mrs. Haywood was not imitating *Pamela* and *Tom Jones* but taking advantage of a newly perceived taste, that of Defoe's public steering another course : the stress still falls on life as known to the reader (*a*), even in the most popular fiction, but the reader's interests have shifted from the regulation of property to the regulation of the feelings (they are nevertheless the same kind of interests). These writers are as firmly based as Defoe. Instead of the romantic idealism the modern reader expects they display sensibility controlled by decorum, a decorum directly related to Addison's sedateness, and which in some form or other is found discreetly restraining

(*a*) Not, of course, life measured by events, but by scope and intensity.

eighteenth-century taste in every field. A typical utterance of the *Idler* may explain what is meant:

> It is very difficult to determine the exact degree of enthusiasm that the arts of painting and poetry may admit. . . . An intimate knowledge of the passions, and good sense, but not common sense, must at last determine its limits (*a*).

Now this voices an attitude completely antithetical to that described on p. 68. And it explains the discomfort, a succession of slight shocks and jars, which the modern reader of eighteenth-century novels finds he has exposed himself to. The eighteenth-century novelist is continually pulling up the reader, disappointing his expectations or refusing him the luxury of day-dreaming and not infrequently douching him with cold water. When in *The History of Miss Betsy Thoughtless*, on Betsy's unfaithful husband sending for her to comfort his last hours and her responding with great good nature, we learn of her old admirer Trueworth : 'when he heard this cruel husband was no more, and, at the same time, was informed in what manner she behaved, both in his last moments, and after his decease, nothing, not even his love, could equal his admiration of her virtue and her prudence'; or when at the happy ending of *The History of Jemmy and Jenny Jessamy*, Jenny composedly declares to Jemmy before marrying him : ' I shall not be so unreasonable as to expect more constancy from you, than human nature and your constitution will allow '; then one seems for a moment to put one's finger on the eighteenth-century virtue, predominant in any novel till the death of Smollett, the source equally of Jane Austen's strength and of Maria Edgeworth's, disguised

(*a*) *Idler*, No. 80.

by romantic trappings in Scott and finally lost to the succeeding age. It consists in the absence of romantic idealism, and in consequence the presence of a rational code of feeling; words really mean something, and a particular vocabulary is at the novelist's disposal that enables him to deal with any situation with dignity. The temperature of even the critical scenes is decidedly cool, for the rhetoric of sensibility employs an abstract vocabulary which effectually maintains an emotional decorum. When Mrs. Haywood retires from an avowal of love with—' After this a considerable time was passed in all those mutual endearments which honour and modesty would permit' (a), or Jane Austen disposes of a delicate interval in the history of her hero and heroine so—' I purposely abstain from dates on this occasion, that every one may be at liberty to fix their own, aware that the cure of unconquerable passions, and the transfer of unchanging attachments, must vary much as to time in different people ' (b), or when Maria Edgeworth describes some one as ' pressing her hand with all the tenderness which humanity could dictate ' (c), they are preserving their distance from the emotional situations they are handling, and the reader's own mode of feeling is not tampered with. It is essentially the critical temper that produced and maintained this code of good taste and good sense—a sense of standards even in the realm of emotion. The ideal of ' a well-regulated mind ' explicitly mentioned by Maria Edgeworth and Jane Austen [74] is implicit in the works of their immediate predecessors; in comparison with any of them the

(a) *The History of Miss Betsy Thoughtless.*   (b) *Mansfield Park.*
(c) *Belinda.*

novels of Charlotte Brontë, for instance, exhibit a shameful self-abandonment to undisciplined emotion which makes these latter seem the productions of a schoolgirl of genius. The critical reader is never in any novel before 1820 made uncomfortable by crudities of feeling as he is in reading Dickens, Charlotte Brontë, Kingsley, or by the vulgarity and puerility that he winces at in Dickens, Thackeray, Kingsley, Meredith . . . indeed almost any Victorian novelist except Emily Brontë, Mrs. Gaskell, George Eliot. The decline and disappearance of the eighteenth-century code is part of the history of the reading public.

It is the sudden growth of the reading, and particularly the novel-reading, public in the second half of the eighteenth century that started a series of changes in such important matters as the relation of author to publisher, the scope and nature of the periodical, the expectations of the reader, and the aims and object of the novelist. The change may be noticed, for instance, in the difference between the tone of the *Tatler* and of the *Idler*, the one talking at his ease to a circle of friends and the other consciously raising his voice for the benefit of a public assembly ; or it may be more forcibly brought home by the fact that the average daily sale of newspapers practically doubled between 1753 and 1775 in a nearly stationary population. Such statistical evidence as is available that bears on the growth of the reading public at this period has been collected by Mr. A. S. Collins in his two works, *Authorship in the Age of Johnson 1726-1780* and *The Profession of Letters 1780-1830*, but to the literary critic the internal evidence is even more con-

vincing as well as more interesting. Briefly, the case
was that the *Spectator* with its general popularity had
given a fillip to the taste for fiction, as Addison himself
noted, and Richardson's opportune discovery of a
technique for examining the heart that should also
make improving reading finally decided the direction
of popular taste. So great was the demand for such
novels that the book clubs and subscription libraries
that existed up and down the country to serve a timid
but solid taste for literature were metamorphosed into
the modern circulating library. They increased
enormously, and in addition the booksellers seeing
their chance set up their own, so that in 1761 the
Annual Register remarks as a matter of course that ' the
reading female hires her novel from some County
Circulating Library, which consists of about a hundred
volumes ' and Sheridan in *The Rivals* (1775) makes
Lucy report to her mistress, ' I don't believe there's a
circulating library in Bath I haven't been at.' Now so
long as there were good novels to provide the circulating library was an excellent institution, and, fortunately,
for many years there were four serious novelists at
work who kept the standard of fiction at a very high
level. As we have seen, when a Mrs. Haywood sat
down to write a novel she could produce admirable
fiction, because she was in touch with the best work of
her age ; the Mrs. Haywoods changed their technique
as soon as a Richardson or a Sterne provided them with
a new one ; they were quick to seize the advantage of a
fresh method, which is what only a genius can invent :
the journalist of fiction can only create literature when
he has a living tradition to work in. In the light of the
situation discussed in Part I., it is interesting to notice

the simplicity of the eighteenth-century literary map. The bestsellers of the twentieth century do not change their courses because D. H. Lawrence, Virginia Woolf, or James Joyce has written; indeed they have probably never heard of these novelists, and as we have seen, their readers certainly have not. The eighteenth-century public was still homogeneous : in the depths of the country those who could read read *Pamela* aloud to those who could not, and Lackington the book-seller writes in his autobiography in 1791, rather surprisingly :

> I cannot help observing, that the sale of books in general has increased prodigiously within the last twenty years. According to the best estimation I have been able to make, I suppose that more than four times the number of books are sold now than were sold twenty years since. The poorer sort of farmers, and even the poor country people in general, who before that period spent their winter evenings in relating stories of witches, ghosts, hobgoblins, &c. now shorten the winter nights by hearing their sons and daughters read tales, romances, &c., and on entering their houses, you may see Tom Jones, Roderick Random, and other entertaining books stuck up on their bacon racks, &c. If *John* goes to town with a load of hay, he is charged to be sure not to forget to bring home Peregrine Pickle's Adventures; and when *Dolly* is sent to market to sell her eggs, she is commissioned to purchase The History of Pamela Andrews. In short all ranks and degrees now READ.

But a taste for novel-reading as distinct from a taste for literature is not altogether desirable. In this case it meant that when Smollett died and there was no writer of any considerable ability to succeed him, the insatiable demand for fiction—now the publisher's mainstay—had to be satisfied by the second-rate.

Hacks were employed to provide the circulating library, which now became a symbol for worthless fiction, with constant supplies of fresh novels. The process is somewhat telescoped and the facts greatly exaggerated in the following extract from Clara Reeve's *The Progress of Romance* (1785), but it shows in what light a cultivated woman regarded the circulating library in the last quarter of the century :

> Euphrasia. ' They [novels] did but now increase upon us, but ten years more multiplied them tenfold. Every work of merit produced a swarm of imitators, till they became a public evil, and the institution of Circulating Libraries conveyed them in the cheapest manner to every bodies hand.'
>
> Hortentius. ' I rejoice that you do not defend Circulating Libraries,—if you had, I would have fought against them with more success, than I have ever met with hitherto, when I have been your opponent.'
>
> Euph. ' I am entirely of your opinion, they are one source of the vices and follies of our present times.'
>
> .   .   .   .   .   .
>
> Euph. ' The year 1766 (*a*) was very prolific in the Novel way, and indeed they seem to have over-run the press, till they became a *drug* in the *terms* of the *trade*.—The Reviewers complained bitterly of the fatigue of reading them, it became necessary to have an Annual Supply for the Circulating Library, in consequence the manufacturers of Novels were constantly at work for them, and were very poorly paid for their labours.' (*b*)

The change that the circulating library made in the

(*a*) Clara Reeve has antedated the process.

(*b*) On the contrary, for at this period novels even by unknown writers fetched nearly as high prices as poetry was to command in the next generation. *Vide* A. S. Collins, *The Profession of Letters*, p. 97, etc.

reading habits of the semi-educated, but particularly of women, the chief novel-readers, had far-reaching effects. A comparison of bestsellers of the 1770-1795 period with those of the previous twenty years will reveal a narrowing down process: Sterne is replaced by Henry Mackenzie and his imitators, Richardson by writers like Mrs. Sheridan (*a*), Henry Brooke and Richard Cumberland, Fielding and Smollett by Mrs. Radcliffe, Mrs. Inchbald, Charlotte Smith (and eventually Scott). That is to say, whereas the response of the reader of the 'fifties had been a complex one, it now became a simple response to the extremely unskilful and clumsy call for tears, pity, shudders, and so forth. The immense popularity of Sterne, which elicited one volume of *Tristram Shandy* after another, is astonishing to the twentieth century, in which its only readers are probably those specifically concerned with literature, for to the general reader it is interminably dull, without either plot or point. Sterne requires careful and persevering reading, but the reward is an extremely subtle kind of pleasure, since Sterne's success consists in harmonising a variety of moods and bringing off chameleon-like changes of feeling (*b*) with a juggler's dexterity; a whole public that clamoured for more and more parts of *Tristram Shandy* is now almost inconceivable. But it did not last long. A proof of what happened to that public lies in a little volume entitled ' The BEAUTIES of STERNE; including all his Pathetic Tales, and most distinguished OBSERVATIONS on LIFE. Selected for the Heart of

(*a*) Mrs. Sheridan's *Memoirs of Miss Sidney Biddulph* was published in 1761, but she is an early instance of the disintegrating process that later set in all round.

(*b*) ' Feeling,' *vide* Pt. III.

Sensibility.' The compiler, a Mr. W. H., explains in
the preface :

> I intended to have arranged them alphabetically, till I
> found the stories of *Le Fever*, the *Monk*, and *Maria*, would
> be too closely connected for the *feeling reader*, and would
> wound the bosom of *sensibility* too deeply : I therefore placed
> them at a proper distance from each other.

This one-sided version of Sterne was so popular that
by 1782 it had reached a fourth edition (*a*), and it
proves how much easier it was found to read Sterne for
the wrong reasons than for the right ones—that is, to
make a partial instead of a complete response. The
heart of sensibility could be as satisfactorily catered for
by Henry Mackenzie, who separated out of Sterne's
balanced whole the most popular elements. In consequence, whereas to read *Tristram Shandy* is a bracing
mental exercise, *The Man of Feeling* represents only a
refined form of emotional self-indulgence. The same
kind of relation exists between them as between *Don
Juan* and *Prometheus Unbound*, *Tristram Shandy* being
just such a hit-or-miss switchback performance as
Byron's. *Don Juan* can be read in various ways (one
of them will yield precisely the same kind of pleasure
as Shelley's poetry), but when read so as to give a
complete response the poem is peculiarly invigorating ;
Prometheus Unbound can only be read in one way, and
its characteristic effect is the opposite of invigorating—
one might describe it as intoxicating or boring according to the suitability of the reader.

The history of the influence of Richardson is rather
different, and Richardson himself assisted the circulating library novel to take shape. *Grandison*, though

(*a*) And by 1793 a 12th edition.

hardly *Pamela*, paved the way for the kind of fiction that Hannah More attacked in her *Cheap Repository* penny tracts. Her objections are those of a sound eighteenth-century realist, and though they dispose of the successors of Richardson, it is important to realise that they leave Richardson himself almost untouched.

' The people talk such gibberish as no folks in their sober senses ever talked, and the things that happen to them are not like the things that ever happen to any of my acquaintance. They are at home one minute, and beyond the sea the next. Beggars to-day, and Lords to-morrow. Waiting-maids in the morning, and Dutchesses at night. You and I, Master Worthy, have worked hard many years, and think it very well to have scraped a trifle of money together, you a few hundreds, I suppose, and I a few thousands. But one would think every man in these books had the Bank of England in his scrutore. Then there's another thing which I never met with in true life. We think it pretty well, you know, if one has got one thing, and another has got another. I'll tell you how I mean. You are reckoned sensible, our Parson is learned, the Squire is rich, I am generous, one of your daughters is pretty, and both mine are genteel. But in these books (except here and there one, whom they make worse than Satan himself) every man and woman's child of them, are all wise, and witty, and generous, and rich, and handsome, and genteel. Nobody is middling, or good in one thing, and bad in another, like my live acquaintance, but 'tis all up to the skies, or down to the dirt. I had rather read Tom Hickathrift, or Jack the Giant Killer.' [*The Two Wealthy Farmers*, 1795 (?).]

But the effect of the circulating library habit was deeper than this suggests. The readiness to read a good novel had become a craving for fiction of any kind, and a habit of reading poor novels not only destroys the ability to distinguish between literature and trash, it creates a positive taste for a certain kind of writing, if only because it does not demand the effort of a fresh response, as the uneducated ear listens with pleasure only to a tune it is familiar with.   The function of the popular novel of the late eighteenth century is adequately dealt with by Coleridge in *Biographia Literaria*, Chapter XXII. :

> For as to the devotees of the circulating libraries, I dare not compliment their pass-time, or rather kill-time, with the name of reading.   Call it rather a sort of beggarly daydreaming, during which the mind of the dreamer furnishes for itself nothing but laziness, and a little mawkish sensibility; while the whole *material* and imagery of the doze is supplied *ab extra* by a sort of mental *camera obscura* manufactured at the printing office, which *pro tempore* fixes, reflects, and transmits the moving phantasms of one man's delirium, so as to people the barrenness of a hundred other brains afflicted with the same trance or suspension of common sense and all definite purpose.   We should therefore transfer this species of amusement from the genus reading, to that comprehensive class characterised by the power of reconciling the two contrary yet co-existing propensities of human nature, namely, indulgence of sloth, and hatred of vacancy.

And he explains himself in more detail in the first of the *Lectures on Shakespeare and Milton* :

> I will run the risk of asserting, that where the reading of novels prevails as a habit, it occasions in time the entire destruction of the powers of the mind; it is such an utter loss to the reader, that it is not so much to be called pass-time as kill-time.   It conveys no trustworthy information as to facts; it produces no improvement of the intellect, but fills the mind with a mawkish and morbid sensibility, which is directly hostile to the cultivation, invigoration and enlargement of the nobler faculties of the understanding.

Now such a charge could not possibly have been levelled at the novel before Henry Mackenzie began to write. *Tristram Shandy, Peregrine Pickle, Tom Jones, Jemmy and Jenny Jessamy*, to take a few of the out-standing popular successes, are extremely wide-awake productions. They are written in accordance with the principles of the contributor to the *Idler* quoted above —'an intimate knowledge of the passions, and good sense, but not common sense' are assumed to be qualities possessed by both author and reader. Even *Pamela* is not merely the serving-maid's version of 'Cinderella,' as a bare account of its plot might suggest; compare *Pamela* with *The Sheik*, which in the year of its publication was to be seen in the hands of every typist and may be taken as embodying the typist's day-dream, and it is obvious that *Pamela* is only in-cidentally serving the purpose for which *The Sheik* exists and even then serving it very indifferently. And apart from Richardson, no other novelist of that age even provides a scaffolding for castle-building. On the contrary, as we have seen, these novelists and such of their successors who did not write for the circulating library—Maria Edgeworth, Jane Austen, Hannah More—are concerned to destroy any comforting illusions the reader may cherish, to make the reader more aware of, more fully alive to, and therefore better fitted to cope with, the world he lives in.

It was inevitable that the popular novel should become stereotyped, and that it should hit out the constituents of the commonest form of fantasying; it was the easiest kind of plot for a hack to produce—just as day-dreaming is infinitely easier than thinking—and the pleasantest for a lazy reader to take in.[75] The hero or heroine with whom the reader can identify himself, the romantic love-story with a happy or else a movingly tragic ending, the naïvely good and bad characters and the romantic jargon, became the inevitable foundation of any but a highly exceptional novel for the next hundred years. It became impossible for a novelist not to conform with this convention ; Scott could not— the introduction to *Waverley* and the conclusion to *Old Mortality* suggest he dared not—refuse to give the public what it wanted, and he was no genius, merely, as an inspection of Mrs. Radcliffe's novels shows, another Mrs. Radcliffe. So he put his novels together in the easiest way, and his originality consisted in finding new backgrounds to set off the old conventions, as hers had been. Nothing is more obvious than that he was bored with his central characters, his plot and situations. His interest was driven out on to the margins of his story, where he could slip in a character or two he had observed and relapse from the language of romance into the dialect that was spoken around him and to which his ear was therefore sensitised. Smollett's freedom was complete: his interest is visible in every line he wrote ; beside him Scott appears hemmed in, his prose is curiously fatigued—the clumsy, unrealised descriptions of thrilling actions, the rhetorical outbursts in ' the language of passion,' the conscientious oil-paintings of historical scenes and characters, drag their slow lengths along often ridiculously (*a*). He not only wrote fast and carelessly— Smollett did that too, and Smollett's vigorous prose runs freely without being slipshod—but he gave his work a merely perfunctory attention. The popular novel at that date had no room for a writer's interests.

(*a*) *Vide* especially the dramatic scene from *Ivanhoe* in *The Oxford Book of English Prose*, p. 532.

And so the eighteenth-century idiom, so admirably suited for the literature of a society that abhorred ' enthusiasm,' began to lose its edge : in Addison and Fielding it is everything, in Scott it has become a wearily sustained convention. It was said previously that in the eighteenth century words really meant something, and yet in the early nineteenth century the same words seem to have become counters. Take the most simple instance : Fielding's aim, in his own words, was ' to recommend goodness and innocence ' (a); by Scott's time, while the same object was still the avowed one of every novelist, yet the phrase has no longer any precise meaning—the idiom has become a conventional currency like that of the Musical Banks. Or to put the case more glaringly, one may compare the heroines of the two ages who embody this ideal, Clarissa, Sophia, and the Emily of *Peregrine Pickle* on the one hand, and any Scott young lady heroine on the other. Mrs. Radcliffe represents the intermediate stage, where though the circulating library conventions are in full possession yet there is still something alive in the body of the book. The superb absence of any historical sense is the saving of *The Mysteries of Udolpho*.[76] It proves conclusively that late eighteenth-century taste was still sure of itself, that there was a culture strong enough to absorb everything alien. Mrs. Radcliffe has no perceptible misgivings in treating a story of the year 1568 as the history of a contemporary young lady of delicate sensibility ; the French and Italian aristocracy meet to discuss over tea and coffee the opera and Parisian fashions, while Emily's papa has an exquisite taste for Gothic ruins.

(a) *Joseph Andrews.*

But the elasticity of the idiom handled by Sterne and Richardson is gone for ever. The language has hardened, it forms itself into lumpy periods—whereas Addison and Fielding write as they spoke, Johnson and Jane Austen compose on paper.

While the popular novel was bleaching the diction of the age a corresponding change was inevitably taking place in sensibility. The robust, clear-headed reader of Sterne and Fielding became and ever after remained prudish and romantic—nothing bears better witness to the startling change than that *Pamela* is employed by the would-be seducer in *The Sylph* (1779) to corrupt the mind of the village maiden. Plenty of similar evidence exists—Scott's grand-aunt with her ' Take back your bonny Mrs. Behn,' [77] Tom Moore's rather startled note on the eccentric peer of the old school who lived at Ditchley 'reading aloud of an evening all " the good old coarse novels," *Peregrine Pickle* particularly ' (*a*), Jane Austen's astonishing censure of the *Spectator*,[78] all summed up by Coleridge as ' the greater purity of morality in the present age, compared even with the last.' He continues :

> Let me ask, who now will venture to read a number of the *Spectator*, or of the *Tatler*, to his wife and daughters, without first examining it to make sure that it contains no word which might, in our day, offend the delicacy of female ears, and shock feminine susceptibility? Even our theatres, the representations at which usually reflect the morals of the period, have taken a sort of domestic turn, and while the performances at them may be said, in some sense, to improve the heart, there is no doubt that they vitiate the taste (*b*).

It was not that the multiplication of female readers

(*a*) *Diary*, May 30th, 1829.
(*b*) *Lectures on Shakespeare and Milton*, The First Lecture.

made it necessary for the novelist to consider feminine delicacy and susceptibility; in the days when Lady Mary Wortley Montagu received in one box *Peregrine Pickle*, *Roderick Random*, *Clarissa*, and *Pompey the Little*, among others (*a*), there was a large public of women to admire Richardson and Sterne as well as, like her, to criticise them. The limitation of all the complicated appeals that the novel can make to a specific simple few—an appeal that arouses only noble and pathetic feelings, for instance—means not only a serious limitation of the novelist's scope, it must mean ultimately, where fiction is the chief or only form of art that the general public encounters, an all-round impoverishment of emotional life.

It must not be supposed, however, that so drastic a change took place instantly. It only appeared at the time as a sudden drop in the novel's prestige and the definition of a way in which the novelist understood he had to tread if he wished for popularity. There was still the same high level of cultured opinion, represented and sustained by the reviews—the *Gentleman's Magazine* started in 1731 was soon followed by the *London Magazine*, in 1749 the *Monthly Review* inaugurated a new phase in the history of the Press, and in 1756 a rival, the *Critical Review*, appeared, and so to the more formidable *Edinburgh* (1802), the *Quarterly* (1809), and the specifically *Literary Gazette* and *Blackwood's* (1817). As late as 1817 Isaac D'Israeli was writing on ' Literary Journals ' in this vein :

> The invention of Reviews, in the form which they have
> at length gradually assumed, could not have existed but in
> the most polished ages of literature; for without a constant

(*a*) February 1752.

supply of authors, and a refined spirit of criticism, they could not excite a perpetual interest among the lovers of literature. These publications are the chronicles of taste and science, and present the existing state of the public mind. . . . Multifarious writings produced multifarious strictures, and public criticism reached to such perfection, that taste was generally diffused. . . . To the lovers of literature these volumes, when they have outlived their year, are not unimportant. They constitute a great portion of literary history, and are indeed the annals of the republic. . . . The *Monthly Review*, the venerable mother of our journals, commenced in 1749, *etc.* (*a*).

This not only suggests the authority and standing of the literary periodical, it shows that the eighteenth-century idiom was still current in 1817; in fact, eighteenth-century modes of feeling and thinking lasted, along with the Georgian architectural style, well into the nineteenth century. The phraseology of the periodical of the age is significant—'elegant literature,' 'polite learning,' 'polished society,' 'the polite world,' 'a refined spirit of criticism'; it is the idiom of a society with critical standards so firmly imposed from above (it is essentially an aristocratic culture) that the mere idea of any serious challenge to them was almost unthinkable. So the circulating library novel became a subject for general ridicule—'branded as a mere vehicle for frivolous, or seductive amusement . . . a species of writing which [is] never mentioned, even by its supporter, but with a look that fears contempt' (*b*)—in spite of the lip-service paid by every aspiring novelist to criticism in the form of a preface, or even an introductory chapter to each book,

(*a*) *Curiosities of Literature*, p. 5.
(*b*) Fanny Burney, dedication to *The Wanderer* (1814).

devoted to a discussion of such elementary points as the object of the novelist, his moral justification, the rules of novel-writing, and so forth. Yet this degree of seriousness seems remarkable in popular novelists, even though, as has been suggested, a fashion for such critical tit-bits had perhaps been set by *Tom Jones* and *The Tale of a Tub*. There was still only one public, which through the reviews took its standards from above. The reviews were intelligent, serious, and critical; moreover, novels were still being published in manageable numbers, so that every novel received notice and all novels were criticised by the same standards. Whatever objections to those standards we may raise, the advantages of this state of affairs is apparent when compared with the state of anarchy described in Part I. Chapter II. The reviewers then were at least in agreement as to what was worth doing in fiction and what was not. I open the *Monthly Review* for the 1790's at random, and find Mrs. Radcliffe's *The Italian* under consideration. The writer as a preliminary to ' placing ' the book begins by a description of ' the genuine novel '—

> The most excellent, but at the same time the most difficult, species of novel-writing consists in an accurate and interesting representation of such manners and characters as society represents. [March 1797.]

—and he is thus able to recognise *The Italian* as an ingenious example of the second-rate. In the next number another novel, *Memoirs of Emma Courtney* by Mary Hays, is approved because:

> These memoirs rise above the class of vulgar novels, which aspire only to divert the unoccupied mind, by occasional

illusion, from an irksome attention to the daily occurrences
and trivial incidents of real life. [April 1797.]

The number of novels published began to go up in
the middle of the 1780's; in 1796 the *Monthly*
noticed twice as many as in the previous year, and by
1800 novels had become so numerous and in such bad
repute that the *Scots* and *Gentleman's* magazines had
practically ceased to notice them at all (*a*). Of the
1300 odd novels noticed by the *Monthly* and the
Critical reviews between 1770 and 1800, only four—
Evelina, Vathek, Castle Rackrent, and *Humphrey Clinker*
—have survived, and these are for different reasons
exceptional to the period. Throughout the 1790's the
reviewers can be seen struggling to retain one set of
values; in the end they gave up for the time being not
their respectability but the novel (*b*).

What helped to stave off the demoralising effect of
the circulating library was undoubtedly the technical
incompetence of the novelists. After Richardson had
shown the way they of course knew, as no one had
known before, roughly how to evoke a certain kind of
response. But they rather blundered towards their
goal than went all out for it; not even the most
efficient of them—Mrs. Radcliffe—shows a trace of
the cunning business methods of the twentieth-
century bestseller.[79] In consequence one can read the
novels of Scott and his predecessors without forfeiting
one's self-respect, whereas, as indicated in Part I., it is
often impossible to say as much for their modern

(*a*) I am greatly indebted for factual matter used here to an unpublished
M.A. thesis of London University by W. H. Husbands, entitled ' The
Lesser Novel 1770-1800.'

(*b*) But a generation later the novel industry had become organised, with
dire effects on the reviewers.

counterparts. And an additional brake on progress was the important fact that a fair proportion of the population could not read : it received its education through hand and eye and word of mouth and did not complicate matters by creating a separate semi-literate public to interfere with the book market. Those who had a desire for learning could rise hand over hand like the Lackingtons and Drews considered in the previous chapter : the rate of absorption of the lowest class into the middle class was slow enough to prevent any lowering of standards.

Three illustrations of the common reader's background at the end of the century may be useful here. One is that when social workers began to teach the poor to read in large numbers, Hannah More was the writer who catered for the new public. Her delightful tales and novels issued as penny numbers (*The Cheap Repository*) from 1794 to 1797 deal with the shepherds, farmers, labourers, servants, poachers, small shop-keepers, and their families whom she knew ; they are marked by what the *Edinburgh Review* called her ' amiable good sense,' and the more ambitious of them are excellent examples of the sub-acid critical attitude that characterises the best eighteenth-century writers ; [80] and they sold two millions in the first year (1795).[81]

Another is Eliza Fletcher's autobiography (*a*). She was born at Oxton in Yorkshire in 1770, the daughter

(*a*) '*Autobiography of Eliza Fletcher*. Edited by the survivor of her family' (1875). The autobiography was written 1838 to 1857. She died in 1858, and the editor supplemented the memoirs with family letters and the younger generation's recollections of their mother's tales and anecdotes. The volume is of great interest to the literary historian, since Mrs. Fletcher was one of the great Edinburgh hostesses.

of a yeoman farmer, and of the formative influences of her childhood she wrote:

There were then no books for children but fairy-tales and Æsop's and Gay's Fables. My father's library was upon a small scale—the Spectator, Milton's Works, Shakespeare's Plays, Pope's and Dryden's Poems, Hervey's Meditations, Mrs. Rowe's Letters, Shenstone's Poems, Sherlock's Sermons, with some abridgements of history and geography, filled his little bookshelves. To these Mrs. Brudenell's [a neighbour's] store added a few other works, such as Robertson's History of Scotland, Sully's Memoirs, Pope's Homer, etc. . . . Music and story-telling, recitations from Pope's Homer or Shakespeare's Plays, with sometimes a pool at commerce or a game of blind-man's buff, were our evening recreations. . . . [Of her visits to her maternal grandfather's] Mr. Hill was a man of very superior understanding, and an elegant classical scholar, a perfect gentleman in manners, with a mildness and quietness approaching to Quakerian. He had an utter contempt for the vanities and frivolities of life. He lost his wife when his four daughters and his only son were very young, and he then took as inmate a niece of his own, to be their guardian and companion. My mother, his eldest daughter, was the only one he ever sent to a boarding school. He cultivated in them all a love of reading, a taste for simple pleasures, and a strong sense of usefulness and public good.

A third is a communication from an anonymous correspondent in the *Gentleman's Magazine* for June 1852 on 'Country Book-Clubs Fifty Years Ago':

I thought of the quiet but deep influence which the Review and Magazine, and the few but well-selected books supplied by the Country Book-Club to the twenty-five or thirty families among which they circulated, exercised in their day. . . . Mostly the *new* books were read aloud, *en famille*; but this was only the case with those which were still passing through the hands of the members of the club, and were to be given up at the end of a stated time. . . .

The orders issued to the bookseller of the market-town where the club assembled were not inconsiderable. In fact nearly all the new publications of English origin which were really worth having, in general literature and popular science, were included, and the families we have noted were never without a fair amount of books. But the greatest advantage by far to these families sprung from the yearly accumulation of all those among the books which were not absolutely worthless in a library kept at the aforesaid market-town. From thence the families of members were privileged to take them unrestricted. . . . By the time I had myself arrived at the years of literary appetite and enjoyment, the club had been in existence a considerable time, and the accumulations were very respectable. But there was a great deficiency in our *older* literature. The library was in fact only a reflection of the years of its own life, which extended perhaps no further back than ninety years ago [*i.e.* to 1765 *c.*]. We had many good books, however: Burke, and Gibbon, and Hume, and Robertson, and Dr. Johnson, and a long series of Annual Registers, Monthly and Critical Reviews, and Monthly and Gentleman's Magazines. Of voyages and travels there was no lack; and, as I remember, the literature connected with the stirring period of the French Revolution occupied considerable space. Works of fiction were not numerous. We had neither Fielding nor Richardson, nor, I think, Smollett. To the best of my belief we began with Madame D'Arblay, with Madame de Genlis, and Dr. Moore, whose *Zeluco* and *Edward* were well read. Godwin also, with his political speculations and his powerful novels, Miss Edgeworth, in due time, with her exquisite fictions. . . . [He goes on to speak of what ' the youthful readers of that day ' owed to such periodicals as the *Gentleman's Magazine*.] I remember clearly what a respect I felt for the anxiety about accuracy in details which I there saw displayed. . . . I liked the reverential tone of the whole, and did not find it so very dull after all; for there were curious anecdotes here and there, and some pretty pictures,—and then, at that time, children's books were not so abundant; we, at least, had very few indeed. The father's food was that of the family.

Scarcely anything was ever ordered at the club which a gentleman would have hesitated in reading to his daughters; and this being well known, the children were left to select their own congenial matter. They took or left as they pleased. At all events, they had not a set of books ' written *down* ' to children's supposed capacities, but a manly stamp was upon all.

The most interesting part, indeed, of the whole subject of Country Book Societies at the period to which I refer is their strong influence on domestic and individual character. The absence of much outward stimulus at a time when country-houses were few and far between, when people were not always running up to London, and rarely even visiting the county-town, gave more time for this influence to operate. Very few books were bought by farmers, or even gentlemen. Cheap literature was not, and some trouble was occasioned by the transit and exchange of one's volumes. Therefore, when the eight or ten miles of dull road had been passed over and the treasure obtained, one's mind was disposed really to make good use of what came. Then the book furnished material for conversation. It became a family friend, and its least details were matters of discussion.

It is then only to a small portion of the reading public that the changes apply, to the patrons of the seaside resorts and watering-places, to Farmer Bragwell's daughters and the Catherine Morlands. To oppose the circulating library there was a tradition whose strength was undiminished, since it depended on family life, which in essentials was scarcely different from what it had been for generations. The bulk of the educated class was scattered up and down the country forming little centres of culture from Edinburgh to Cornwall, each pursuing its own sober round of duties and pleasures, meeting in the evenings to sing and play, read aloud the latest books from the town, recite poetry, discuss politics, and keeping in touch through the critical review and the dignified news-paper. That is to say, the governing class was cultivated.

Nevertheless, a menace to the old standards had appeared, voiced apologetically enough as early as 1770 by Charles Jenner in *The Placid Man* :

> Life is full of cares and anxieties; man has occasion for, and a right to make use of, many expedients to make it pass with tolerable ease. Various are the schemes to which he applies for that purpose; one hunts, one shoots, one plays, one reads, one writes. Scarcely any one expects his mind to be made better by every one of them; happy if it is made no worse; and in this light what more pleasant, what more innocent, than that amusement which is commonly called Castle-building? . . . For which amusement nothing affords so good materials as a novel.

IV

THE DISINTEGRATION OF THE READING PUBLIC

§ 1

Economic Developments making for Disintegration

THE last chapter ended by announcing the discovery of a new use for fiction—the second of the four in the list on p. 48—but added that this applied only to the leisured class, and particularly to the more leisured sex. The general public read to improve or inform themselves, since a real social life saved them from the vacuity described in Part I.—the way of life of the Dashwood family in *Sense and Sensibility* (1811) is still that of the Edmonstones in *The Heir of Redclyffe* (1853). As for the lower orders, the draining of the country into the cities had begun in earnest with the nineteenth century, and the horrors of a brutal industrialism (*a*) left no time, even if there had been facilities, for the traditional amusements and occupations of the folk, and equally of course no leisure for novel-reading, while in rural England the halcyon age had passed away, succeeded by wars, a run of bad harvests and the enclosure of the commons,[82] which left the independent peasant a farm labourer as wretched as the factory hand ; such conditions could produce painfully self-educated men like Francis Place and Thomas Cooper, but not a Boots Library public. For that a higher standard of living is necessary.

(*a*) Fully described by J. L. and Barbara Hammond in *The Age of the Chartists*.

What saved the lower middle-class public for some time from a drug addiction to fiction was the simple fact of the exorbitant price of novels. Scott, trading on his immense popularity, had forced the price up to half a guinea a volume or 31s. 6d. a novel, which was adopted by Colburn, who specialised in publishing fiction, and remained the fixed rate for a new novel until the 'nineties. The ordinary public could not afford to buy, and circulating libraries were not so organised that they could borrow until Mudie opened his Bloomsbury house in 1842, and for a subscription of a guinea a year sent out his box of novels to thousands of country houses. But in the mid 'forties the invention of various processes (especially of ink-blocking on cloth) made cheap books a profitable speculation (a), and publishers immediately began to exploit the poorer public by first a six-shilling one-volume novel, and then in the 'fifties and 'sixties by the cheaper Railway Library and 'Yellow Back' novels. But this is to anticipate.

The turn of those who early in the century were thus deprived of the novels of fashion [83] came with Dickens and periodical publication—a form in which Pierce Egan's *Tom and Jerry* swept the town in 1821, causing *Pickwick* to be written. The instalments in sum only reduced the price of the entire novel by a third, but it meant an immediate outlay of only a shilling or even sixpence instead of an impossible guinea and a half; *Pickwick* sold 40,000 copies a number, and for twenty-five years novelists published in paper-covered parts. In January 1845 the *Literary Gazette* observed in reviewing No. 1 of Chapman and Hall's Monthly

(a) *Vide* Michael Sadleir, *The Evolution of Publishers' Binding Styles 1770-1900*, p. 612 and footnote.

Series of Original Fiction: 'The plan of serial publishing has now taken almost every shape: weekly, fortnightly, monthly, biennial, quarterly, half-yearly, annually, irregularly.' The shilling number presently had a rival in the shilling magazine, which ran several novels as serials—*Blackwood's*, *Fraser's*, the *Cornhill*, *Macmillan's*, Dickens' *All the Year Round*—giving better value and soon driving the monthly numbers out of the field.[84] All these were as popular as the substantial story magazines of the *Strand* class are to-day (it was worth the *Cornhill's* while to offer the comparatively unknown Trollope £1000 for a suitable serial, which as *Framley Parsonage* established him as a novelist); the *Cornhill* with 90,000 subscribers, and *Macmillan's Magazine* with nearly as many (in a reading public half the size of to-day's), suggest the extent of the middle-class public, Dickens' 70,000 subscribers to *Master Humphrey's Clock* of a lower class—one has only to remember the tone of the references to Dickens in *Cranford* and *The Heir of Redclyffe* to realise that his serial numbers were considered the fiction of the uncultivated and inherently ' low.'

The effect on the novel of serial publication—the publisher's attempt to reach a new public in the absence of facilities for cheap editions—was of course the well-known one of forcing authors to construct in instalments each of which closed with a curtain. But this means a good deal more, the discovery for instance of all that is implied in the term ' sensation novel ' which was scornfully coined by the critics about this time. The sensational novel seems to be and is explained by literary historians as being a direct descendant of the Mrs. Radcliffe-Byron school, but there is an essential difference between the novel of Mrs. Radcliffe and the novel of Dickens. Mrs. Radcliffe makes an appeal less to the nerves than to the imagination, using as we have seen the desiccated idiom of the age, like Scott, and she does achieve a total effect. The sensation novelists make a brute assault on the feelings and nerves in quite another way. Richardson and Sterne, we have said, were the originators of the subsequent popular fiction.[85] In them one sees a highly specialised interest in the workings of what was called the heart. It is like the interest of a previous age in heroic drama, a stylisation of life having been set up in which ' sensibility,' like the point of honour, became a convention with a set of laws of its own, which it required a training to appreciate. No one made the mistake of confusing the subject-matter of this kind of art with ' life '; the emotions aroused by it (we know they *were* aroused from Richardson's correspondence and Sterne's imitators) might be called intellectual since they required an intellectual stimulus. The reader wept because she knew she ought to weep, like the young ladies who were punctually moved to tears by the name Missolonghi. We can discover the nature of the interest by examining *Clarissa* to see where the stress falls : it is not on the seduction, rape, and similar events, where the modern reader would naturally expect it, but on the long-drawn-out dying of the heroine who, like the Man of Feeling, is a martyr to an exquisite code of *mœurs*. As in the case of heroic drama the convention lost interest, and once the code that supports such a convention has been scrapped the work is found to be boring and ridiculous. There exists a remarkable letter from Lady Louisa Stuart to Scott which illustrates this point admirably :

One evening a book was wanted to be read aloud, and what you said of Mackenzie made the company chuse *The Man of Feeling*, though some apprehended it would prove too affecting. However we began: I, who was the reader, had not seen it for several years, the rest did not know it at all. I am afraid I perceived a sad change in it, or myself— which was worse; and the effect altogether failed. Nobody cried, and at some of the passages, the touches I used to think so exquisite—Oh Dear! They laughed. . . . Yet I remember so well its first publication, my mother and sisters crying over it, dwelling upon it with rapture! And when I read it, as I was a girl of fourteen not yet versed in sentiment, I had a secret dread I should not cry enough to gain the credit of proper sensibility. This circumstance has led me to reflect on the alterations of taste produced by time. What we call the taste of the Age, in books as in anything else, naturally influences more or less those who belong to that Age, who converse with the world and are swayed by each other's opinions. But how comes it to affect those who are as yet of no Age, the very young, who go to an author fresh and, if one may say so, stand in the shoes of his first original readers? What instinct makes them judge so differently? In my youth Rousseau's *Nouvelle Heloise* was the book that all mothers prohibited and all daughters longed to read: therefore, somehow or other they did read, and were not the better for it if they had a grain of romance in their composition. Well! I know a young person of very strong feelings —one ' of imagination all compact,' all eagerness and enthusiasm. She lately told me she had been trying to read the *Nouvelle Heloise*, but it tired and disgusted her, so she threw it by unfinished. I was heartily glad to hear it; but, I own, a good deal surprised, for if she, the same she, had lived fifty years ago, she would have been intoxicated and bewildered and cried her eyes out (a).

(a) Lady Louisa Stuart to Scott, September 4, 1826, collected by Wilfred Partington in *The Private Letter-Books of Sir Walter Scott*, p. 272.

Clarissa is only saved because it just touches tragedy—as heroic drama is apt to do—and because, like *Pamela* and parts of *Grandison*, it has some of the eighteenth-century virtues. But like Henry Mackenzie's novels, it will never squeeze a tear from posterity. The difference between the popular novels of the eighteenth century and of the nineteenth is that the new fiction instead of requiring its readers to co-operate in a sophisticated entertainment discovers ' the great heart of the public.' Whereas Sterne's successors at any rate represent a cultivation of the emotions founded on a gentle code, Dickens stands primarily for a set of crude emotional exercises. He discovered, for instance, the formula ' laughter and tears ' that has been the foundation of practically every popular success ever since (Hollywood's as well as the bestseller's). Far from requiring an intellectual stimulus, these are the tears that rise in the heart and gather to the eyes involuntarily or even in spite of the reader, though an alert critical mind may cut them off at the source in a revulsion to disgust.

This is the root of the difference between the bestseller before *Nicholas Nickleby* and after, between ' *The Secrets of Sensibility* in four volumes ' (*a*) and *Trilby, Comin' Thro' the Rye, The Constant Nymph*. The new kind of fiction flourished because it was written for a new, a naïve public, not that of the old circulating libraries or that could afford to buy Scott but for the shopkeeper and the working man. It is Defoe's public, and the completeness of its reorientation is of

---

(*a*) '. . . the leddy I saw the day comin' intil a circulation leebrary to ax for the Secrets o' Sensibility, in four volumes.'—*Noctes Ambrosianæ* (January 1827).

some importance. It is being catered for by a new kind of novelist. The peculiarity of Dickens, as any one who runs a critical eye over a novel or two of his can see, is that his originality is confined to recapturing a child's outlook on the grown-up world, emotionally he is not only uneducated but also immature. When he is supplying the *sine qua non* of the popular novel—the young lovers who have traditionally to be of good birth and breeding and their background of upper middle-class life—he does not merely fall back on conventional situation and character, like Scott, he produces them at the level of Sir Leicester Dedlock and Dr. Strong—the painful guesses of the uninformed and half-educated writing for the uninformed and half-educated. The eighteenth-century novelist's was a mature, discreet, well-balanced personality. Dickens is one with his readers; they enjoyed exercising their emotional responses, he laughed and cried aloud as he wrote. We miss equally in Reade and the Kingsleys the adult and critical sensibility of the older novelists, who wrote for the best, because it was the only, public.

The novelist who made his living by cheap serial publication had necessarily to abandon cumulative effect for a piecemeal succession of immediate effects. This was not only generally practised by the popular novelists of the 'forties, but explicitly recognised by them. Any possibility of a total effect to which every part contributes is negatived by this formula, and since experience seems to show that to accustom oneself to read on a kind of penny-in-the-slot-machine principle is to lose the ability to read in any other way, another phase in the history of the reading public began in which the newly acquired habits, as they gained

ground, were to break down the old and presently
change the face of the world of letters.

For the time being this only affected the Dickens-
Reade-Collins public, since the sensation novel with
its violent incident, stagey dialogue and melodramatic
use of coincidence and the wildly improbable was
despised by the Trollope - Thackeray - George Eliot
public. So we now have two levels of reading public,
though with no such sharp division between them as
was noticed between the various strata in Part I.—the
numbers of *Master Humphrey's Clock* and *Household
Words* crept into such upper middle-class homes as the
Edmonstones' in *The Heir of Redclyffe*, to be read
apologetically by the younger generation; *All the Year
Round* contained not only serials by Dickens, Collins,
and Reade, but a novel of Mrs. Gaskell's as well, and
whereas Thackeray, for instance, with his 'Adsum' and
Amelia only too frequently evokes the same responses
as Dickens in his set pieces, Dickens himself has a
personal outlook and idiom which, though elsewhere
only present in patches, succeed in getting the upper
hand in *David Copperfield* and *Great Expectations*
sufficiently for these novels to be called literature. We
have no occasion, therefore, to talk of a ' lowbrow ' and
a ' middlebrow ' public here. All that can be said is
that because of new commercial conditions the beginnings of a split between popular and cultivated
taste in fiction is apparent. As yet the people were
not by any means restricted from reading and enjoying the ' better ' fiction, since it too was running as
serials in the shilling magazines and even in Dickens's
twopenny weeklies, and though addressing itself to
a gentler and more serious audience it nevertheless

employs the same alphabet; in the twentieth century, as we saw, the language and methods of the serious novelists are hieroglyphic to the reader of Edgar Wallace or even of Hugh Walpole.

But the production of cheap editions mentioned earlier drove a wedge between the educated and the general public. In 1848 the astute W. H. Smith secured the right of selling books and newspapers at railway stations, and a new style of popular literature was needed for his stalls; ten years later he issued Charles Lever's works as one-volume novels in the famous yellow covers, other publishers followed the 'Yellow Backs' with cheap shilling novels, either reprints or specially written for the purpose, which had enormous sales; Routledge's Railway Library was so successful that in 1853 Lytton got £20,000 from them for the right to issue cheap editions of his already published works for ten years, and at the end of that period they found it profitable to renew the contract (*a*). The flood, of course, swept the Harrison Ainsworths and Lyttons rather than the Trollopes and George Eliots into popular esteem,[86] for the new public had formed its taste on Dickens's numbers. And that public now acquired the regular reading habits of the class which subscribed to the circulating libraries. By 1863 the threat to literature had forced itself on the *Quarterly's* notice, and the *Quarterly* did its duty. Two dozen of the popular novels were collected for an article on 'The Sensation Novel,' in which the writer observes:

A class of literature has grown up around us, usurping in many respects, intentionally or unintentionally, a portion

(*a*) Quoted from F. Mumby, *Publishing and Bookselling*, p. 325.

of the preacher's office, playing no inconsiderable part in moulding the minds and forming the habits and tastes of its generation; and doing so principally, we had almost said exclusively, by ' preaching to the nerves.' . . . Excitement, and excitement alone, seems to be the great end at which they aim. . . . A commercial atmosphere floats around works of this class, redolent of the manufactory and the shop. The public want novels, and novels must be made—so many yards of printed stuff, sensation-pattern, to be ready by the beginning of the season. . . .

Various causes have been at work to produce this phenomenon of our literature. Three principal ones may be named as having had a large share in it—periodicals, circulating libraries, and railway bookstalls. . . . This institution [the circulating library] is the oldest offender of the three. . . . It is more active now than at any former period of its existence. . . . The manner of its action is indeed inseparable from the nature of the institution, varying only in the production of larger quantities to meet the demand of a more reading generation. From the days of the ' Minerva Press ' (that synonym for the dullest specimens of the light reading of our grandmothers) to those of the thousand and one tales of the current season, the circulating library has been the chief hot-bed for forcing a crop of writers without talent and readers without discrimination. . . . The railway stall, like the circulating library, consists partly of books written expressly for its use, partly of reprints in a new phase of their existence . . . generally of the sensation kind. . . . The exigencies of railway travelling do not allow much time for examining the merits of a book before purchasing it; and keepers of bookstalls, as well as of refreshment-rooms, find an advantage in offering their customers something hot and strong, something that may catch the eye of the hurried passenger, and promise temporary excitement to relieve the dulness of a journey.

Cheap novels not only brought to popular notice a kind of fiction which would otherwise not have been accessible, but ultimately drove out the expensive three-decker. The class that could afford to buy novels at a guinea and a half each had been the main support of literature, and it was not a small class: it could absorb on publication 10,000 copies of a guinea poem by Byron or Scott, and 16,000 copies of *Adam Bede*. Moreover, the three-volume novel carried with it a certain profit since the circulating library took at least a fixed number and the cost of production was very much lower than it is to-day (not to speak of the difference in price between 7s. 6d. and 31s. 6d).[87] But the three-decker, when publishers had taken to re-issuing their novels in a five-shilling one-volume form as soon as the first demand was over, was seen to be uneconomic; the powerful circulating libraries led by Mudie and Smith issued a circular to the publishers on June 27th, 1894, declaring that after six months had elapsed they would pay only four shillings a volume for novels in sets, and by 1897 there were only one-volume novels on the market. This made all the difference to the novelist with no popular appeal. Whereas in George Eliot's time literature had paid,[88] that is to say, a serious novelist could make a handsome living without surrendering anything, by Conrad's it had ceased to do so. Novelists of the stamp of Gissing and Henry James cannot find publishers easily to-day,[89] and they cannot in any case hope to make a living from their novels.

The sudden opening of the fiction market to the general public was a blow to serious reading. It has previously been suggested that the reading of the general public had been from necessity or choice largely serious. Constable's scheme in 1826 for a popular series which should stand in every humble inglenook did not include fiction, and when carried out consisted chiefly of history, travel, and works of scientific interest; when two years later Murray's Family Library was launched as a rival it also was confined to 'useful knowledge and elegant literature,' and sold some 30,000 copies of the forty-seven volumes, and Knight's Library of Entertaining Knowledge, also started in 1829, was a similar venture in history, biography, voyages and travels, science and natural history. When Railway Libraries and 'Yellow Backs' offered a kind of reading that needed little exertion, it was not likely that any other would stand a chance except with the few determined on self-improvement. The change had indeed begun before cheap novels, with the serial numbers and magazines. Knight's Weekly Volume series of useful literature for the poor, published between 1844 and 1846, was a comparative failure, and he wrote of this later:

> Although very generally welcomed by many who were anxious for the enlightenment of the humbler classes, the humbler classes themselves did not find in them the mental aliment for which they hungered. They wanted fiction, and the half-dozen historical novels of the series were not of the exciting kind which in a few years became the staple product of the cheap press. . . . At the time of the issue of the Weekly Volume, the sale of books at railway stations was unknown. Seven years afterwards it had become universal. Then, in the vicinity of great towns where there was a railway station, the shelves of the newspaper vendor were filled with shilling volumes known as the 'Parlour Library,' the 'Popular Library,' the 'Railway Library,' the 'Shilling Series' (a).

The fiction habit, therefore, had been acquired by the

(a) Charles Knight, *Passages of a Working Life during half a century*, vol. III.

general public long before the Education Act of 1870, the only effect of which on the book market was to swell the ranks of the half-educated half a generation later (until then educated taste had managed to hold its own).[90] How strongly the habit had taken root the content of the *Fortnightly Review* shows. Founded in 1865 as 'the organ of liberalism, free-thinking and open enquiry . . . of all the serial publications of the day probably the most serious, the most earnest, the least devoted to amusement, the least flippant, the least jocose,' as Trollope wrote, the Board of Directors nevertheless decided at the outset that it must always contain a novel.

In effect, cheap novels meant a temptation for the novelist to specialise that Scott, for example, had never been subjected to. It could never occur to a novelist of Scott's day that there could be any other public to address than his peers, and Scott exhibits accordingly the dignity of a well-bred man who is sure of himself and his audience, he has none of Thackeray's uneasiness. For all his yawns and indolence and stiffness Scott has a splendid self-assurance which Lytton in the next generation woefully lacks, but then Lytton had discovered how to exploit the market, as a mere list of his novels proves (*a*). And this lowering of the level of appeal makes Lytton the first of modern bestsellers, with Marie Corelli and Gilbert Frankau as his direct descendants. Compare his diction with Scott's;

(*a*) 1828, *Pelham* (novel of fashion); 1829, *Devereux* (historical romance); 1830, *Paul Clifford* (novel with a thesis); 1832, *Eugene Aram* (idealisation of crime); 1833, *Godolphin* (philosophical, fashionable); 1834, *Last Days of Pompeii* (historical), and also *Rienzi* (1835); 1837, *Ernest Maltravers* (realism and philosophy), and also *Alice* in the next year . . .; 1842, *Zanoni* (supernatural), etc. Lytton's career has a remarkable parallel in that of Hugh Walpole, who is a bestseller at about the same level.

it is the difference between the latter's verse and the poetry of any second-rate Romantic.   Lytton's inflated language means an inflation of sentiment, and his pseudo-philosophic nonsense and preposterous rhetoric carry with them inevitably a debasing of the novelist's currency.   But they were taken seriously by the general public.   Scott, who though he had no artistic conscience had had the benefit of an eighteenth-century education, observed of Lytton's novels : 'There is, I am sorry to say, a slang tone of morality which is immoral.'   To make a useful generalisation, best-sellers before Lytton are at worst dull, but ever since they have almost always been vulgar.   A similar distinction is to be made between periodicals before and after Northcliffe entered Fleet Street.

The direction Lytton gave to popular fiction caused it to set its face away from literature; in fact, as the century grows older the bestseller becomes less a case for the literary critic than for the psychologist [91]—in place of Aphra Behn we have Ouida with the voluptuous day-dream instead of the dispassionate narration of a complicated plot.   It was Lytton who taught the novelist to use what is now called uplift, best defined in terms of its use as strictly a device for rendering acceptable to the reader a fable which his instincts urge him to enjoy but his acquired social conscience would otherwise oblige him to take exception to (Lytton used it, for instance, in *Eugene Aram* to divert attention from his idealisation of a criminal).   This is the ' slang tone of morality ' Scott found distasteful.   Defoe, of course, had hit on a similar but less dangerous trick (*vide* pp. 102 *sqq.*).   More generally uplift can be described as a device for giving in itself emotional satisfaction, *e.g.* in the novels of the late Gene Stratton Porter, and *in excelsis* in Hollywood films, so that forms of entertainment in which uplift now figures are largely masturbatory. The history of uplift in nineteenth and twentieth-century fiction is worth looking into. A distinction was made in Part I. Chapter III. between the Victorian and the Georgian bestseller, and it can now be substantiated. Victorian uplift is associated with a liking for the word ' noble ' (as in the verse of Elizabeth Barrett Browning, Tennyson, and Alice Meynell, the essays of Ruskin and the novels of Charles Kingsley); it is not merely sentimental since it was bound up with a genuine desire to lead a useful life, serve humanity, etc., as well as to visualise oneself in a noble attitude. It led to keeping commonplace books and doing good works,[92] and incidentally to the novels of Mrs. Humphry Ward and Marie Corelli, both of whom and for this reason attracted the admiring attention of Gladstone.

Their success shows too how far the reading public's capacity had shrunk since Lackington. It was suggested earlier that the fiction habit had discouraged serious reading, and through the Victorian era there is evident in consequence a gradual inclusion in the novelist's function of what had formerly been left to writers on history, philosophy, science, religion, ethics, politics . . . everything, in fact, which demands concentration and does not offer the bait of a story. A class of popular novelists noticed in Part I. Chapter III. as serving to convey cultural news to the lower levels came into existence at this time, and in consequence of this closure of the man in the street's communications with the ideas of his age. The condition of success for such a novelist is that he should be at the same level of development as his public; then alone can he maintain that burning enthusiasm in treating what for the more educated is a matter of commonplace or *vieux jeu* or merely childish non-sense.[93] Marie Corelli described the reception met by her first novel *The Romance of Two Worlds* (1886) thus :

> [It was] the simply worded narration of a singular psychical experience, and included certain theories on religion which I, personally speaking, accept and believe. . . . Ignored by the Press, it attracted the public. Letters concerning it and its theories began to pour in from strangers in all parts of the United Kingdom. . . . I attribute my good fortune to the simple fact that I have always tried to write straight from my own heart to the hearts of others (*a*).

Nothing can better illustrate the immense drop from the highly critical and intelligent society led by Charles Fox to later Victorian taste than the nature of Marie Corelli's success. She was not merely the idol of the man in the street; Tennyson, Theodore Watts-Dunton, Queen Victoria, and the Prince of Wales were equally enraptured, *Ardath* ' brought both Gladstone and the British ambassador at Madrid to her feet ' (*b*), the Dean of Gloucester wrote expressing his admiration, Dean Wilberforce and Dean Farrar testified that her novels made for sweetness and light, the Dean of Westminster read from *Barabbas* from the Abbey pulpit on Easter Sunday, Lord Haldane wrote to tell her that her style was brilliant and her range of imagination very great, Lord Charles Beresford seriously envied her her gift of ' incisive English,' Mr. Asquith begged for an autographed copy of one

(*a*) *My First Book* (1894), edited by Jerome K. Jerome.
(*b*) *Memoirs of Marie Corelli*, Bertha Vyver.

of her books, Father Ignatius (described as ' a prophet in his generation ') preached on *The Sorrows of Satan* and the hall was packed, streams of private carriages discharging far more of Marie's readers than could be accommodated so that a similar sermon had to be delivered on the following Sunday, she was invited to lecture to the Edinburgh Philosophical Society and the lecture was enthusiastically received, she was invited to be the first lady to read a paper to the Royal Society of Literature, Ella Wheeler Wilcox literally did homage on her knees to the inspired novelist, and the Master of Magdalene and the Rector of St. Andrews University were among her firmest admirers.   Marie's own conception of her work is elaborately set forth in *The Sorrows of Satan (a)*, where the novelist heroine Mavis Clare is obviously less a day-dream than what she thought herself to be in fact.   This ' woman of genius with a thinker's brain and an angel's soul ' though sneered at by the critics, who are all in league against her (jealous of her ' mental superiority,' her success, and her moral purity), has a vast popular following ; she attacks ' modern science ' (identified with ' atheism ' and ' animalism '), the abuses of high life and contemporary literature, is noted for ' the intellectual grasp and power ' of her novels and all the while preserves ' a child's heart and a child's faith.' It is safe to say that no novelist before so visualised himself.   But once Hall Caine and Marie Corelli had

(a) First published November 1895 ; 10th ed., 1895 ; 32nd ed., 1896 ; 36th ed., 1897 ; 39th ed., 1898 ; 42nd ed., 1900 ; 50th ed., 1905 ; 56th ed., 1910 ; 59th ed., 1914 ; 63rd ed., 1918.   The continued popularity of her novels is somewhat surprising. *The Master Christian,* for example, first published in 1900, reached a 19th edition in 1921 ; and the 20th, a popular edition, came out in 1924.

—for reasons best explained by a psycho-analyst—discovered the novel as a means of satisfying their suppressed desires and so, since they were themselves emotionally uneducated, the starved desires of the vast bulk of the public, it was easy for other writers, eager to make money and not restrained by such a degree of fineness as to make the means distasteful, to imitate their accents.

Meanwhile intercourse with the French school of novelists had a remarkable influence on English writers whose attention had been attracted by the experiments of Flaubert, Zola, Maupassant, Turgeniev, Balzac, even of Victor Hugo, and for the first time in history we have a whole body of English novelists determined to write novels which should be works of art—*Notes on Novelists* and the painful cogitations and revisions of George Moore, Henry James, and Conrad are the fruits of this intercourse; even Hardy for all his simplicity was affected by two at least of the French artists. Trollope in his *Autobiography* observes with dignity in the course of censuring Wilkie Collins for his ungentlemanly attention to detail (as a writer of detective fiction Collins had of course to plan his novels), ' When I sit down to write a novel I do not at all know, and I do not very much care, how it is to end.' This light-hearted attitude is in fine contrast to the implications of *Notes on Novelists*, and though the former had not assisted to produce great novels it had meant that no barrier was placed between the best novelists of the age and the ordinary reader. It has previously been pointed out that any one who could read Dickens (the Edgar Wallace of his time) could also, subject to a little self-discipline, read and understand George

Eliot, Charlotte Brontë, Thackeray, Trollope, the novelists of the educated. So it had always been. But the conscious cultivation of the novel as an art meant an initiated audience. The economic causes noted in this section as tending to separate the homogeneous reading public of the eighteenth century into the severely stratified public of Part I. were reinforced by the appearance of the highbrow novelist, who, unlike the merely serious novelists of the past, aiming like George Eliot, for instance, at moral ends easily comprehended by the half-educated, set out to develop the possibilities of his medium for ends outside the understanding of the ordinary reader, and which far from being ' moral ' only too often appeared to him the very opposite. Dickens and George Eliot were near neighbours, but there is an unbridged and impassable gulf between Marie Corelli and Henry James. And so the great novelists of the age pass out of the common reader's field of vision. There is a well-substantiated story (a) of how when Scott was to visit a great London house the servants petitioned to be allowed to stand in the hall and watch him pass; we cannot flatter ourselves of the possibility of that having happened even with Conrad or Hardy, who for different reasons seem likely to be the last novelists of repute known to the general public even by name.

§ 2

Repercussions on the Periodical

In 1829 an article appeared in the June number of the *Edinburgh Review* whose acuteness is scarcely

(a) Rogers told it to Macaulay (*vide* Trevelyan's *Life of Macaulay*, p. 157).

disguised by the stately periods in which it was framed. Under the heading ' Signs of the Times ' the writer declares :

> Were we required to characterise this age of ours by any single epithet, we should be tempted to call it, not an Heroical, Devotional, Philosophical or Moral Age, but, above all others, the Mechanical Age. . . . What wonderful accessions have thus been made, and are still making, to the physical power of mankind; how much better fed, clothed, lodged, and, in all outward respects, accommodated, men now are, or might be, by a given quantity of labour, is a grateful reflection which forces itself on every one. . . . But leaving these matters for the present, let us observe how the mechanical genius of our time has diffused itself into quite other provinces. Not the external and physical alone is now managed by machinery, but the internal and spiritual also. Here, too, nothing follows its spontaneous course, nothing is left to be accomplished by old, natural methods. Has any man, or any society of men, a truth to speak, a piece of spiritual work to do, they can nowise proceed at once, and with the mere natural organs, but must first call a public meeting, appoint committees, issue prospectuses, eat a public dinner; in a word, construct or borrow machinery, wherewith to speak or do it. Without machinery they are hopeless, helpless—a colony of Hindoo weavers squatting in the heart of Lancashire. . . .
>
> These things, which we state lightly enough here, are yet of deep import, and indicate a mighty change in our whole manner of existence. . . . To us who live in the midst of all this, and see continually the faith, hope, and practice of every one founded on Mechanism of one kind or other, it is apt to seem quite natural, and as if it could never have been otherwise. . . . At no former era has Literature, the printed communication of thought, been of such importance as it is now. The true Church of England, at this moment, lies in the Editors of its Newspapers.

So remarkably modern an utterance would pass—

apart from the style—for a complaint from the next century, were it not for the closing sentences. No one in the twentieth century so aware as this writer would look to literature and the Press for salvation; and it is the Press that has contributed most to put literature out of the question. A short history of the periodical in the last hundred years is essential to that explanation of the situation described in Part I. which it is the object of this study to attempt.

The first daily paper in the language addresses itself, like the *Tatler*, to a discriminating public, or rather, is not aware of any other public. The first number of the *Daily Courant* (March 11th, 1702) assures the reader that in reporting foreign news the Author will not ' take upon him to give any Comments or Conjectures of his own, but will relate only Matter of Fact; supposing other People to have Sense enough to make Reflections for themselves.' And for a century and a half there is no radical change to report in the tone of the Press: the journalist of every reputable periodical continued to use the same methods— the methods of Defoe, Addison, Swift, Johnson, Jeffrey . . . to influence the reader by appealing to his good sense, good taste, and social morality. Even when popular agitation had produced, in defiance of the stamp-tax, an illegal cheap Press at the end of the eighteenth century, Cobbett is its typical journalist. Journalists not only wrote well, they were not uncommonly men of letters.

The typical periodical of the first half of the nineteenth century was the *Edinburgh Review*, as that of the eighteenth century was the *Spectator*. They occupied an important place in the social consciousness of the

English nation : they had a more important office than the provision of news or literary gossip. The *Spectator*, for example, in a small, highly centralised community, where every one of account knew every one else and where the London coffee-houses served as foci for the exchange of ideas, held the community together by stabilising the ideal standard of taste, and served, as we have seen, to bring together the various classes whose interests and outlooks might well have been incompatible. Even after the lapse of over a century, when a number of quarterlies and monthlies existed, nevertheless each, with pretty nearly the same sense of responsibility and authority, could be relied on to preserve the standard of opinion. From the beginning of an organised reading public till the late nineteenth century tradition and authority were guarded by a consciously civilised Press.

There is obviously something to be said for this kind of centrality (compare Part I. Chapter II.). It is not merely that men of genius could maintain themselves by journalism without degradation. It meant that the reading public was homogeneous, and in consequence a genuinely original author could in general count on instant recognition, a good thing not merely for himself but for the state of literature. There is now necessarily no equivalent of the *Edinburgh Review* in its prime. Twenty-three years after its foundation, ' to have the entry of its columns was to command the most direct channel for the spread of opinions, and the shortest road to influence and celebrity . . . his article on Milton appeared in the August number (1825). The effect on the author's reputation was instantaneous. Like Lord Byron, he awoke one morn-

ing and found himself famous. . . . Murray declared
that it would be worth the copyright of *Childe Harold*
to have Macaulay on the staff of the *Quarterly*. The
family breakfast table in Bloomsbury was covered with
cards of invitation to dinner from every quarter of
London ' (*a*).

When ' The Taxes on Knowledge ' were reduced,
but before they were finally abolished, it is interesting
to see how the working class was catered for. Take
1850 as the date before the new conditions in fiction
discussed in § 1 had time to affect the periodical, and
let us examine a few examples of successful popular
periodicals. In 1832 Charles Knight produced the
Penny Magazine for Brougham's Society for the Distribution of Useful Knowledge, and it found 200,000
regular purchasers straightway. Its nature is described
by Knight himself in the preface to the first volume :

> If this incontestable evidence of the spread of the ability
> to read be most satisfactory, it is still more satisfactory to
> consider the species of reading which has had such an ex-
> tensive and increasing popularity. In this work there has
> never been a single sentence that could inflame a vicious
> appetite; and not a paragraph that could minister to preju-
> dices and superstitions which a few years since were common.
> There have been no excitements for the lover of the mar-
> vellous—no tattles or abuse for the gratification of a diseased
> personality—and, above all, no party politics. The subjects
> which have uniformly been treated have been of the broadest
> and simplest character. Striking points of Natural History
> —Accounts of the great Works of Art in Sculpture and
> Painting—Descriptions of such Antiquities as possess his-
> torical interest—Personal Narratives of Travellers—Bio-
> graphies of Men who have had a permanent influence on
> the condition of the world—Elementary Principles of Lan-

(*a*) Trevelyan, *Life and Letters of Lord Macaulay*, p. 85.

guage and Numbers—established facts in Statistics and Political Economy—these have supplied the materials for exciting the curiosity of a million readers. This consideration furnishes the most convincing answer to the few (if any there now remain) who assert that General Education is an evil. The people will not abuse the power they have acquired to read, and therefore to think. Let them be addressed in the spirit of sincerity and respect, and they will prove that they are fully entitled to the praise which Milton bestowed upon their forefathers. . . .

There was poetry in the *Penny Magazine*—Chaucer, Surrey, and Wyatt, seventeenth century, eighteenth century, and Romantic poetry—but no fiction. Other papers of the same kind, nearly or quite as popular, such as *Chambers's Journal* and the *Saturday Magazine*, in general contained a story in each number. This then is the equivalent of the ' Sunday paper ' of Part I. (*a*).

The monthly magazine for the home (class *g* on p. 11) had its forerunner too. Taking a random dip, there is in 1848 ' *The Family Economist*: A Penny Monthly Magazine Devoted to the Moral, Physical, and Domestic Improvement of the Industrious Classes,' with a picture of a contented industrious family on the cover surrounded by such mottoes as ' Education is Second Nature, ' Labour Rids Us of Three Great Evils, Irksomeness, Vice and Poverty.' It contains useful advice, stories after the model of Hannah More's *Cheap Miscellany*, is unpretentious and rational without being in the least patronising, and is above all well written.

(*a*) ' So long as the Penny Magazines make a good selection of articles from the best works, they are beneficial. None can long accustom themselves to just and elegant compositions, without being disgusted with that which is vulgar and mean.'—*Autobiography of Sir Egerton Brydges* (1834), p. 208.

In 1846 G. W. M. Reynolds, the Northcliffe of his age, discovered the existence of a potential periodical public which, not yet catered for by the newspaper, was not equal to the magazines edited by Dickens and his acquaintance; he supplied them with *Reynolds' Miscellany*, carefully designed to meet their taste. The circulation was enormous. Reynolds was the author of many bestsellers which often ran as serials in his *Miscellany* before being republished in penny weekly parts—*The Mysteries of London, The Necromancer, Wagner the Wehr-Wolf, Pickwick Abroad, Louise the Orphan*, and so on, whose sales Thackeray estimated must have run into millions. The first number, November 7th, 1846, contains an address:

To Our Readers

Stimulated by the growing improvement in the public taste, and convinced that the readers of Cheap Literature are imbued with a profound spirit of inquiry in respect to Science, Art, Manufacture, and the various matters of social or national importance, the Projector of this MISCELLANY has determined to blend Instruction with Amusement; and to allot a fair proportion of each Number to Useful Articles, as well as to Tales and Light Reading. Cheap Literature has become respectable, because the immense class that supports it has latterly made a wonderful intellectual progress; and those Periodicals which hope to gain, and secure the favour of that class, must provide a literary aliment suited to the improved taste of the present day.

And the contents bear out this interesting assertion. Volume one contains—

(*a*) Instalments of a serial by the editor—' Wagner: the Wehr-Wolf.'

(*b*) 'The Anatomy and Physiology of Ourselves Popularly Considered,' in nineteen serial chapters.

(*c*) 'Popular Papers on Science'—mechanics, electricity, inventions, astronomy.

(*d*) Six 'Letters to the Industrious Classes,' by the editor, in the style of Cobbett.

(*e*) Reviews and essays and topical articles—*e.g.* 'How to Read,' 'The Moral Elevation of the People.'

(*f*) 'The Provincial Press of the United Kingdom,' criticised and described in forty-two paragraphs.

'All with Numerous Wood-Engravings.' The advertisements are of technical works for artisans and such elementary text-books as *Sessions in Natural Philosophy, The Catechism of Music, The Plain and Easy Grammar for the Industrious Classes.*

Now all this seems to show (1) that the readers were at least as often men as women; (2) that a genuine interest in rational affairs and an insatiable desire for self-improvement were taken for granted in the reader; (3) that the sempstress and servant-girl, the mechanic and artisan, for whom G. W. M. Reynolds admittedly concocted his penny weekly, wanted only one instalment of a penny novelette to a magazine otherwise devoted to improving reading—if they had wanted more the *Miscellany* would not have been so popular or Reynolds and his wife would have provided more fiction. There is an impressive decorum about the *Miscellany* which the age of the Northcliffe and the Beaverbrook Press can hardly understand. Its most striking feature is a complete absence of any emotional appeals. Even ' Wagner, the Wehr-Wolf,' with its Rosicrucians, Inquisitors, and ' Wehr '-wolves, its borrowings from *Faust* and *Don Juan* and *Robinson Crusoe*, and its setting in the high life of medieval Florence, is in the tradition of Mrs. Radcliffe and Scott that looks back to the eighteenth century—the stilted idiom leaves the reader everything to do if he wishes to be thrilled—it bears no relation to Lytton. The references to ' the march of mind,' the proud self-label of ' the industrious classes,' the advertisements of improving works for ' the million,' suggest how well the Lackingtons of the new era were managing for themselves. There is nothing pathetic or ridiculous in the ambitions of the million.[94] The constant insistence on open-mindedness in politics and non-material standards in living without any appeals to religious sentiment or anything cheap in the radicalism for which Reynolds stood, is a considerable achievement. It is a heritage from the eighteenth-century revolutionary idealists and the vogue of Godwin and Tom Paine. The prevailing note is ultimately seen to be a demand for ' the amelioration of the condition of the industrious millions ' by general education. It is a tragic fact that State education, when it came, could only damp this amazing enthusiasm for ' enlightenment ' or else side-track it—at best, turn the potential Lackingtons into Lewishams.

The popular Press about 1850, then, has the dignity of the best papers of the age. The standards of journalism were set from above, and the characteristics of the periodicals tabulated in Part I.—their glorification of food, drink, clothes, and material comforts, their determined inculcation of a higher standard of living, their appeal to prejudice, snobbism, and herd instinct, their facetious denigration of serious values—were unknown. The daily papers catered for the governing and professional classes, intelligently interested in politics, the money market, the law, and current affairs, adopting towards their readers the only tone which those readers would have permitted, and if other classes found them dull, they must go without, there was no choice. The discovery by several men towards the end of the nineteenth century that the periodical, like the novel, could be made profitable by treating it as a business concern changed all this. W. T. Stead contributed to that change when his thirst for political influence found an outlet in journalism, but his methods, though only a faint anticipation of those of later editors,[95] and serving chiefly, as Northcliffe patronisingly remarked, ' to relieve the tedium of the dull newspapers of the 'eighties,' were coldly received by the better part of the public and always found distasteful by them; and he never succeeded, either, in achieving the large circulations of his successors. The three men who created the modern Press went differently to work. Newnes with *Tit-Bits* in 1881 hit on the principle of supplying ' what the Public wants '—a want, of course, which is not felt until supplied, and the still more enterprising Northcliffe realised the importance of the discovery [96]; in 1888 he followed with *Answers*, and two years later *Pearson's Weekly* commenced a successful career : that is to say, there was room for three very similar weeklies which supplied miscellaneous news items without any object other than that of holding for a brief while the

attention of the newly literate. All three were average
men who applied the ordinary business methods to
what had formerly been a profession, and all three
were, significantly, as uncultured as the man in the
street for whom they catered—' " I *am* the average
man," Sir George Newnes would say. " I am not
merely putting myself in his place. That is the real
reason why I know what he wants " ' (*a*) ; ' A better
educated Northcliffe would have been unable to
produce either an *Answers* or a *Daily Mail* so ex-
quisitely suited to the minds of those who welcomed
them ' (*b*). They were unable to understand, and so
contemptuous of the old journalistic tradition in which
educated men devoted their best powers to maintain
the standard of responsibility of the daily paper—
Hamilton Fyfe reports Northcliffe as saying ' To think
that they took all this trouble and went through all
these contortions for something that would be read by
very few people and in a few hours would be dead as
Queen Anne ! ' (*c*). ' They thought the way to sell a
newspaper was to have first-class criticisms of books
and pictures and music and plays ' (*d*). And this brings
out the essential change, in attitude ; the balance-sheet
now became the test of a paper's standing (*e*), and
owner, editor, and reporter had a common end—to sell
as many copies as possible, irrespective of the means.
For the new journalism did not confine itself to
Tit-Bits : in 1890 Newnes started the first modern

(*a*) Hulda Friederichs, *The Life of Sir George Newnes.*
(*b*) Hamilton Fyfe, *Northcliffe.*
(*c*) *Ibid.*, p. 59.   (*d*) *Ibid.*, p. 86.
(*e*) ' The balance sheet is the only honest test of a paper's soundness.'—
Northcliffe's right-hand man, Kennedy Jones, *Fleet Street and Downing
Street*, p. 323.

magazine, the *Strand*, which was followed in 1893 by the *Pall Mall Magazine* (now *Nash's*), in 1895 by the *Windsor*, 1898 by the *Royal* and others; in 1894 Northcliffe bought the *Evening News*, in 1896 he started the first ha'penny paper, and in the course of the next ten years he and Pearson and Newnes got possession of most of the popular Press, inventing such important new kinds of periodical as the *Daily Mirror* or reorganising older papers on the model of the *Daily Mail*.

The competition for circulation meant inevitably an appeal to the numerically greatest public, as had happened in fiction already, and an appeal, therefore, by such means as the novelist practised. It is not so much the competitions, publicity stunts, free insurance, and so forth, nor the lowering of the tone of political controversy, that characterise the modern Press: it is the use of applied psychology to secure readers. Northcliffe in directing the *Daily Mail* seems almost entirely to have concentrated on the appearance of the paper, the manner in which features and news were treated, and the production of 'talking-points' in every number —'the direction of its policy was in the hands of smaller men. Northcliffe left it almost entirely to them. In his daily messages he seldom even mentioned their treatment of the matters which concerned the welfare of nations; he confined himself almost entirely to the technical side of their activities. In truth he did not think it much mattered what was said in leading articles, nor how the public were misled by the colouring and suppression of facts' (*a*). It has been pointed out in this chapter that the characteristic of the old

(*a*) Hamilton Fyfe, *op cit.*, p. 294.

journalism, whether designed for the governing class or the masses, was its assumption of a reader humane, rational, free from superstition and prejudice and interested in the major activities of his age. The new type of journalist that the new journalism created is worth studying—for instance, in the text-books of journalism and journalistic college courses, particularly in Michael Joseph's *Journalism for Profit*, where a final chapter contributed by successful journalists on 'How I make Journalism Pay' is of considerable interest. A significant extract has already been made (*vide* p. 26); others are useful illustrations here:

> I write as simply as possible on the things that both charm and amuse me, trying to appeal to the 'kiddy' heart that is in every one of us 'grown-ups.'
>
> . . . More and more the public asks to be amused and interested rather than informed.
>
> The most practical method I know of how to make free-lance journalism pay is to deliberately write what is known in Fleet Street as 'tosh.' I say this not as a cynic but as a philosopher . . . for the average adventurer in the lists of 'literature' who writes for his living will soon learn to take things as they are and to profit by them to the best of his ability. By 'tosh' I mean the kind of innocuous twaddle which a very large number of perfectly respectable newspapers and periodicals require for the immense lower-middle class public upon which they depend for their existence.

The old journalist was controlled by a sense of the dignity of his profession; the modern 'cynical,' cheaply sophisticated journalist who gives the public what it wants, is, and considers himself, a business man,[97] and he has precisely the same code and outlook as the next man who is out to sell his goods.[98]

The process by which a tradition is killed is always

instructive, and perhaps nowhere can it be more easily studied than in the history of the Press, where the whole process was effected in one generation.[99]   There were two main tendencies at work : the one by which independent concerns are perforce bought out by combines (so that in 1922 Amalgamated Press Limited, only one of the Harmsworth companies, controlled nearly eighty weeklies and monthlies), the other by which, as costs of publication rose and periodicals became dependent on advertisers, who naturally placed their advertisements in the papers with the largest circulations (other things being equal),[100] those periodicals that tried to sell under the old colours were obliged to adopt the new technique or perish.   So even while this study was writing, the *New Statesman* (highbrow Labour) and the *Nation and Athenæum* (highbrow Liberal, and itself the tomb of a first-class literary review, the *Athenæum*) have been obliged to combine resources as *New Statesman and Nation*, while at a lower level the comparatively dignified Liberal *Daily Chronicle* has been swallowed up by the *Daily News*. The non-commercial *Daily Herald* necessarily succumbed : ' It is no longer a Labour propaganda paper —it is just successful journalism of the Odham variety,' the London School of Journalism instructs its pupils.

The new journalism, then, did succeed in turning every working man into a newspaper-reader ; it also incidentally induced him to exchange the old personal active interests for a new set of communal passive ones, assisting to bring about the state of affairs to which allusion has been made in Part I. Chapter III.[101] ; and it necessarily affected his reading habits.   The previous section of this chapter suggested that the flood of cheap popular novels had produced a nation of novel-readers, and we have to consider in what way, if at all, a nation of newspaper-readers differs from that. Consider the contemporary newspaper, or better still, let us see how its prototype, the *Daily Mail* of Northcliffe's early experiment, differs from the Victorian novel in its demands on the reader. One of the most important innovations Northcliffe made was to establish a system of short leaders—three to a column—in his new paper. The traditional editorial style—the rounded and majestic period, the elaborate argument, the moderate tone—had to go; it was replaced by the bright snappy style that picks out the ' human ' features of a topic in three simple paragraphs. It was Northcliffe's discovery of ' tabloid journalism,' [102] which is in fact only an application of the principle of *Tit-Bits* to greater issues. The *Daily Mail*, and the Press generally ever since, have presented to the reader an irresponsible collection of scraps, each designed complete with headlines and captions to catch the eye, like a poster, and like a poster too to ' put across ' its contents at a glance. So that all educated people now have two more or less conscious ways of reading—one that in theory at least they reserve for books, the other, with the eye, which they automatically adopt for newspapers and magazines (*a*). The uneducated have only one, for the former, which they are of course taught at school, is soon abandoned in a world in which all their reading is of the latter kind (reinforced by the pictorial papers and the cinema). And there are signs that even the

(*a*) The effect on the language of the journalistic technique of shock appeal is brilliantly discussed in Chap. VIII. of William Empson's *Seven Types of Ambiguity* (1930).

educated are, as might be expected, tending to substitute the easier reading habit for that demanding a considerable effort. The law of natural selection, by which a novelist who does not write the kind of novel that can be looked through will be less popular than the novelist who does, is leading to a state in which only the latter kind of novel can get published.

The advice, now a commonplace, which schools of journalism conscientiously give their pupils—

> Avoid the solid block of type. It is the modern fashion to split up articles into a series of vivid sub-paragraphs. Solid chunks of print weary the reader's eyes, and eventually tire the brain (a).

—has not found the publisher of popular novels deaf:

> The pages of a novel must not even look solid. If a publisher sees the proofs come back from the printer with more than a few inches of unbroken matter in a page he is quite capable of taking the law into his own hands and breaking up the paragraphs himself. Only the few authors labelled as 'literary' have been permitted a little latitude in this respect—perhaps because they were found to be incorrigible or because their sales were so inconsiderable any way that it was not considered worth while to trouble about them (b).

If one considers successively a few pages of Mrs. Radcliffe or Scott, of George Eliot, of Mrs. Humphry Ward, and finally of Hugh Walpole or Wells or Galsworthy (to restrict the test to the reading of the educated), one is impressed both with the sudden atrophy of the attention in the reader and his reduced reading capacity. He has now to be helped by spacing out ideas and reiteration. But apply the same test to

(a) Quoted from London School of Journalism correspondence with pupils.
(b) E. H. Lacon Watson, *op. cit.*

the reading of the uneducated—Dickens, Marie Corelli, Edgar Wallace—and it is even more striking. The thinness and surface liveliness of the writing, the crude, elementary prose, carefully constructed in phrases and simple sentences so as to read with the maximum ease, of modern popular novelists at all levels approximates as nearly as possible to the style of the journalist, and this is not surprising when we recollect how close is the connection between popular novel and magazine story and between magazine and newspaper. In fact, the line between journalist and novelist can no longer be drawn. The typical bestseller is also a successful and regular contributor to the magazines (*e.g.* Gilbert Frankau) or has been trained on the staff of a big daily paper (*e.g.* Philip Gibbs). And both journalist and bestseller are now closely akin to the copywriter.

§ 3

Levelling down

What Northcliffe had done was in fact to mobilise the people to outvote the minority, who had hitherto set the standard of taste without any serious challenge. And Northcliffe did this—how far consciously it is impossible to say, for his acuteness was the superficial variety that can hardly be called intelligence—by working upon herd instinct (*a*). A description of the methods of the new journalism is unnecessary, they are sufficiently well known and any popular daily will furnish examples; the nature of the new technique can most easily be demonstrated by a comparison

(*a*) ‘ Successful journalists understand the popular mentality and exploit it.’—London School of Journalism.

between the forces in journalism before and after the advent of Northcliffe : on the one hand there are such figures as Addison, Swift, Johnson, ' Junius,' Cobbett, Jeffrey, and on the other, with corresponding influence, Bottomley (during the war *John Bull* was selling a million copies weekly), James Douglas, the Northcliffe and Beaverbrook Press. The *Pall Mall Gazette* edited by Morley, the last of the old order, with W. T. Stead as assistant editor, was a microcosm worth examining. ' Morley and I approached almost everything from a different standpoint,' declared Stead. ' We disagreed, as I often said, on everything from the existence of God to the make-up of a newspaper ' (*a*). Moreover, consider the tone in which Northcliffe's colleague and biographer writes of the change :

> The props of the Old Journalism feel bewildered. Their task, they believe, is to enlighten such of the public as can profit by enlightenment on political questions, on foreign policy. Their duty, they maintain, is to guide opinion concerning matters which may affect national well-being, cause changes of Government, raise the issue of peace or war. They have nothing to do with increase of circulation. They call this ' pandering to mob interest in trivialities,' commercial, undignified. Their standard of importance is set by the chiefs of political parties, Foreign Office, and the Treasury; by the famous Clubs (Reform, Carlton, Athenæum); by the great country houses, the country rectories; by the Universities, by Bench and Bar. Now the standard is to be set by the mass of the people ; the New Journalism will put in the foreground whatever is of interest to them, whatever will make them ' hand the paper about ' (*b*).

(*a*) Quoted from *The Making of Modern Journalism*, p. 25.
(*b*) Hamilton Fyfe, *Northcliffe*, p. 84. Cf. too, *ibid.*, p. 270 : ' He knew what the newspaper readers wanted and he gave it to them. He broke down the dignified idea that the conductors of newspapers should appeal to the

Now the tone of this passage, in which it is impossible to overlook a certain triumphant note, can be shown to recur in innumerable connections in post-war civilisation. Viewed from the opposite side from that of Northcliffe's admirers, the change between this and the civilisation of the English people hitherto can be summarised in the words of Sir Egerton Brydges (whose autobiography provides a remarkable seismogram of the period up to 1830 which destroyed the eighteenth-century tradition): 'Formerly, no doubt, the mob had a lower class of books than at present, but then they did not set them up for the best' (a). It is, above all, the collapse of authority that marks the reading public described in Part I. The history of the overthrow of authority must be briefly sketched at this point.

The Puritan conscience implied a seriousness, an habitual occupation of the mind by major questions, and this had been the shaping factor in the lives of the middle-class and respectable poor from Bunyan's age till well on into the nineteenth century, when, as we have seen, it was side-tracked into a path which has more and more widely diverged from that of the arts. But before this had happened the rapid increase in the reading public seems to have suggested fears for the future to thinking men, though they were doubts only entertained for the moment, jotted down and then probably forgotten. For instance, a prophetic idea

intelligent few. He frankly appealed to the unintelligent many. Not in a cynical spirit, not with any feeling of contempt for their tastes ; but because on the whole he had more sympathy with them than with the others, and because they were as the sands of the sea in numbers. He did not aim at making opinion less stable, emotion more superficial. He did this, without knowing he did it, because it increased circulation.'

(a) *The Autobiography, Times, Opinions and Contemporaries of Sir Egerton Brydges* (1834).

had occurred to Tom Moore, and he had thought it worth mentioning to Wordsworth and entering into his diary in 1834—' Broached to him my notions (long entertained by me) respecting the ruinous effects to literature likely to arise from the boasted diffusion of education ; the lowering of the standard that must necessarily arise from the extending of the circle of judges ; from letting the mob in to vote, particularly at a period when the *market* is such an object to authors. Those " who live to please must please to live," and most will write down to the lowered standard. All the great things in literature have been achieved when the readers were few ; " fit audience find and few." In the best days of English genius, what a comparatively small circle sat in judgment ! ' Shortly before, Sir Egerton Brydges had recorded his impressions of the effect of a wider public—' It is a vile evil that literature is become so much a trade all over Europe. Nothing has gone so far to nurture a corrupt taste, and to give the unintellectual power over the intellectual. Merit is now universally estimated by the multitude of readers that an author can attract. . . . Will the uncultivated mind admire what delights the cultivated ? Will the rude and coarse enjoy what is refined ? Do the low endure the reasonings which justify subordination ? . . . In all good writings nothing ought to be uttered contrary to truth and wisdom. But the mob do not love truth—they relish only what feeds their appetites and passions. If genius had only reason, integrity, feeling, and taste to appeal to, it would be safe ; but it has to appeal to corruption, prejudice, selfishness, and ignorance. . . . The public now, perhaps, read a great deal, but in so confused and immethodical a manner that they retain no impressions ; it is like an evanescent stamp upon moist sand. All they learn is to deface what they once had been taught, and to have no opinions at all—except that every one may think after his own fashion, and that all old-received principles are narrow and unenlightened prejudices.' But the very tone in which he deplores the state of affairs shows how secure he felt his order was : the low did in fact endure the reasonings which justify sub-ordination and his style is the proof, it is as unshaken as Gibbon's. Another proof is that he can write un-questioningly of 'the control of taste and judgment,' of 'reason and sentiment,' of 'sound thinking' and 'true feeling '—as his style implies a sympathetic back-ground so his terms postulate a cultivated public with an accepted scale of values. And even in *Culture and Anarchy* (1869) there is the same inner assurance. Arnold's critical idiom betrays the conviction that certain important terms essential to his argument— 'culture,' 'right reason,' 'the will of God,' 'the best self,' 'perfection '—do not need defining ; he addresses himself to the general reader (*Culture and Anarchy* was soon brought out in a sixpenny pocket edition and later in the still cheaper paper form) and yet can assume that his idiom will be intelligible to them. No chasm has opened between him and the public, for however Philistine or barbarous sections of it might be, and though Arnold could accurately point to the sources of danger, there was a strong tradition of respect for the things that Arnold felt to be valuable : there is no sense of isolation in his cheerfully ironic ' we poor disparaged followers of culture.' Twenty years later it was still open to Sir Edmund Gosse to con-

template as a distant possibility the anarchy which
Arnold had envisaged :

> One danger which I have long foreseen from the spread
> of the democratic sentiment, is that of the traditions of literary
> taste, the canons of literature, being reversed with success by
> a popular vote. Up to the present time, in all parts of the
> world, the masses of uneducated or semi-educated persons,
> who form the vast majority of readers, though they cannot
> and do not appreciate the classics of their race, have been
> content to acknowledge their traditional supremacy. Of
> late there have seemed to me to be certain signs, especially
> in America, of a revolt of the mob against our literary masters.
> . . . If literature is to be judged by a plebiscite and if the
> plebs recognises its power, it will certainly by degrees cease
> to support reputations which give it no pleasure and which
> it cannot comprehend. The revolution against taste, once
> begun, will land us in irreparable chaos (a).

But the quotation on page 186 shows that the possibility has now become a fact, and for a typical member
of the journalistic profession a fact to dwell on with
satisfaction. So complete a revolution in the outlook of
the reading public cannot be lightly passed over. Some
at least of the contributory factors must be mentioned.

Undoubtedly the new journalism played a major
part, reinforcing the more gradual influence of the new
bestseller, but a corresponding series of social changes,
less evident because extending over a longer period,
helped at least as much ; without them the immediate
success of the Northcliffes and Frankaus would have
been impossible. The first is, of course, the more or
less complete transformation of the upper and middle
classes effected by the modern Public School system,
which has replaced the famous ' eccentric ' Englishman

(a) ' What is a Great Poet ? ' (1889) in *Questions at Issue*.

of the Augustan and Georgian ages by the ' simple but virile ' type, imposing upon a nation whose governing class had been for several centuries noted as having pronounced (because highly developed) personalities and keen intellectual interests, an ideal whose key-words are correctness and sport.[103] This ideal has had the effect of arresting the development of whole generations at adolescence ; the first expressions of it in fiction are the novels of Thomas Hughes and the Kingsleys— there is nothing like their writings in the language before them, but a very great deal after. Another social change of some cultural importance is that in the status, antecedents, and acquirements of the clergy ; it used to be said for the Established Church that at least it put a scholar and a gentleman in every parish, a function which it has for some time ceased to fulfil. A parallel is provided by two other professions formerly open to the serious and disinterested—it is no longer possible for an intelligent man to make politics his career, like Balfour, or to earn by journalism a hand-some living while preserving his self-respect, like ' Honest John ' Morley. In addition, scientific interests have alienated a large proportion of the more intelligent of the community from culture. Altogether the character of the governing and professional classes has radically altered. The people with power no longer represent intellectual authority and culture.

Authority depends on the recognition of standards other than those of *l'homme moyen sensuel*, and after many centuries of unquestioning assent to authority the natural man has reasserted himself. We thus have a situation closely resembling that of the United States, marking a new phase in our history and one which, as it is likely to continue indefinitely, is perhaps worth dwelling upon. Most noticeable is the extension of business ethics and all that the word ' business ' implies to fields of activity which had formerly non-commercial values,[104] for since the business man is the average man, the ' worth while ' measure must be applied all round. Journalists, advertising agents, editors of magazines, and popular authors were naturally the first to discover that it is more profitable to make use of man's suggestibility as a herd animal than to approach the reader as if he were what used to be called ' the thinking man '; fear of the herd, approval of the herd, the peace of mind that comes from conforming with the herd, are the strings they play upon and the ideals that inform their work.[105] The practical effects of the triumph of the business ethos are—to the anthropologist, at least—exciting. For example, it has already been mentioned that the Press now depends on the advertiser—' To-day the newspaper is, in its commercial aspect as a matter of pounds, shillings, and pence, a by-product of Advertising' (*Commercial Advertising*, Thomas Russell, 1919). It is to the interest of the advertiser that the public should be kept from any kind of alarm so that it will spend without hesitation, therefore the contents of newspaper and magazine must create confidence, preserve the *status quo*, reassure and divert attention from political and economic troubles. Hence the insistence, illustrated in Part I. Chapter II., on cheerful stories, bright articles, happy endings, and the avoidance of any ' unpleasant ' (*i.e.* disquieting) note. Reinforced by the average man's preference for a comfortable outlook, this has brought about a public sentiment overwhelmingly in favour of blind optimism. An inspection of the slogans displayed on Wayside Pulpits [106] (they represent one of the popular substitutes for religion and their success makes them a reliable index) reveals that they are largely devoted to denunciation of an attitude described as pessimistic, or easy assurances of everything turning out well if let alone. This is not without significance.[107] The Wayside Pulpit posters are tags collected from such sources as newspaper headlines and articles, 'songs sung over the Wireless,' etc. (a), and they are representative of the mental stock-in-trade of the general public; such tags are expressive of an attitude that they have formed, an attitude, it must be noted, which is not based on personal experience. Yet they are what the man in the street now lives and shapes his life by; they rise irresistibly to the lips in an emergency, for instance. Contrast them with the local and national proverbs which till recently (*i.e.* till such standardising forces as the cinema, radio, large-circulation newspapers and magazines destroyed traditional culture and local differences) served as a rule-of-thumb for dealing with the major as well as the minor situations of life. [Plenty of samples may be found in *Adam Bede* and *The Mill on the Floss*, where the speech of the lower and lower-middle classes is largely composed of traditional similes and dicta. And *vide* note 56.] They are the growth of ages of individual experience (the experience, that is, of the shrewdest and most intelligent of the community) tested by generations of use and pooled to form a stock of social wisdom. And they suggest that the standardising forces just mentioned

(a) I am indebted for information about the Church Publicity Section, and in particular about the choice of Wayside Pulpit posters, to the courtesy of the Church Publicity Secretary, Mr. Geo. S. Hirst.

have destroyed something worth preserving, if only for utilitarian reasons.

The extent to which the attitude approved by the herd is fixed by such agencies for imposing conformity as the Public Schools, advertising, and the Press, cannot be overestimated. It is more than difficult, it is next to impossible, for the ordinary uncritical man to resist when, whichever way he looks in the street, from poster and hoarding, and advertisement in bus and tramcar, whichever paper or novel he picks up, whatever play or film he attends for amusement, the pressure of the herd is brought to bear on him. Not the least effective, and certainly the most subtle part of the campaign, is the use of the indubitable fact that it is pleasanter to be one of the herd, *i.e.* less wear and tear is involved in conforming than in standing out against mass sentiment; righteousness and goodwill are accordingly arrogated to the man who behaves like his fellows, the lowbrow, who accepts uncritically the restrictions imposed by the herd, while the highbrow, who does not, is vilified as a ' superior ' or arrogant person. This has a direct bearing on literature. Skim through the bound volumes of *Punch*, and it becomes evident that from baiting the merely rich, the vulgar, and the stupid, it now reserves its powers, and they are by no means negligible,[108] for attacking nonconformity in manners and originality in ideas and art. There has recently grown up a whole *Punch* literature—*Punch* humour, *Punch* essays, even *Punch* fiction—and all markedly anti-highbrow. This becomes serious when one remembers that whereas a century ago there was a solid body of opinion behind the Reviews, which organised and expressed the attitude of the cultured minority—

'no genteel family *can* pretend to be without it,' Scott wrote of the *Edinburgh Review*—perhaps the only periodical every genteel family can now be counted on to take is *Punch*. Such a *volte-face* has innumerable indirect effects on the life of the nation.[109]

It follows that in such a society the critic's office is not popular, criticism of any kind appearing to be disloyalty to the herd. The more subtle implications of literary criticism are equally distasteful, for since genuine criticism demands from the reader a real effort and continual readjustment, and above all asserts the standards of a severe taste, it is felt to be insulting to the natural man. Thus criticism has been—in general esteem at least—replaced by belles-lettres (writing about writing); a comparison between the reception accorded to the collection of light essays so popular now (a representative one would include essays on writers with the status of Boswell and Lamb, Masefield, Coventry Patmore, Beddoes, Humbert Wolfe . . .), and of a book attempting a critical appraisal of serious writers or a discussion of fundamental critical problems, will put this point beyond dispute. It is not merely that the former is invariably reviewed too kindly, but that animus is betrayed against the latter, a state of inflammation which was noticed in Part I. Chapter II. as characterising the Book Clubs and the middlemen of literature generally.[110] Herd values in art (what the natural man likes in books or pictures or tunes is literature or art or good music) tend to be supported by denying distinctions. This is a fair example, though more subtle (and insidious) instances are commoner:

Poor is the man (and the critic, too) whose spirit is so illiberal as to restrain him from being on good terms simultaneously with Job and Jacobs, Boccaccio and Francis of Assisi, Milton and Edgar Wallace, Donne and P. G. Wodehouse.

[*Twentieth Century Literature*, A. C. Ward, 1928.](*a*)

Here one notices the accent of hearty good-fellowship employed to reinforce the suggestion that any one who denies the P. G. Wodehouses and Edgar Wallaces a place in literature along with Milton and Donne is mean-spirited as well as arrogant. The same accent, the mark of 'a good mixer,' is an essential part of the equipment of the writer who supplies periodicals and newspapers with a regular weekly essay. The stock facetiousness about highbrow art, novel and drama, and ' modern ' poetry, that *Punch* popularised has now been taken over by weeklies with more serious pretensions. Rather more subtle expressions of herd animus are to be found scattered throughout low- and middlebrow fiction :

In 1910, the year of his most difficult and obscure volume of poems, *Troilus*, he had suddenly, obeying an impulse that he did not understand, and that did not seem to be his, published at intervals in the columns of the august *Daily World* a number of poems about the man in the street. They had been rather colloquial, slangy, poems, and some of the higher critics had denied that they were poems at all, but they had immense force and energy and were as simple as Tennyson's ' Mr. Wilkinson ' . . . He delighted a wide public, because he provided something very rare now in England and always acceptable—literature that was acknowledged to be fine superior literature, and that yet could be understood by everybody (*b*).

Kit and Mr. Porteus sat opposite each other, for when Kit was at work on Latin prose and algebra, Mr. Porteus

(*a*) ' Judex damnatur cum nocens absolvitur ' was the motto of the *Edinburgh Review*.

(*b*) Hugh Walpole, *Hans Frost*.

would be amusing himself with Einstein's theory or a book of MacDougal's psychology.

'Psycho-physical parallelism. What's that, Sorrell?'

'Don't know, sir.'

'As a matter of fact it's rot. To be able to realise a theory is rot saves one a lot of trouble. Now what about ten minutes boxing?' (a)

The chief difference appears to be that the middlebrow is anxious to get the best of both worlds while the lowbrow is concerned only to speak of the other with sufficient 'knowledgeableness' (as the advertising agents call it) to be able to deny its value. The quality of knowledgeableness is very noticeably present in the writings of three of the most successful and representative modern bestsellers, Kipling, Arnold Bennett, and Gilbert Frankau. Gilbert Frankau's would have to be the name to fill the last place in the list that includes Defoe . . . Richardson . . . Scott, Lytton, Dickens . . . Marie Corelli, Florence Barclay; Arnold Bennett's weekly articles in the *Evening Standard* exhibited in the most concentrated form the spirit of contemporary reviewing; while, as the *Publishers' Circular* says, 'Rudyard Kipling is the only author whose new poems are news events to be cabled to every quarter of the civilised globe.' It is significant that these three writers share the idiom and ideology of the copywriter, and that all three possess to perfection the 'note of authority and "knowledgeableness"': it is this which principally accounts for their success as purveyors of what the public wants.[111] Gilbert Frankau's novels play upon the same appeals as the modern advertisement—his heroes are to be visualised as the fault-

(a) Warwick Deeping, *Sorrell and Son.*

lessly groomed strong silent men with the shaving-soap
advertisement chins, their eyes are always narrowing to
pin- or needle-points, great play is made with the words
' purposeful,' ' vision,' ' urge,' ' personality,' the business man's self-dramatisation is the unvarying ideal
(' calm with that peculiar frozen calmness which serves
big men in big issues,' ' a mind trained to deal instanter
with the minds of its fellow-men ' (a)), and so on.
These, however, are only surface indications of the
trend of this fiction. A suggestion was made in
Part I. Chapter III. that the twentieth-century bestseller is concerned with supporting herd prejudices, and
in fact it will be found that this kind of writing caters
for the Babbitt element of society. Marie Corelli, Hall
Caine, Florence Barclay, Edna Lyall, start from the
assumption that the reader, like the writer, is passionately in favour of the Christian ethic, the accepted
social and moral code, family affection, altruism, and
self-sacrifice. Their successor pulls another set of
strings, the loyalties of the club, the regiment, and the
Public School. So the idiom employed by Arnold
Bennett and the Book Clubs is not critical, it merely
sizes up a work by the business man's criterion—' a
big book,' ' value for money,' ' a worth-while experience,' ' *Rogue Herries* is a real full-time man's job in
fiction '—the only criterion known to Mr. Frankau
whose heroes are always aiming at ' the big things of
life—money and power ' (b). The body of a magazine
is now carefully selected to endorse the ' message ' of
the advertisements, and it looks as though a general
infection has taken place. It would be impossible to
find a more complete illustration of what might be

(a) Gilbert Frankau, *Gerald Cranston's Lady*.   (b) *Ibid.*

called the magazine outlook of modern fiction than Bennett's last novel, *Imperial Palace*.[112] It is full of ' entrancing, perfect,' and ' fabulously expensive' women, millionaires, luxurious living, and bluff man-of-the-world horse-sense masquerading as psychology and insight. The author frankly identifies himself in tastes and standards with the hero (head of the most wonderful hotel in the world):

> And he liked her expensive stylishness. The sight of a really smart woman always gave him pleasure. . . . Surely in the wide world that night there could not be anything to beat her! Idle, luxurious, rich, but a masterpiece! Maintained in splendour by the highly skilled and expensive labour of others, materially useless to society, she yet justified herself by her mere appearance. And she knew it, and her conscience was clear.

> And he thought what a shame it was that such a woman, such a cunning piece of femininity, should be compelled by fate to knit her brows over business when she ought to be occupied solely with her ageless charm, the attractions of her boudoir, and the responsiveness of men to her fine arts.[113]

Enough attention has perhaps been given to the effects of the overthrow of minority values, but a few stray threads must be drawn in before dismissing the subject. One is the high-level bestseller status achieved by Ernest Hemingway in this country (*a*), traceable to the acceptability of the formula in which he so ingeniously works. The glorification of the ' regular man,' the figure set up by twentieth-century bestsellers, magazine writers, journalists, and advertisers in opposition to the highbrow, naturally prepared a sympathetic public for the simplification of existence

(*a*) *A Farewell to Arms* was selected by the Book Society, besides achieving a considerable reputation in higher circles.

achieved by the hero of *A Farewell to Arms* and expressed in the crude idiom of the he-man. More surprising is the fact that Hemingway has become something of a cult in highbrow circles, and this suggests how strong is the temptation to adopt an easy (because popular) attitude (*a*) : in contemporary society man separates himself from the herd at his peril. Then there is the effect on publishing of the triumph of materialistic standards. In *The Commercial Side of Literature* Michael Joseph defends the best-seller on the grounds that without him the publisher would be unable to print literature :

> One publisher of my acquaintance said to me recently, ' I prefer to publish fiction of quality, what most people call " highbrow " novels, even if the margin of profit is very small, rather than concentrate on slush; but I must admit I couldn't afford the luxury of pleasing myself if it weren't for So-and-so and So-and-so '—and he named two very popular writers in his list—' who pay my rent and salaries and overhead charges.'

This is well enough as a *faute de mieux* so long as the tradition that connects the publishing profession with literature survives, but there are signs that it is preparing to snap, and when that profession too becomes a trade contemporary literature stands an excellent chance of ceasing to exist for the public at large :

> Moreover, once the standards of publishing success became purely pecuniary ones, the author who merely brought honour or glory to the house would be dropped from the books: when Standard Books, Inc., took over half a dozen firms, they would naturally ' write off ' such authors, and take good care that they did not appear again on the lists. I remember the ominous words of a capable advertising executive, one of the

(*a*) Similarly, the highbrow cult of detective fiction.

best in that unfortunate trade, when I discussed the publishing business with her a few years ago. ' If I consented to handle a publisher's advertising, I would do exactly what I do with other manufacturers. " How many lines do you produce? " Perhaps he will answer, thirty. I would say : " Cut them down to five and advertise them." That's the way to put books across ' (a).

It has already become practically impossible to get a book reviewed unless it is advertised, and highbrow novels, which return little or no profit, cannot stand the enormous cost of advertising. We may well see a return to the primitive circulation of manuscripts among a select company.

A final point must be made to prevent misunderstanding. Throughout Chapter III. of this part numerous references were made to the formative force of society, while in Chapter IV. an apparently identical force described as the herd is alleged to have overthrown the work of the previous ages. ' Society ' was to be interpreted in the eighteenth-century sense in which, like ' the world,' it meant a select, cultured element of the community that set the standards of behaviour and judgment, in direct opposition to the common people. Thus the highest definition of man was that of a social animal : the gregarious instinct he shares with sheep and wolves. The ameliorating influence of associating with the well-bred and cultivated was universally acknowledged [114]—it accounts for the horror of being confined in the country, away from ' the world,' so noticeable in the literature of the Restoration and eighteenth century, until the Romantic

(a) ' Publishing, Old and New,' by Lewis Mumford (*The New Republic*, October 1st, 1930). The Book Clubs are, of course, just such engines of standardisation.

poets discovered the superiority of solitary to social man. If one accepts the argument (*a*) that ' In any period it is upon a very small minority that the discerning appreciation of art and literature depends : it is only a few who are capable of unprompted first-hand judgment. . . . The accepted valuations are a kind of paper currency based upon a very small proportion of gold. To the state of such a currency the possibilities of fine living at any time bear a close relation,' then it becomes evident that the individual has a better chance of obtaining access to the fullest (because finest) life in a community dominated by ' society ' than in one protesting the superiority of the herd.

(*a*) Vide *Mass Civilisation and Minority Culture*, F. R. Leavis (Minority Press, 1930).

PART III

THE SIGNIFICANCE OF THE BESTSELLER

The work of Charles Garvice has little artistic importance; but he was a thoroughly competent craftsman. . . . Mr. Murry says that he can sympathise with my ' evident desire to disconcert the preciousness of the aesthete.' But when he says that things such as Charles Garvice made were ' simply not worth making well,' etc., I charge him with precisely the preciousness of the aesthete. Was it not worth while to give pleasure to the naïve millions for whom Charles Garvice catered honestly and to the best of his very competent ability? Ought these millions to be deprived of what they like, ought they to be compelled to bore themselves with what Mr. Murry likes, merely because Mr. Murry's taste is better than theirs? The idea is ridiculous. The idea is snobbish in the worst degree. Taste is still relative.

Things that Have Interested Me, ARNOLD BENNETT.
(2nd Series.)

When I take up one of Jane Austen's books, such as ' Pride and Prejudice,' I feel like a barkeeper entering the kingdom of heaven. I know what his sensation would be and his private comments. He would not find the place to his taste, and he would probably say so.

MARK TWAIN.

Le cinéma matérialise le pire idéal populaire. . . . Il ne s'agit pas de la fin du monde, mais de la fin de la civilisation.

ANATOLE FRANCE.

THE SIGNIFICANCE OF THE
BESTSELLER

I

THE NOVEL

THE object of this essay has been previously stated as an attempt to find an explanation of the situation described in Part I., a description which ended by raising the question whether such a state of affairs was common to other ages or, if unique, in what way it differed and how it had come to pass. Part II. was devoted to these problems, and it should now be sufficiently obvious that 'things' have not 'always been the same': perhaps it would be insulting not to leave the reader to make for himself the detailed comparison between Parts I. and II. which should prove the point. Only general conclusions will be noted here, with a view to sketching an answer to the vital question, How does the reader of our own time compare with his predecessors?

First, we can hardly avoid noticing that the function of fiction has varied considerably through the last three and a half centuries, and that the rôle of fiction has borne a close relation to the use the reader has been accustomed to make of his leisure. Thus Nashe had to compete with the stage, Defoe with edifying literature; by the time the eighteenth century had evolved the fiction appropriate to its needs, novels

had become, in Lackington's phrase, ' excellent productions ' that ' tend to polish both the heart and the
head.' Fiction, from being a matter of sporadic
attempts to provide ingenious journalists with a living,
had found a place in the life of a society whose ideal of
' true taste and good manners ' (*a*) made it a useful
means of disseminating the mode of feeling of the
cultivated. The history of the next century of fiction
is that of a rapidly growing public, an organised profession to serve it, and then inevitably of writers
specialising in a way unknown to Defoe, studying the
market in order to exploit it. But this would not have
been possible unless some radical change had taken
place in the life of the reader. The novel of Deloney
and Defoe provided admirable amusement for a small
part of the leisure of a people sufficiently in command of
wide first-hand experience to be independent of fiction
and sharing too a social life of no mean interest, so that
in their reading they did not ask to be turned away from
life and no journalist dreamt of ' writing down ' to
them. Even after the Industrial Revolution, as long as
the Puritan tradition survived, we find the same conditions hold : the journeymen and peasants and trades-
men of the first half of the nineteenth century did not
go to books for an escape from their lives but to qualify
themselves to live to more purpose—they devoted part
of their leisure first to poetry, history, and criticism,
by way of education, and then to ' the best novels,'
though unfortunately Scott had by then superseded a
number of the novelists in Lackington's list (*b*). It is
only a world run by Big Business that has produced a

(*a*) Matthias, *The Pursuits of Literature*, 1794-97.
(*b*) *Vide* p. 109.

civilisation whose workers must have recourse to substitute living.[115]

Changes in environment, then (using 'environment' broadly to mean all external circumstances which determine the pattern of the average life), are seen to be primarily responsible for the kind of fiction the general public requires and gets.[116] But the environment is ultimately responsible for a great deal more: it determines the extent to which the man in the street has access to literature, the market that the serious novelist can count on; that is to say, in the last event, the quality of living and the solvency of literature. Thus conclusions about Parts I. and II. can be marshalled most serviceably in three divisions—(a) Changes in environment, (b) Changes in the book-market, (c) Changes in reading capacity. A composite picture has been offered of what has happened to the reading public in three centuries, with an attempt to state the bare facts and suggest relations and causes without involving value-judgments. The reader will not need to be abnormally acute to detect instances where this attempt has necessarily broken down. For the significance of the whole subject is the questions it raises (one of them is posited by the first extract attached to this section) which must be faced by any one aspiring to candour. It had better be admitted straightway that there are no simple answers to these highly complicated questions—a fact on which people like the late Arnold Bennett triumphantly trade—but with patience and goodwill a satisfactory agreement between those genuinely interested can be arrived at or at any rate a tenable position found. Since most of us are rather concerned to defend our own attitude, which from laziness or indifference or worse is more likely than not to be the anti-highbrow ' taste is still relative,' than to take part in the strenuous process of justifying our finer awareness, it is as well to state in advance that whatever case may be made out from the findings of this study, the wholehearted Rotarian, the comfortable believer in optimism and the idea of Progress, the upholder of the joys of having a good time, and their equivalents in the world of letters, are not likely to be moved. It is as much as can be expected if they are made uncomfortable.

In what terms, by what scale, one asks, can decline or improvement be assessed? How can the reading public of the early seventeenth century be compared with that of the twentieth? Here the three categories devised above come in useful, for if we want an impersonal standard to measure by we should start by showing that the market is now, owing to popular fiction, in a less healthy state for literature (*vide* note 35, p. 161 and notes, pp. 31-2, p. 172, p. 200), whose importance can be assumed to need no demonstrating to any reader of this essay. Then, with these facts in hand, to Arnold Bennett's rhetorical questions, ' Was it not worth while to give pleasure to the naïve millions for whom Charles Garvice catered . . .? Ought these millions to be deprived of what they like because . . .? ' etc., one will be in a position to reply, without more exaggeration than is justified, ' When any one buys a volume of Charles Garvice he is doing harm to literature.' [It has then to be shown that when he reads it he is doing harm to himself. But this must be left till last.]

While we are all no doubt agreed that it is desirable

that literature should flourish, it is perhaps not as evident that the average man suffers from exclusion from the world of art. But when it was found in Part I. (pp. 38-9) that the man in the street is now cut off from literature, the statement had more serious implications than might have been supposed—for, it will be argued, Defoe's and Bunyan's public too were outside 'the circumference of wit' and generations of country folk have lived to some purpose without the aid of books other than their Bible. But these had a real social life, they had a way of living that obeyed the natural rhythm and furnished them with genuine or what might be called, to borrow a word from the copy-writer, 'creative' interests—country arts, traditional crafts and games and singing, not substitute or kill-time interests like listening to radio and gramophone, looking through newspapers and magazines, watching films and commercial football, and the activities connected with motor cars and bicycles, the only way of using leisure known to the modern city-dweller—for it is now only the suburban or urban dweller who counts (*vide* note 31), the average man is 'the man in the street.' When

> The pianola replaces
> Sappho's barbitos,

national life suffers : fantasy-fiction [117] is the typical reading of a people whose normal impulses are starved of the means of expression.[118] The old culture of the English countryside (it still lingers on in diminished vigour in the few remote parts to which even the motor coach has not yet penetrated) (*a*) was a great deal more

---

(*a*) Cf. *Small Talk at Wreyland* (Cecil Torr), in which a dying culture is mirrored, just caught in time, with *Change in the Village* (' George Bourne '),

inclusive than we are inclined to suppose ; it had room for local variations in the tempo of living, and it provided a ritual and a code which made possible even for the illiterate a decent, a comely, and a satisfying existence. As a proof, compare the idiom of such people, as recorded for example in the novels of Hardy and George Eliot and T. F. Powys, the notebooks of Mr. Cecil Torr and the writings of Mr. George Sturt, with the suburban idiom spoken around us and used by journalists. It is the latter that is inflexible and brutal. The cottager was far from being inarticulate : from Bunyan's day to our own there is plenty of evidence that the Authorised Version provided a medium of self-expression (without displacing the sound pagan philosophy of the folk), the biblical idiom serving as a mould into which their feelings could be poured and so richly and finely take shape. The newspaper and radio have destroyed this, and the suburban culture with its absence of a personal life and a personal idiom has failed to produce anything like as subtle a medium (a) (vide p. 57 and note 39). The new idiom is less adequate since it is incapable of flexibility, it has no fine rhythms to draw upon, and it is not serious (i.e. has no room for expression of spontaneous personal

and ' *England's Green and Pleasant Land* ' (Anon.), where two once vigorous agricultural communities are shown, reflecting the general plight of the English countryside, the one destroyed by enclosure of the commons and subsequent suburbanising, the other drained of its best stock by the city and struggling against the resultant anæmia.

(a) An otherwise undistinguished novel, *Spring Darkness*, by John Metcalf (1928), is interesting since it conveys the emptiness and meaningless iteration of the suburban life ; so also, but unconsciously, does *The English Miss*, R. H. Mottram (1926). *The Suburban Young Man* and other novels of E. M. Delafield (popular circulating library fiction) are excellent illustrations of the idiom of that life, in which everything said has a stale flavour of having been acquired from the newspaper or magazine.

feeling) : it is not only formed to convey merely crude states of mind but it is destructive of any fineness.

So whereas for the type represented by Bunyan literature did not matter, it is of the gravest importance that what the twentieth century reads should modify and correct the influence of environment. It is only by acquiring access to good poetry, great drama, and the best novels, the forms of art that, since they achieve their effects through language, most readily improve the quality of living, that the atmosphere in which we live may be oxygenated. But poetry no longer exists for the general public (*vide* note 7); still less drama of any significance, and the bestseller, the magazine story, and the circulating library novel are all that is read in the way of fiction. What the average reader now goes to fiction for was discussed in Part I. Chapter III., and of the four reasons why people read novels summarised on p. 48, only the last was not investigated —for the last is the highbrow's, and popular fiction does not afford occasion for that approach.

The distinction between a great novel and a bestseller is analogous to the distinction between good poetry and successful bad poetry. [A poem may be bad for two reasons : because it fails to be a good one— *e.g.* some of Shelley and Wordsworth ; or because it does with complete success something that is not beneficial—most popular poems come in here, *e.g.* the work of successful bad poets like Chesterton, Kipling, Ella Wheeler Wilcox.] Great novels are frequently doing something like good poetry, the bestsellers of verse and of fiction are also doing something comparable, but quite different from the effect of the great novel and good poem—if they were not doing something for the class of reader who forms the general public they would not be bestsellers. They are, in brief, engaged in establishing undesirable attitudes (*a*) (*vide* Part I. Chapter III., Part II. Chapter IV. § 1 and § 3). It remains to find what the great novel does for the reader, how it works, and, most important for purposes of this inquiry, what capacities it demands from the reader.

In so far as a novel, like a poem, is made of words, much of what Mr. Richards says of poetry (*b*) can be adapted to apply to the novel, but even so the critic does not get much help, for there is an important difference between the way a novel and a poem takes effect. A poem is so much more delicate and compact an organisation than a novel that the whole depends on the quality of the part—in criticising a poem one can safely bear out one's general impression by examining particular passages, the poem succeeds or fails at every point. But the novel is diffused, it cannot be read through at a sitting, and the whole is apt to be lost sight of in the immediacy of the parts. It is more like a poem seen in sections through a microscope—so highly magnified that to perceive its total rhythm and so estimate its value with conviction is a feat attended with the greatest difficulty. [The novel has, however, in consequence of this difference, some advantages—one is that it can be read more easily; another is that it can be translated, so that while *Faust* or *Le Cimetière Marin* cannot be apprehended as works of art in English, we can get something comparable to the original experience and so make a rough guess at the value of *Anna*

(*a*) In the sense of attitude = imaginal and incipient activities or tendencies to action, as defined by Mr. I. A. Richards, *Principles of Literary Criticism*, Chap. xv.

(*b*) In *Principles of Literary Criticism*.

Karenina or *The Possessed* or *A la recherche du temps perdu* in another language than that in which it was written.] The critic of a poem can usually cite his poem, or at least specimen stanzas and crucial passages, and the question What is a poem? has been settled, in *Principles of Literary Criticism*, to the satisfaction of most of us and the relief of the critic. The critic of the novel is not in this happy position. He cannot even cite a chapter (the equivalent of a stanza or a line), and the paragraph or two that he may reasonably quote is too short an extract to set up the rhythm of the book. The novel does not stand or fall by its parts ; it has room for bad writing, dull spells, and feeble interludes, and can carry them all off—George Eliot, Conrad, and Hardy, to take notable instances, are guilty of all this and yet are serious and important novelists—and the critic cannot safely dismiss *The Return of the Native* because the staple of its prose is abominable and because when a climax is reached (Book V. Chap. III.) the writing collapses into ludicrous melodrama. Such a collapse in a poem would betray an instability of poise and a fundamental falseness of feeling in the poet, on the strength of which we need have no hesitation in finding the poem a failure. But in a novel it may only show that this is where the novelist's interest ceases, it merely demonstrates a limitation of the novelist's make-up which may be fatal, as in the case of Scott, or may not if the novelist is wise enough, like Hardy, to keep his subject-matter as far as possible within the limits of his experience (he is admirable so long as he is not dealing with educated people or describing what he is not interested in). By the time the fifth book of *The Return of the Native* is reached Hardy has set up his rhythm which carries the reader unfalteringly over the weak spot, for with the expectation aroused by the first chapter and satisfied for long stretches, a break here and there does not matter.

The novel's effect, then, is cumulative, and such a form demands from the reader a prolonged expenditure of effort. To be equal to this demand is the first requisite in a reader. The other constituents of reading capacity can be lumped together as ability to cope with the ' meaning,' adopting the division of Meaning into Sense, Tone, Feeling, and Intention made in *Practical Criticism* (*a*). To the degree that the reader has these capacities he is free of literature. And the reading capacity of various ages may be gauged by the demands made on each by its popular fiction, which since it was by definition widely read is the fairest test of the general reading level at any given time.

(*a*) *Practical Criticism*, I. A. Richards, pp. 181-2, where Tone signifies the attitude of author to reader and Feeling the attitude of author to what he has to say.

II

READING CAPACITY

THE writer will probably have been thought to lay undue stress throughout Parts I. and II. on certain aspects of civilisation which may have appeared to have only the loosest connection with the object of this study; but the attention paid to the nature of the society of each age, its idiom, *mœurs*, and preoccupations, can now be justified. Where the general reader is concerned, the capacity for cumulative reading is formed or destroyed by environment; ability to follow the sense of an author depends on mental habits less personal than social; susceptibility to tone is finally a test of manners; the quality of the popular novelist's feeling about what he writes is an indication of the degree of seriousness the age permits, and the nature of his intention is conditioned by the degree of familiarity with literary technique at which the general public has arrived. All but a few novelists, then, are dependent on the extent to which the reader can be expected to co-operate.

The kind of demand made by Elizabethan prose was outlined in Part II. Chapter II. (*vide* pp. 87-8), where Nashe was selected as the journalist whose style is most intensively characteristic of the popular writing of the time. It is 'difficult' prose, that is, the modern reader cannot absorb it as easily as the prose with which he is provided by contemporary journalists and popular authors. It is necessary to enquire why the common reader of the sixteenth century found no impediment where his twentieth-century descendant is barred out. Consider two later novelists who are also now reckoned difficult, Sterne (*vide* p. 134) and Virginia Woolf (*vide* pp. 60-61). It will be convenient to reproduce the sentence already quoted from *The Unfortunate Traveller* in order to compare it with a specimen of the last novelist (it is no use inspecting a fragment of Sterne, for reasons that will be explained presently):

(a)   Verie devout Asses they were, for all they were so dunstically set forth, and such as thought they knew as much of God's minde as richer men: why inspiration was their ordinarie familiar, and buzd in their eares like a Bee in a boxe everie hower what newes from heaven, hell, and the land of whipperginnie, displease them who durst, he should have his mittimus to damnation *ex tempore*, they would vaunt there was not a pease difference betwixt them and the Apostles, they were as poor as they, of as base trades as they, and no more inspired than they, and with God there is no respect of persons, onely herein may seeme some little diversitie to lurk, that *Peter* wore a sword, and they count it flat hel fire for anie man to weare a dagger: nay, so grounded and gravelled were they in this opinion, that now when they should come to Battell, theres never a one of them would bring a blade (no, not an onion blade) about hym to dye for it.

(b)   The gruff murmur, irregularly broken by the taking out of pipes and the putting in of pipes which had kept on assuring her, though she could not hear what was said (as she sat in the window), that the men were happily talking; this sound, which had lasted now half an hour and had taken its place soothingly in the scale of sounds pressing on top of her, such as the tap of balls upon bats, the sharp, sudden bark now and then, ' How's that? How's that? ' of the children playing cricket, had ceased; so that the monotonous fall of the waves on the beach, which for the most part beat a measured and soothing tattoo to her thoughts and seemed consolingly to repeat over and over again as she sat with the children the words of some old cradle song, murmured by nature, ' I am guarding you—I am your support '; but at other times suddenly and unexpectedly, especially when her mind raised itself slightly from the task in hand, had no such kindly meaning, but like a ghostly roll of drums remorselessly beat the measure of life, made one think of the destruction of the island and its engulfment in the sea, and warned her whose day had slipped past in one quick doing after another that it was all ephemeral as a rainbow—this sound which had been observed and concealed under the other sounds suddenly thundered hollow in her ears and made her look up with an impulse of terror.

It is evident that the difficulty the reader has with the passage (a) is in a great part due to an incoherence in the author's mind and a complete absence of consideration for the reader in the way he chooses to express himself. With Nashe, as with his contemporaries generally, everything that comes to the author's mind irresistibly provokes an illustration and is only too likely to blaze up into a metaphor, which is then pursued for its own sake until it palls or is deserted for another more tempting; ultimately there is a leap back to the point of departure and a fresh dart forwards, with the same result as before. Such prose is the outcome of a restlessly active mind, that, distracted by the tug-of-war of its many interests, and childlike, cannot bear to stop to sort out or to abandon anything where all are treasures. Nashe's reader is following a hare-and-hound trail, and the twentieth century is out of training for cross-country work, so long has it been accustomed to writers who take pains to make their line of thought apparent; for it is a difficulty of *sense* only. But the public Nashe addressed was admirably trained in such exercise. Sermon and drama and music (*vide* Part II. Chapter I.) had accustomed it to follow attentively and alertly, and with the workings of Nashe's kind of mind it was, through the medium of its amusements, familiar. The term ' nimble wits ' is a catchword of the period—this quicksilver quality of the mind was evidently prized and cultivated by the Elizabethan, and there are everywhere signs that both author and public enjoyed exerting their powers in this direction. Since that time we have cleared up our habits of punctuation, spelling, paragraphing, and sentence-construction, and in the process have removed a large part of the difficulty Nashe's reader was exposed to. On the other hand, that reader had to concentrate, and an author who could count on this—as the Elizabethan clearly could and did—could allow himself far more licence than any popular author of the nineteenth or twentieth centuries; the sixteenth and seventeenth centuries sat down to read with different expectations from the readers observed in Part I. Reading was then almost inseparably associated with reading aloud (punctuation, for instance, was for the voice and not the sense), as it seems to have been with the Romans, and this would tend not only to slow down the tempo of reading but also to disentangle the threads.

Yet the kind of ability manifested by the Elizabethan reader is not incompatible with naivety (*a*) : Nashe's public would have been bewildered if faced with the modern magazine story or such a recent bestseller as *Gentlemen Prefer Blondes*, whose slick technique is the product of centuries of journalistic experience and whose effect depends entirely on the existence of a set of stock responses provided by newspaper and film.

(*a*) *Vide* pp. 89-91.

Nor could Sterne's novels have been written in any earlier age.   There is no possibility of illustrating by quotation the kind of difficulty presented by *Tristram Shandy*, for it is not at all a difficulty of sense.   Nashe's writing is a display of undisciplined mental vigour, whereas Sterne's art is essentially conscious and studied; he is all along playing a game with the reader in which all his cards are on the table—see, for instance, the last part of Book VI., Book I. Chapter XXII.—

. . . In this long digression, which I was accidentally led into, as in all my digressions (one only excepted) there is a master-stroke of digressive skill, the merit of which has all along, I fear, been overlooked by my reader,—not for want of penetration in him,—but because 'tis an excellence seldom looked for, or expected indeed, in a digression;—and it is this: That tho' my digressions are all fair, as you observe,—and that I fly off from what I am about, as far, and as often too, as any writer in *Great Britain*; yet I constantly take care to order affairs so that my main business does not stand still in my absence.

I was just going, for example, to have given you the great out-lines of my uncle *Toby's* most whimsical character;—when my aunt *Dinah* and the coachman came across us, and led us a vagary some millions of miles into the very heart of the planetary system: Notwithstanding all this, you perceive that the drawing of my uncle *Toby's* character went on gently all the time;—not the great contours of it,—that was impossible,—but some familiar strokes and faint designations of it, were here and there touch'd on, as we went along, so that you are much better acquainted with my-uncle *Toby* now than you was before, *etc.*

—and Book II. Chapter IV. which opens:

I would not give a groat for that man's knowledge in pen-craft, who does not understand this,—That the best plain narrative in the world, tacked very close to the last spirited apostrophe to my uncle *Toby*—would have felt both cold and vapid upon the reader's palate;—therefore I forthwith put an end to the chapter, though I was in the middle of my story.

Such a technique requires a far more subtle under-standing between author and public than was possible in the early period described in Part II. Chapter I.; it depends on the establishment of a social tone.[119] Sterne's eccentric style, with his blank, black, and marbled pages, his dots and dashes, asterisks, paren-theses and curious type-setting, is essential to his intention ; his progress, like Byron's in *Don Juan*, is not structural but consists in rapid variations in the scale of *feeling*, in unexpected changes in the emotional pressure. There is no other pattern in *Tristram Shandy* or *The Sentimental Journey* (or *Don Juan*), and so no reason, as Sterne himself was perfectly aware (*a*), why they should ever stop. His public read and admired him for this virtuosity. It could do so since it had the ad-vantage of a social literature (Pope and Addison were both the classics and bestsellers of the eighteenth century) which had previously developed the possi-bilities of the civilised emotions (*vide* pp. 121-5). It is always, in Pope, Addison, Sterne, an elegant tear, a delicately poised smile, a distribution of emotion and a reservation of the critical faculty—this poise is in-compatible with tragedy but neither is it susceptible to ridicule : it is equally removed from the naïve humour and full-bodied tragic passion of the Eliza-bethan audience on the one side and from the undis-criminating surrender to bursts of laughter and storms

(*a*) *Vide* Book I. Chap. XXII.

of tears of Dickens's public on the other. Unless one is prepared to work steadily through fantastically distorted sentences about nothing, chapters of digressions and pages of irrelevancies, with no reward but the satisfaction of a taste for virtuosity, Sterne will yield nothing. Part of this highly sophisticated entertainment is that the reader's expectations are constantly teased, threatened with frustration, and finally fulfilled only to be burlesqued immediately afterwards. Sterne's prose exhibits another kind of high spirits than Nashe's, and just as the latter required certain capacities which were provided for by the contemporary background, so, without such a social and literary education as the *Tatler* and Pope's poetry stand for, Sterne would have had no public. As it was, each fresh volume of Sterne's was rapturously received; it was a public prepared to take some trouble for its pleasures, and the function of the novel was recognised as something more than an amusement—' to polish the heart and the head.' The last three or four books of *Tristram Shandy* are actually more perversely irrelevant and have even less story content than the previous books. A generation later (*vide* pp. 134-5) the reading public had become less athletic, for reasons discussed in Part II. Chapter III.; it exhibited a tendency to select those portions of *Tristram Shandy* and *The Sentimental Journey* which elicit merely the responses ' How touching ' and ' How true.' In Sterne's imitators and successors we completely miss that exploration of diverse planes of feeling that make Pope and Sterne at once so mobile and so assured.

There is no reason, therefore, why both Nashe and Sterne, ' difficult ' writers as they now are, should not

have been popular in their own day : the conditions of
the age made them accessible to the common reader.
But the difficulty presented by *To the Lighthouse* is not
only more formidable and complex than that of *The
Unfortunate Traveller* or *Tristram Shandy*, it is especially
calculated to baffle the general public of the twentieth
century. First, comparing the style of the passages
quoted above, one notices that it would be impossible
to rearrange (b), as (a) could be rearranged, for the
greater convenience of the reader, nor could (b) be
pruned and adjusted, to the same end, without altering
its substance. Whereas Nashe's metaphors are explanatory, piquant, humorous, etc., Virginia Woolf's
are on a higher level of seriousness—the Elizabethan
prose writer was unable to resist running off into
similes and metaphors (a form of self-indulgence
uncommon in subsequent less virile ages), but the
latter's thoughts and perceptions inevitably flower into
images, like a poet's. The complex mode of feeling
can only be conveyed thus in images, with just as much
indication of the sense as will serve for a spring-board
to the reader. Thus to a public accustomed to nothing
more ambitious than the elementary prose of the
journalist (*vide* pp. 184-5) the style of *To the Lighthouse*
is formidable in the extreme. Again, the *tone* is pro-
hibitive to any one who does not share the author's
cultural background, and the subtle play of *feeling*—a
matter here of intonation and stress, less easily grasped
than Sterne's plain dealing—baffling to an age that
does not read poetry. Above all, the *intention* is the
final barrier—the usual complaints of would-be readers
of Mrs. Woolf's novels are ' She doesn't write about
anything,' ' Her characters aren't real,' and ' There

isn't any story' (*a*). The novels are in fact highbrow art. The reader who is not alive to the fact that *To the Lighthouse* is a beautifully constructed work of art will make nothing of the book (*vide* pp. 60-61). And it is not an easily perceived structure, as in *Tom Jones*, where it is a matter of frank engineering, or in *The Awkward Age* and *The Ambassadors*, where it is a question of a fairly obvious architectual design (*b*). The full force of the novel is only perceived in the third part, where almost everything refers back and gives significance to earlier passages. Passage (b) quoted above to illustrate the complexity of the style is one of the central significant moments (it is constantly caught up in the third part of the novel). The technique and the intention (*c*) are poetic, and *To the Lighthouse* requires that the reader should have had a training in reading poetry.

To the Lighthouse is not a popular novel (though it has already taken its place as an important one), and it is necessary to enquire why the conditions of the age have made it inaccessible to a public whose ancestors have been competent readers of Sterne and Nashe. The sixteenth, seventeenth, and eighteenth centuries, we

(*a*) Variations actually confided to the writer were : ' I don't seem to get any kick out of Virginia Woolf' (from a bestseller); and ' She doesn't get anywhere.'

(*b*) Compare the movement of (a) and (b)—(a) is irresponsible, behind (b) is a complex sensibility—eyes, nerves, intelligence, are controlled and directed to an end.

(*c*) ' Phrases came. Visions came. Beautiful pictures. But what she wished to get hold of was that very jar upon the nerves, the thing itself before it has been made anything. Get that and start afresh ; get that and start afresh ; she said desperately, pitching herself firmly again before her easel. It was a miserable machine, an inefficient machine, she thought, the human apparatus for painting or for feeling ; it always broke down at the critical moment ; heroically, one must force it on.'—*To the Lighthouse*, p. 297.

have seen, trained certain capacities, gave a certain education to the average man. The training of the reader who spends his leisure in cinemas, looking through magazines and newspapers, listening to jazz music, does not merely fail to help him, it prevents him from normal development (*vide* Part II. Chapter IV.), partly by providing him with a set of habits inimical to mental effort. Even in small matters it gets in his way : for example, the preconceptions acquired from the magazine story and the circulating library novel are opposed to any possibility of grasping a serious novelist's intention.[120] Northcliffe's interference with reading habits alone has effectively put literature out of the reach of the average man. Chapters II., III., and IV. of Part II. make it apparent that whereas the eighteenth century and nineteenth century helped the reader, the twentieth century hinders—whereas the tide was with a man born between 1740 and 1840 seeking self-cultivation, it is now against him (cf. Part II. Chapters II. and IV. § 2, § 3), in spite of the machinery for passing him from elementary to secondary school and university (it is, of course, comparatively easy for the modern Lackington to become a prosperous Babbitt or even one of the Book Club public). Consider the ease with which the Lackingtons absorbed works of the dimensions and density of *Clarissa*, *Tristram Shandy*, *Paradise Lost*, Gibbon's *Decline and Fall*, Pope's Homer, Johnson's essays. This meant, stating it in the lowest terms, an inability to be bored and a capacity to concentrate,[121] due in part, no doubt, to the fact that there was no competition of amusements provided. Life was not then a series of frivolous stimuli as it now is for the suburban dweller,[122] and there was time for the less immediate pleasures. The temptation [123] to accept the cheap and easy pleasures offered by the cinema, the circulating library, the magazine, the news-paper, the dance-hall, and the loud-speaker is too much for almost every one. To refrain would be to exercise a severer self-discipline than even the strongest-minded are likely to practise, for only the unusually self-disciplined can fight against their environment and only the unusually self-aware could perceive the neces-sity of doing so. For Lackington's contemporaries the discipline was imposed by circumstance without refer-ence to the individual, which is partly what was meant by the assertion that the age was in their favour. ' My father's library was on a small scale,' wrote Eliza Fletcher (a) : fewer books came the way of the common reader (for one thing far fewer were published, so that less sifting of rubbish had to be done), but they were almost invariably literature, and a large proportion non-fiction. It will have been noticed in Part II. Chapter II. how inferior a place the novel occupied in comparison with solid reading—good poetry (Shakespeare, Milton, Dryden, Pope), good criticism (Johnson, the Reviews) good prose (Swift, Addison, Gibbon), serious thinking (Locke, Hume, Berkeley, the seventeenth-century divines). An apposite quotation from Coleridge may serve to make the point more effectively than an argument :

It is noticeable, how limited an acquaintance with the master-pieces of art will suffice to form a correct and even a sensitive taste, where none but master-pieces have been seen and admired: while on the other hand, the most correct notions, and the widest acquaintance with the works of excel-

(a) *Vide* p. 147.

lence of all ages and countries, will not perfectly secure us against the contagious familiarity with the far more numerous offspring of tastelessness or of a perverted taste. If this be the case, as it notoriously is, with the arts of music and painting, how much more difficult will it be, to avoid the infection of multiplied and daily examples in the practice of an art, which uses words, and words only, as its instruments (a).

Now compare the environment described in Part I. and Part II. Chapter IV. The mere appearance of the printed page has altered, in the direction determined by Northcliffe, so that its contents are to be skimmed : the temptation for the modern reader is *not* to read properly —*i.e.* with the fullest attention (the practice that died only with the last generation of reading aloud in the family circle was the best possible insurance of good reading habits—and mere trash, moreover, will not stand this test). We have no practice in making the effort necessary to master a work that presents some surface difficulty or offers no immediate repayment ; we have not trained ourselves to persevere at works of the extent of *Clarissa* and the seriousness of Johnson's essays, and all our habits incline us towards preferring the immediate to the cumulative pleasure. Hence one of the few valuable novels of the twentieth century, Lawrence's *The Rainbow*, whose intention required that it should move in a slow, laboured cycle, is hardly read : it takes so long to set up its rhythm (in spite of the magnificent opening) that few readers are willing or able to give it the time and energy it requires. A novel that cannot be taken in at one reading stands little chance of a public in the twentieth century.

So for a nation of newspaper-readers a substitute

(a) *Biographia Literaria,* Chap. XXII.

literature has appeared : instead of Gibbon the public
of Part I. has the school of amusing biography; instead
of Johnson intimate little volumes of belles-lettres;
even science must be popular and theology bright for
an age which demands that its reading shall be light
and explicitly disavow seriousness. The recent tendency of publishers to produce works on religion,
morality, history, politics . . . by getting the more
notorious members of Church and State and Science to
contribute their views, or even by reprinting such views
from the columns of the popular Press and from B.B.C.
talks, is significant. Anthologies and symposia are
infinitely more 'readable' (a) than complete works,
but very much less valuable mental training (cf.
pp. 86-7). In Part II. Chapter II. it was noticed how
the models of good writing were for so long generally
recognised to be Swift, Addison, Goldsmith; a critic
a century hence consulting the prose anthologies of the
post-war age for data would have reason to conclude
that the twentieth-century equivalents are Chesterton,
Belloc, and the factitious peroration of *Queen Victoria*.
Certainly the popular ideal of ' style ' has completely
changed. That change began when the mannered
writing of the Romantic essayists, and later on of
Pater, Meredith, and R. L. Stevenson, filtered down
through the Press as the higher journalese: style
became then something recognisably literary as distinct
from educated speech-idiom (cf. pp. 122-3). Hence
the thick-and-rich prose reeking with personality of
twentieth-century favourites [124]—not merely middlebrow stylists like Chesterton, Belloc, C. E. Montague,

(a) Post-war books are apt to be praised by reviewers and advertised as
' readable.' The implications of this term cannot be exhausted in a footnote.

Maurice Hewlett, but bestsellers of widespread popularity such as A. S. M. Hutchinson, Kipling, Michael Arlen. The kind of advertisements that appear in *Punch* and the luxurious weeklies (class (*d*), p. 11) to advertise high-class products tend to employ persuasive copy rather than mere illustrations, and on this account are worth inspecting ; they reveal that the copywriters have formed their notions of good writing on the stylists just mentioned and have reason for supposing that the public they aim at reaching shares their taste.[125] Now this taste is allied to the need for stimulant—it helps to hold the reader's attention,[126] it is partly the product of the new magazine and newspaper (whose influence has been discussed in Part II. Chapter IV. § 2), and it still further removes the common reader from literature. A taste formed on mannered prose at the journalist's level is certain to find the classics of the language and the best contemporary literature insipid and dull.

His environment is even more subtly against the twentieth-century reader than this account may suggest. It was affirmed on p. 71 that in the postwar civilisation ' the rate at which cultural news penetrates is surprisingly slow '—surprisingly, that is, considering the elaborate machinery for disseminating such news which that civilisation possesses. But when this machinery is examined, the newspaper, the cinema, and so on are seen actually to form and accentuate the stratification which was noticed as a striking peculiarity of the twentieth-century public, whatever their function may be in theory they do in fact harden their public, not render it adaptable, conserve popular prejudice, not correct it, above

all, induce attitudes which they may profitably exploit. Similarly the Book Clubs described in Part I.
Chapter II. are instruments not for improving taste
but for standardising it at the middlebrow level, thus
preventing the natural progression of taste that in the
later eighteenth century, for instance, was assisted.
Now, considering this background and these formative
influences, it is not difficult to account for the disappearance of poetry from the average man's reading.
Poetry was widely read throughout the seventeenth
and eighteenth centuries and for at least the first half
of the nineteenth century : not only the acknowledged
classics—Shakespeare, *Paradise Lost*, Dryden, Pope—
but the successive new poets—Gray, Goldsmith,
Johnson, Cowper, Burns, Wordsworth, Coleridge,
Byron, Keats, Shelley, Tennyson; *Don Juan* reached
even the strict Puritan households (for Byron's
prestige *Praeterita* is the best witness, in which even
Ruskin's evangelical parents are described as regularly reading aloud to the family Byron's poetry, and
Pope's, and Johnson's works, as well as Shakespeare
and the Bible, and their ambition for their son was that
he should become as great a poet as Byron). The
eighteenth-century reader, we have seen, was prepared
to give as much as an author could demand : the
suppleness, concentration, and critical awareness demanded (and at that time received) by *Tom Jones*,
Tristram Shandy, Gibbon, Swift's irony and Johnson's
criticism, are exactly what are required of the reader of
the eighteenth-century poets, from Dryden to Crabbe.
The general public were then qualified to make the
acquaintance of the best poetry as well as of the best
novels and the best criticism of their time, coming to

that poetry in the right attitude and with adequate reading habits. The work of Shelley, Spenser, Keats, and Tennyson, and eventually of the Pre-Raphaelites, which, with the ballads and Milton's minor poems, in the next century superseded the eighteenth-century poetry, required (at any rate in the way they were generally read) less scrupulous attention. They yielded a warm, sensuous gratification to the most careless perusal, while at the same time limiting to the later Romantic convention of the poetical the scope of the poet's interests and so of the reader's sympathy. To read any of the popular poetry of the eighteenth century it is at least essential to keep awake in order to follow the sense, and above all necessary to respond as an adult. The loss in maturity and poise noticeable between Pope and Shelley is paralleled by the same disparity between Sterne and Thackeray, Jane Austen and Charlotte Brontë, Smollett and Dickens. The nineteenth-century writers appeal at a different level, they require far less from the reader and they repay him abundantly in inferior coin. Just as the poetry of the Victorian Romantics appealed to adolescent and childhood sensibility and worked in a soporific medium, so the Victorian popular novelists accustomed the reading public to habits of diminished vigilance, provoked an uncritical response and discovered the appeals which have since made the fortunes of Sir James Barrie and Mr. A. A. Milne, the reputation of the Poet Laureate, and the success of most later nineteenth-century and twentieth-century bestsellers. The process by which reading habits were being changed was accelerated by the machinery mentioned earlier : the reader of the popular Press is now only fit for the

Kipling kind of verse, the Book Club public is incapable of any more arduous exercise in reading than Georgian poetry demands. As a consequence, the important poets of the twentieth century, like its novelists, are unknown to and hopelessly out of reach of the common reader; and so are most of the artists of the past. The affirmation in *Practical Criticism* that it is through poetry alone that humanity may improve itself seems as desperate as the blackest pessimist could wish, though it is there made the foundation for a pious hope. To be seriously interested in contemporary developments of poetry is to be stigmatised as a highbrow, and in the face of such an environment, with discouragement of every kind, even the educated are scarcely willing—or able—to make the painful effort required in reading good poetry.

The reading capacity of the general public, it must be concluded, has never been so low as at the present time. And what bearing this has on the individual sensibility will be discussed in a final chapter. It will be necessary, in spite of what has been said in the previous chapter of even a very good novelist's liability to write below his level, to illustrate generalisations by extracts, and the writer realises that this will require some justification. Inevitably it is difficult if not unfair to demonstrate what is essentially a pervasive quality without exhaustive page-by-page comment of the kind that would require the reader to work through the novel with the writer, but apart from such considerations as that few of the novels under discussion are subtle enough to merit such close scrutiny or are worth reading save for anthropological reasons, mere considerations of space and time insist on some more economical critical method. It is useless (though, as the established practice, it must be found generally convincing) to carry on a discussion in terms of such abstractions as 'plot,' 'character,' 'setting,' 'theme,' 'action' . . . which, it cannot be too often repeated, are only abstractions, convenient enough for the reviewer whose office is to recommend for the library list, but if taken as starting-points for criticism fatally misleading—criticism based on a demand for convincing 'character' implies that a novel's value depends on the lifelikeness of the personæ (*vide* Part I. Chapter III)[127]; if based on theme or subject-matter it leads to the fallacious conclusion that Wells is a greater or 'better' novelist than Henry James or Jane Austen because he is apparently concerned with every side of human activity and they with nothing but what Henry James himself described as 'the human passion' (*a*); or if on plot, that *Wuthering Heights* and *Clarissa* are as preposterous as the novels of Ethel M. Dell, and so on. These abstractions, however, are the only terms that tradition has provided for the critic, with a few more of the same kind that Mr. Lubbock in *The Craft of Fiction* and Mr. Forster in *Aspects of the Novel* have tried to put into circulation. But these terms unfortunately are useless for purposes of valuation, though they have no doubt a certain limited significance in a discussion of technique, of the kind referred to in the introduction as academic, which asks of a novel that somehow impresses as a great one, How is it put together? But to take *Madame Bovary* or *Vanity Fair* to pieces does not help: a discussion of the mechanics of successful novels (except for professional

(*a*) Mr. Wells himself made this mistake. Vide *Boon*, Chapter IV. § 3.

novelists) is pointless and profitless. The essential technique in an art that works by using words is the way in which words are used, and a method is only justified by the use that is made of it; a bad novel is ultimately seen to fail not because of its method but owing to a fatal inferiority in the author's make-up. The technical perfection of the novels of Mr. George Moore does not prevent them from being faultlessly dead, and therefore as insignificant as the novels of Mr. Thornton Wilder, which they so suggestively resemble.

Henry James's ' very obvious truth that the deepest quality of a work of art will always be the quality of the mind of the producer. . . . No good novel ever proceeded from a superficial mind ' is a much more likely critical basis. And though it may be interesting to the professional novelist or the amateur of letters to examine how different authors have solved their respective problems, it must be borne in mind that technical dexterity and complexity are only means to an end and not in themselves meritorious or necessarily proofs of excellence : to extend somewhat the limits of this assertion, the complexities discussed earlier in this chapter do not make Virginia Woolf a greater novelist than Jane Austen—in fact, Mrs. Woolf betrays more limitations than Miss Austen, or rather, more serious limitations, in so far as she is less critical, less spiritually fastidious. She belongs to an order which acquiesces more easily than Jane Austen's did.[128] The soundest method for the critic of the novel would be to reinforce a general impression by analysis of significant passages on the lines of Vernon Lee's *The Handling of Words* (though there the passages are chosen at random and the analysis is carried out too pedantically : it serves to show too that, like all critical methods, this requires sensibility as well as intelligence if it is to be used without disaster—admirable critiques of Hardy and Henry James are followed by an examination of a passage from *Richard Yea-and-Nay*, which, we are told, exhibits the same virtues as the prose of Henry James !). Significant passages, because in these the novelist will be most intensely and so most perceptibly himself. There is no danger of doing injustice either way to bad fiction, because though good novelists can not infrequently be caught nodding, I have never found a bad novelist write above or much below his own general level ; the bestseller's style is uniform and consistent.

III

LIVING AT THE NOVELIST'S EXPENSE

THE last chapter should have made clear what
Parts I. and II. have served to document: that
the general reading public of the twentieth century is
no longer in touch with the best literature of its own day
or of the past, and why. It is almost impossible for
the novel which is an æsthetic experience to become
popular, and, on the other hand, popular fiction cannot
now contain, even unwittingly, the qualities which have
made the work of Defoe, Dickens, and Smollett something more than popular fiction. The public described
in Part I. has discovered that fiction can serve a purpose
quite other than that known to Lackington's age, but,
as we have seen (p. 138), the bestseller of the eighteenth
century does not lend itself to this purpose. The principal difference between the modern bestseller and the
novel of Part II. Chapter III. is that before Lytton
fiction does not invite uncritical reading, it keeps the
reader at arm's length, and does not encourage him to
project himself into the life he reads of by identifying
himself with the hero or heroine (even if he had done
so he would have got little satisfaction out of it). The
technique of the novel of that time rendered such
a process of self-dramatisation impossible: the
eighteenth-century novelist reports (even in Richardson's epistolary convention), that is to say the author
is felt to be present, commenting on the action coolly,
rationally, and often with a malicious pleasure in disappointing the reader's expectations, who is therefore

forced to distance the subject-matter. In the bestseller as we have known it since the author has poured his own day-dreams, hot and hot, into dramatic form, without bringing them to any such touchstone as the ' good sense, but not common-sense ' of a cultivated society : the author is himself—or more usually herself—identified with the leading character, and the reader is invited to share the debauch (*a*). Once the possibilities of fiction as a compensation for personal disabilities and disappointments were discovered, hosts who would never otherwise have thought of writing produced novels—for nothing is now commoner than the ability to write a novel : the points in which a novel differs from a poem (*vide* Part III. Chapter I.) make it so much easier to produce a deceptively good novel than a respectable poem, and technique of the kind that can be acquired by imitation goes much further towards the former than the latter.[129] The great bestseller, the bestseller, that is, whose writing goes straight to the heart of the public, unlike the literary novelist, is actuated by as authentic a passion as the artist, if it is judged by volume and temperature ; hence the degree of conviction that such authors carry to their readers, and it can be established that many of them (*e.g.* Gene Stratton Porter, Marie Corelli) did not in the first place write for money : they were impelled by another kind of need. Even the latest successor of Lytton is quite obviously doing something besides exploiting popular prejudice : any one who will examine *Masterson : A Story of an English Gentleman* will find in the hysterical climax and conclusion evidence of an overwhelming excitement, to be explained by the pervasive self-dramatisation.

(*a*) Cf. p. 53.

This generalisation about the change in the use the novel was put to can be conveniently illustrated by the work of two women novelists, one bred in the eighteenth-century ethos, the other a Victorian Romantic. The advantage Jane Austen had over Charlotte Brontë appears at first sight to be one of personal development rather than of environment. Both in theory were liable to suffer from the same starvation of natural impulses, but there is no trace in the former's work of any such thwarting. She could find material to express her interests and preoccupations in the life around her that she lived and knew, and the attitude of critical detachment that stamps everything she wrote as the product of a mature and balanced personality was a heritage from her environment. *Jane Eyre* is on the contrary a fable of wish-fulfilment arising out of experience, in which figure such common indices as the child's burning sense of injustice, self-idealisation (parallel passages are actually to be found in Marie Corelli), blinding and maiming of the beloved to enhance the value of the subject's devotion, self-abasement to the verge of death followed by dramatic salvation, recognition by enviable relatives, etc., all repeated with little variation in *Villette*. Most bestsellers go on writing the same novel because it is the only one they can produce, and each variant of it is successively popular because the appeal of the commoner day-dreams is inexhaustible— they represent both for author and reader a favourite form of self-indulgence.[130] Considering what has been said above on the effect of a good eighteenth-century novel, it is not hard to understand Charlotte Brontë's distaste for Jane Austen. It is one instance of a widespread popular feeling (*vide* p. 60), and is often the cause of critical bias.

Wuthering Heights is not and never has been a popular novel (except in the sense that it is now an accepted classic and so on the shelves of the educated) (*a*). Though there is evidence enough in the novel that Emily shared her sister's disabilities, *Wuthering Heights* is not an instrument of wish-fulfilment. It proceeds from a stronger mind, a sensibility that has triumphed over starvation and is not at its mercy. The cries of hunger and desire that ring through the book do not distress by a personal overtone, the reader is not made to feel embarrassed by the proximity of an author's face. The emotion exhibited in *Wuthering Heights*, unlike the emotion exhibited in *Jane Eyre*, has a frame round it; it is at least as poignant but it is controlled and directed, how deliberately the bare bones of the novel (admirably dissected by C.P.S. in *The Structure of Wuthering Heights*) show : *Wuthering Heights* is the best example in Victorian fiction of a total-response novel. Charlotte was not master enough of herself to submit her day-dreaming to the discipline of structural organisation.

But it is the Charlottes Brontë, not the Emilies, who have provided the popular fiction of the last hundred years. It is necessary to ask what kind of minds, what is the quality of the sensibility, with which the general public is now in touch through its reading. These are representative passages from bestsellers of classes C and D (*b*).

(*a*) The conventional classification of *Wuthering Heights* with *The Bride of Lammermoor* betrays the quality of the admiration professed for it. A more adequate collocation for it would be Conrad's *Heart of Darkness*.

(*b*) *Vide* Part I. Chapter III.

(a)   Was not here a man trained in the same school of environment in which she had been trained—a man with social position and culture such as she had been taught to consider as the prime essentials to congenial association?

Did not her best judgment point to this young English nobleman, whose love she knew to be of the sort a civilized woman should crave, as the logical mate for such as herself?

Could she love Clayton? She could see no reason why she could not. Jane Porter was not coldly calculating by nature, but training, environment, and heredity had all combined to teach her to reason even in matters of the heart.

That she had been carried off her feet by the strength of the young giant when his great arms were about her in the distant African forest, and again to-day, in the Wisconsin woods, seemed to her only attributable to a temporary mental reversion to type on her part—to the psychological appeal of the primeval man to the primeval woman in her nature. . . .

Again she glanced at Clayton. He was very handsome and every inch a gentleman. She should be very proud of such a husband.

And then he spoke—a minute sooner or a minute later might have made all the difference in the world to three lives —but chance stepped in and pointed out to Clayton the psychological moment (a).

(b)   His father, the Rector of High Stanton, was a thoughtful, literary man, with what used to be called ' high ideals '—it is an old-fashioned phrase now—and a broad humanitarianism. But he was unpopular in his living because he had a touch of mysticism which made him an enigma to the small shopkeepers and middle-class gentry of the little country town. They mistook his reserved nature, absent-mindedness and intellectual culture for pride. The truth is that the man was far above the level of the people among whom he lived, and it was a real torture to him to be impelled day by day and year by year to bring himself down to their small ideals, to limit his vision to the narrow outlook of his parish. . . . They [the Rector and his son] discussed the humour of Molière,

(a) *Tarzan of the Apes*, Edgar Rice Burroughs.

and the wisdom of Dr. Johnson, and the characteristics of other great masters, and Francis never lost his reverence for the wise scholarship, the fine taste, and the prodigious memory of his father. . . . [Francis is at Oxford.] Another surprise was given when it became known that Luttrell was the author of a number of serious little studies in the magazine which revealed a very intimate and rather mystical understanding of nature. . . . [He becomes a journalist] I think few men were ever so quickly inoculated with the subtle poison of Fleet Street as young Frank Luttrell. To a man of his training and temperament Fleet Street was a place of torture. A man who has read poetry and learnt it by heart cannot be content with writing paragraphs about cats at the Crystal Palace and murder in Whitechapel and fat boys at Peckham. Other men of education and ideals would not have suffered so acutely. With stronger fibre they would have resisted more manfully, but Frank was so sensitive that every nerve in him quivered at the least touch (*a*).

And it will be useful to quote also a passage from a novelist who is not popular :

(c)   This clergyman was not a popular man. He had the distinction of being disliked by the people; he was also avoided by Mr. Turnbull and his other well-to-do neighbours, and was treated with extreme rudeness by the farmers. He lived in a house as sombre and silent as the grave. He possessed a housekeeper who did two things: she drank brandy and she told every one about the wickedness of her master.

There were great elm trees round the house, so that in summer only a little corner of the roof could be seen. The place was always in the shade and always cold. It was one of those old church houses through which doubts and strange torments have crept and have stung men for generations, and where nameless fevers lie in wait for the little children. The place was built with the idea of driving men to despair or to God. Inside the house you felt the whole weight cover you. Outside, the trees, overfed with damp leaf-mould, chilled to the bone.

(*a*) *The Street of Adventure*, Philip Gibbs.

. . . Mr. Neville, the vicar, was within, reading; his head was bent a little over his book. Had an artist seen him, an artist like William Blake, he would have thought at once of that romantic prophet, Amos the herdsman. The face was more strong than clever; it had indeed none of those hard, ugly lines, those examination lines, that mark the educated of the world. His beard and hair were grey, and his heart, could it have been seen, was greyer still; and no wonder, for he had found out what human unkindness was.

He had, unluckily for himself, broken down the illusions that the healing habit of custom wraps around men, and especially around the clergy. To tear off this vesture, to arrive at nakedness, was to open, perhaps, a way for heavenly voices, but certainly a way for the little taunts and gibes of the world, the flesh and the devil. . . .

Henry Neville had around him always the hatred of nature and of man. Nature scorned him because he was helpless to dig and to weed and to plant, and because he was always catching cold. He had drawn to himself the malice of man because he had tried and failed to defend the victim against the exploiter. All kinds of difficulties and worries lay about his path like nettles and stung him whenever he moved. Naturally his health was not benefited by this treatment, and he was developing a tendency to cough in the mornings. By reason of all this unkindness Mr. Neville's appearance was certainly very different from the Rev. Hector Turnbull's, and Mr. Neville's smile was not in the least like the smile with which Mr. Tasker greeted his black sow at five o'clock in the morning. There was nothing so different in the world as the smiles of these men. . . .

When he first came down into the country he tried very hard to battle with the place; he tried to cut his own grass, he tried to make his own hay, but he did not succeed any better than Henry Turnbull succeeded with the fir tree. And so he held up his hands and surrendered to the enemy and learned to admire in his prison the beauty of long grass. His polite neighbours saw the long grass, or tried to open the heavy gate, and drove quickly away without calling, poverty in England being regarded as something more vile than the plague.

It was part of Mr. Neville's nature never to retaliate: when the nettle overgrew his garden he let it grow, when his housekeeper robbed him he let her do it, and when this woman told tales in the village about his immorality he never answered them. He knew quite well the kind of men who escape scandal, and he was sure he could never be like them. The people of the village were his warders, the vicarage was his gaol; and to be delivered therefrom, an angel, the dark one, must come to unlock the gate (a).

(a) comes from a bestseller which both as a novel and a film swept England and the United States, (b) from a highly successful novel by the author who was taken (Part I. Chapter III.) as typical of class C (the novelists to whom the general public go for help and advice). Both exhibit a crude, ill-furnished mind trying to interpret the workings of a personality stated but not shown to be cultivated and complex— notice the pitiful attempt at analysis with a set of terms gleaned from some such superficial source as the newspaper and often misapplied. In (a) the author's aim is merely to put across a plausible situation of the kind adapted to the screen (*vide* p. 53), in (b) there is a genuine effort to write on a subtler plane than that on which the author lives—'literary' in the first line means well-read (seen from below), and note the crude use of counters like 'intellectual,' 'ideals,' 'education,' 'mysticism,' the helpless gestures made in the formulas 'and other great masters,' 'poetry,' 'rather mystical understanding of nature,' 'intellectual culture,' also such bad shots as the assumption that straightforward minor reporting would be 'torture' to

(a) *Mr. Tasker's Gods*, T. F. Powys.

'a man of education and ideals' (whereas it would naturally be the more ambitious varieties of journalism, such as those in which the author has specialised, that he would find intolerable). Apart from the obvious inadequacy of the authors to handle the situations they have postulated there is this worth remarking : both are able to depend on stock responses which enable them by a few clumsy strokes to evoke a composite picture that is already stowed away in their readers' minds. The character of the man who is unsuccessful because he is so sensitive or so educated is well known to the C public (compare the hero of *If Winter Comes*), so that the collocation of the words 'absent-minded,' 'literary,' 'mysticism,' 'vision,' and 'ideals' suffices to call up a complete if very hazy story : they are familiar with the details of such a story, having met it on the screen and in their reading nearly all their lives, and are satisfied to believe that the novelist has created what he has in fact merely tricked them into remembering. All this is betrayed by the consistent use of clichés [131] (stock phrases to evoke stock responses (*a*)) —nothing is freshly realised, and of general terms— nothing is concrete and immediate. Contrast (a) and (b) with (c), which, though from an unsuccessful first novel in which the author is only feeling his way towards the stylisation that later produced a triumph of economy in *Mr. Weston's Good Wine* (and has made it impossible to quote from), exhibits a rare sensibility reproducing with exquisite fidelity and sureness a highly personal mode of feeling. Is it not possible to say bluntly that (c) is 'better' than (b) or (a) in so far

(*a*) The reader should have in mind throughout this chapter the account of stock responses in *Practical Criticism*, Part III. Chap. v.

as by way of (c) the reader is in touch with a mind capable of a greater degree of honesty in dealing with experience and a sensibility infinitely more alive to it?

In the writer's opinion it is even possible to go a step further and assert that (a) and (b) had better not be read at all, though in Part I. Chapter III. a case was made out for the C novelist on the ground that communications from one stratum to another must be kept open ; after investigating novels of the C and D type, however, it is difficult to avoid the conclusion that communication at that level had better not be attempted (*a*). It is important to realise that not only the authors of (a) and (b) but nearly all popular novelists are now trying to dramatise problems of feeling and sentiment far too complex for their handling, and in an idiom which inevitably vulgarises whatever it has to convey. They are thus not so much what is often described as ' falsifying life ' as interfering with the reader's spontaneities ; the public of (a) and (b), which is the bulk of the reading public, has no means of knowing what it really thinks and feels : between the mind which has been fed on films, magazines, newspapers, and bestsellers, and a first-hand judgment or prompting, comes the picture of how to think, feel, or behave, derived from these sources [132]—a picture ineluctable because (*vide* Part I. Chapter III.) the illusion conveyed by these agents is that of a more sympathetic and dramatic life and so is peculiarly compelling, and because so often repeated in slightly varying forms as to have become part of the emotional furniture. And the best-

(*a*) A parallel example may enforce the point: some one declared his intention of ' doing the work of the *Criterion* at the level of *John o' London's*,' to which the answer is that *John o' London's* does it already—in the only way it can be done at that level.

sellers of fiction, as of poetry, have commonly been persons convinced of their special fitness to dictate the correct emotional behaviour ; to the uncritical they are fatally persuasive. Attitudes which need very little demonstration to prove socially undesirable have been noticed previously as being created and fixed by post-war bestsellers, and attitudes equally pernicious to individual happiness are conveyed by both Victorian and twentieth-century fiction—*e.g.* the attitudes formed round the words ' noble ' and ' pure,' and the idea of self-sacrifice for its own sake which, entering literature by way of the more popular Victorian poets, was promptly taken over by the novelists and by them incorporated into the popular ideology.[133] The section of *Ulysses* which records subjectively a few hours in the life of Gerty MacDowell is an invaluable reference at this point : for Gerty MacDowell every situation has a prescribed attitude provided by memories of slightly similar situations in cheap fiction, she thinks in terms of clichés drawn from the same source, and is completely out of touch with reality. Such a life is not only crude, impoverished, and narrow, it is dangerous. And it is typical of the level at which the emotional life of the generality is now conducted.[134] How much less efficiently equipped for the business of living such a society is than Bunyan's contemporaries or Mr. Sturt's and Mr. Torr's countrymen, for whom traditional wisdom was available and first-hand experience abundantly provided, must be left to the reader to judge.

Another point : the novels from which (a) and (b) are drawn obviously proceed from minds of no greater calibre and sensibilities as crude and undeveloped as those of the lowest level of reading public. Now Defoe was intellectually on top of his age; with a finger in every interest and a brain spilling over with literary projects, he was not only in touch with the best ideas of his time, as Arnold would say, but in advance of them (a). Even Dickens, to take a leap to the beginning of another phase of popular fiction, was a great deal more than a member of his own public. It is noticeable how composed and firmly planted were the eighteenth-century novelists from Fielding to Maria Edgeworth, on what an unassailable basis of wide and controlled experience their keen discrimination rests. If we postulate a scale (in which (a) would rank at one end and (c) at the other) for determining the point between complete superficiality and complete seriousness that a novel occupies, we may assert that the eighteenth-century novelists exhibit a degree of seriousness in dealing with emotional issues which no *popular* novelist afterwards attains. The author of (b), a favourable specimen of the superior kind of bestseller (*vide* pp. 71-3), is evidently a less adequate medium for introducing the public to life and art than these. Sir Philip Gibbs is not merely a favourable specimen of the bestseller, he is working at the highest level of seriousness known to his readers; it is painful to reflect how much below the level at which it is possible to live (*i.e.* at which the best poetry functions), how much below the level at which even the ordinarily cultivated person lives, how much further from literature than Dickens or even Lytton, this is.

I should like to make some further distinctions between the levels at which the various publics of the twentieth century are supplied with fiction. These

(a) *Vide* his *Essay on Projects* and *The Review.*

three extracts are from representative low-, middle-, and highbrow bestsellers; they were chosen because in them the novelists are explicitly concerned with criticism of life, not as usual indirectly by the communication of experience through dramatic symbols, but almost without disguise in their own persons:

(d) Sorrell philosophised. . . . When the grey chalk-hills showed, Sorrell would think of boundaries and of the finality of a man's experiences. Death, oblivion, extinction—perhaps a melting into soft greyness. And all man's passionate little tricks to escape it, his myths, his gods and his immortalities, his theosophies, and spiritisms. A yearning, a chilliness—after life's full meal. The soft dusk, the obliterating darkness, the unknown and the unknowable.

' Consciousness is less,' he thought, ' than the planks of a boat between you and the deep waters. Some day you will sink, disappear, be forgotten. You will be less than some tree that once grew here.'

' Accept. Do your job. Then, be ready to close your eyes and sleep.'

He was a pragmatist. The satisfaction of life lay in accomplishment. He was content to gaze at the unknown as he looked at the distant chalk-hills, and he felt no urge to climb them. The whole world of the senses might be an illusion, but man's business was to behave as though it were real. The job mattered, the thing you had set out to accomplish, and not for yourself alone. Fighting mattered, striving, enduring, loving the few, disdaining the many. When struggle ceases men cease to be men.

Besides, who would tell where life ended? Death might be the opening of a door, especially to those who climbed to it after a life of stubborn effort. And without effort there might be no door? Or was death like a sieve . . .? (a)

(e) Better not think that out. Some feelings made less trouble if unexamined. . . . No. You couldn't number even the heads. Each head only existed for a second or two. This

(a) Warwick Deeping, *Sorrell and Son*.

was the homogeneous spate of flesh, flowing for thousands of years, for which Christ died. But it didn't know it. Didn't even know now that ships and the sea were under its myriad feet, the interminable and horrific caterpillar. Didn't seem to know anything. The hairs numbered of that tide of heads? Poor little man on a cross! . . . None of the books had ever proved whether it all mattered or whether it did not. Whether everything was happening so because it had to, or whether it was all worse than shove-ha'penny. Cosmic shove-ha'penny? . . . There must be something inherent in this chaos which informed it. Perhaps in the beginning it got the word, and had remembered it, without knowing what it meant. These people were all right. They would work out what had to be done, in spite of all the Perriams, and without knowing what they were doing.

That thought, outside the fruiterer's, gave him the freedom to admire a favourite shop. Better than any Bond Street jeweller's, that place. The greengrocer trafficked with the raw material of the poet. Sonnets and lyrics by the pound. These colours would put it across Helen's artist pals at Hampstead.

. . . Reason! No more reason in it than there was in the hot gas which congealed to a mud ball, on which grew the truth, and crosses and nails for those who dared to mention it. What a joke; and nobody to get a laugh out of it! (a)

(f)   So Mrs. Moore had all she wished; she escaped the trial, the marriage, and the hot weather; she would return to England in comfort and distinction, and see her other children. At her son's suggestion, and by her own desire, she departed. But she accepted her good luck without enthusiasm. She had come to that state where the horror of the universe and its smallness are both visible at the same time—the twilight of the double vision in which so many elderly people are involved. If this world is not to our taste, well, at all events there is Heaven, Hell, Annihilation—one or other of those large things, that huge scenic background of stars, fires, blue or black air. All heroic endeavour, and all

(a) *Gallions Reach*, H. M. Tomlinson.

that is known as art, assumes that there is such a background, just as all practical endeavour, when the world is to our taste, assumes that the world is all. But in the twilight of the double vision, a spiritual muddledom is set up for which no high-sounding words can be found; we can neither act nor refrain from action, we can neither ignore nor respect Infinity. Mrs. Moore had always inclined to resignation. As soon as she landed in India it seemed to her good, and when she saw the water flowing through the mosque-tank, or the Ganges, or the moon, caught in the shawl of night with all the other stars, it seemed a beautiful goal and an easy one. To be one with the universe! So dignified and simple. But there was always some little duty to be performed first, some new card to be turned up from the diminishing pack and placed, and while she was pottering about, the Marabar ·struck its gong.

What had spoken to her in that scoured-out cavity of the granite? What dwelt in the first of the caves? Something very old and very small. Before time, it was before space also. Something snub-nosed, incapable of generosity—the undying worm itself. Since hearing its voice, she had not entertained one large thought, she was actually envious of Adela. All this fuss over a frightened girl! Nothing had happened, ' and if it had,' she found herself thinking with the cynicism of a withered priestess, ' if it had, there are worse evils than love.' The unspeakable attempt presented itself to her as love: in a cave, in a church—Boum, it amounts to the same. Visions are supposed to entail profundity, but— Wait till you get one, dear reader! The abyss also may be petty, the serpent of eternity made of maggots (a).

(e) is a series of extracts from the first half of a novel, and this may be alleged unfair. But the novel consists of the running comments of one man on his various successive experiences : his thoughts, ideas, and comments are the book, they are meant to be not criticised but accepted by the reader, for he is frankly only a

(a) *Passage to India*, E. M. Forster.

stalking-horse for the author (' She was glad Jimmy was different. He was not an intellectual ' (p. 40).) It is only fair to remark in passing that this is at least an honest way to write a novel [135] ; contrast *Point Counter Point* or *Antic Hay*, where the author protects himself by dramatising every possible attitude in order to avoid the necessity of taking up a position and standing by it. And there is nothing more rigorous in the organisation of *Gallions Reach* than is implied in the word succession, so that we are entitled to sample the quality of the author's mind by judicious skimming. To the present writer the two equally evident features of this train of thoughts are their incurable secondrateness ('Poor little man on a cross ! . . . What a joke ; and nobody to get a laugh out of it ! . . . The greengrocer trafficked with the raw material of the poet ') and their confident optimism (' These people were all right. They would work out what had to be done, and without knowing what they were doing '). The popularity of *Gallions Reach* rested on these two characteristics : its ' mysticism ' (' I tell you there are other worlds ' (p. 4). ' Yes, the blessed ghosts we know govern us ' (p. 293)) and its ' thought,' which was found peculiarly congenial by the middlebrow public. Now if the attitude of the authors of (d) and (e) are compared they will be found almost identical. Both toy with possibilities with an engaging appearance of large-mindedness that in fact only covers their incapacity to come to grips with any real problem (' Better not think that out. Some feelings made less trouble if unexamined ')—both are only pretending to be disturbed, to doubt, they are perfectly sure at heart that everything is really all right and the world a jolly place (' He was a pragmatist,' etc. ' There must be something inherent in this chaos which informed it. These people were all right '). And so after our excursion into profundity we come back to the comfortable axioms of *l'homme moyen sensuel*. Although (d) is low-brow, that is, a common bestseller, and (e) middle-brow, a novel much admired by the educated, to the reader of (f) there is little to choose between them (cf. p. 79). It is naturally impossible to apprehend the entire force and significance of (f) out of its context, without having in mind all that has preceded it, but it serves to show up the superficiality of (d) and (e); no one who reads at the level of (f) is likely to read also at the level of (d) or (e). The attitude of the author of (f) is more inclusive than that of the authors of (d) and (e), the considerations with which they trifle have played a formative part in his emotional make-up, his attitude is not to be overthrown by criticism. A sensitive reader apprehends this as much from the tone as the sense of these passages : (d) is the voice of a school-master—an empty solemnity, it is concerned merely to provide what is expected of it; (e), with its alternate queries and exclamation-marks, betrays that the author maintains his altitude as philosopher in the crow's-nest with the utmost difficulty, just as the idiom betrays the inability to discuss with seriousness ; (f) is the tone of the artist who has experienced the spiritual state he is concerned to communicate, not guessed at it. The status of a novelist, his right, that is, to manipulate our minds and impinge upon our sensibilities, is most easily recognised by the tone of his writing. And that is liable to be affected by the conventions of his age and public. When the social code will not admit an important part of experience the right to be mentioned—*e.g.* in the Victorian era there was a tacit convention that what was discussed in the smoking-room did not exist for the drawing-room—there is bound to be an uneasiness in the relation between author and reader.[136] Hence there is something wrong with the tone of almost all the Victorian male novelists. Thackeray's and Trollope's cynicism is one instance; it is meant to pass as realistic (the clear-eyed, unsentimental man-of-the-world, etc.), but it is, of course, the smoking-room sentimentality which is an integral part of the smoking-room attitude.

(g) But it was October before Lord Lufton was made a happy man;—that is, if the fruition of his happiness was a greater joy than the anticipation of it. I will not say that the happiness of marriage is like the Dead Sea fruit—an apple which, when eaten, turns to bitter ashes in the mouth. Such pretended sarcasm would be very false. Nevertheless, is it not the fact that the sweetest morsel of love's feast has been eaten, that the freshest, fairest blush of the flower has been snatched and has passed away, when the ceremony at the altar has been performed, and legal possession has been given? There is an aroma of love, an indefinable delicacy of flavour, which escapes and is gone before the church portal is left, vanishing with the maiden name, and incompatible with the solid comfort appertaining to the rank of wife. To love one's own spouse, and to be loved by her, is the ordinary lot of man, and is a duty exacted under penalties. But to be allowed to love youth and beauty that is not one's own—to know that one is loved by a soft being who still hangs cowering from the eye of the world as though her love were all but illicit—can it be that a man is made happy when a state of anticipation such as this is brought to a close? No; when the husband walks back from the altar, he has already swallowed the choicest dainties of his banquet. The beef and pudding of married life are then in store for him;—or perhaps only the bread and cheese. Let him take care lest hardly a crust remain—or perhaps not a crust (*a*).

A few lines from a topical novel of the seventeenth century will illustrate what is meant :

(h) He had married a virtuous lady, and of good quality. But her relation to him (it may be feared) made her very disagreeable: for a man of his humour and estate can no more be satisfied with one woman, than with one dish of meat; and to say truth, it is something unmodish (*b*).

Trollope's tone is felt to be strained and unconvincing, though he has Thackeray behind him : there is none of the vitality of the second passage, the movement of (g) is suspiciously pompous, while that of (h) is lithe and assured. Aphra Behn's gaiety is something Trollope could not afford ; no Victorian novelist has her aplomb. The smoking-room attitude precludes candour in the most important relations, so that the novelist's mode of living cannot be communicated, he must adopt a false personality and the falsetto voice that goes with it. The smile that the suitable reader of (f) is provoked into giving at (g) destroys it. In the light of (g) consider the betraying prologue and valediction of *Vanity Fair* : on reading them no one can be in doubt about the degree of seriousness he is likely to meet with in the intervening pages. But Aphra Behn's light touch was something she shared with the Augustan age, it is the poise of a whole society (*vide* Part II. Chapter III.) which measured writing by standards that Trollope could not have understood : ' It is written with the Spirit of one who has seen the World enough to undervalue it with good Breeding

(*a*) *Framley Parsonage*, Anthony Trollope.
(*b*) *The Court of the King of Bantam*, Aphra Behn.

. . . and the whole Air of the Book, as to the Language, the Sentiments, and the Reasonings, shews it was written by one whose Virtue sits easy about him, and to whom Vice is thoroughly contemptible.' To say that there is something wrong with the tone is to make a less superficial criticism than might be supposed, for the relation between popular novelist and reader is inevitably decided by the current social relation. A false note here is the sign of a serious limitation in the social life of the time. A sentence in Trollope's *Autobiography* explains everything : Miss Broughton's novels, he wrote, ' are not sweet-savoured as are those by Miss Thackeray, and are, therefore, less true to nature.' This is a result of that narrowing down noticed earlier as the chief effect of the circulating library on fiction. [Thackeray's shocked disgust at the great eighteenth-century writers (*vide* his *English Humourists*) is another.] Similarly a coarsening of tone (coarsening not in morals but in *mœurs*), such as is perceptible between *The Way of All Flesh* and *Death of a Hero*, means a loss on the part of the community at large of something of inestimable value, since fineness of living depends, as we are social animals, very largely on the company we keep and the nature of our intercourse with our fellows.

Such assets as environment can furnish are not part of the post-war novelist's endowment. Addison was neither particularly sensitive nor unusually intelligent, he had only the slenderest of personal talents, and it must be a cause of bitter envy to twentieth-century novelists when they reflect that not the most intelligent and sensitive of them could achieve, like Addison, a work which should at once reflect the finest awareness of their age and yet appeal to the whole public, from ' the circumference of wit ' to the barely literate. Even if the modern set out to defy the stratification which has been demarcated and resolve to address the entire community, the consciousness that the community he was addressing consisted of different reading publics at varying levels would rob him of the complete confidence necessary to a work of art. The novelist who (*vide* note 35) stated that he ' writes to entertain various publics in turn ' is a victim of the literary conditions of his age ; no wonder if his efforts lack conviction.

One of the first difficulties the twentieth-century novelist encounters is the language-problem : to communicate with the general reading public it is necessary to use their language (the *Tatler* was written ' in an air of common speech '). But it is now a language (*vide* Part III. Chapter I.) which has no artistic possibilities. The Elizabethan dramatist (or pamphleteer), we have seen, was able to make use of a rich speech idiom ; with a spoken language that abounded in metaphors, allusions, and proverbs, the idiom of a people that acquired its resources of thinking and feeling from living conversation and not cheap printed matter, he could draw on the resources of the common people's speech without ceasing to be a great artist. The idiom that the general public of the twentieth century possesses is not merely crude and puerile ; it is made up of phrases and clichés that imply fixed, or rather stereotyped, habits of thinking and feeling at second-hand taken over from the journalist. That portion of the vocabulary of the ordinary man which is not concerned with material needs is derived from such sources as those discussed in Part II. Chapter IV. § 2. The set of ideas, for example, attached to the popular use of the words 'vision' and 'ideals' (as in (b)), 'inspiration,' 'personality,' 'creative,' 'human,' 'urge' (as in advertisements and bestsellers), is destructive of them for purposes of serious usage. Just as the vocabulary of 'uplift' and 'ideals' is now indissolubly associated with the order of feeling exhibited in the novels of Gene Stratton Porter and Gilbert Frankau,[137] so the vocabulary of 'vision' and 'inspiration' is the peculiar property of journalism and salesmanship.[138] The generalisations on Life, Love, Marriage, Sex, Woman,[139] etc., which fill the popular novel, the magazine, and the magazine pages of the popular Press, provide film captions and headlines, and so form the popular mind, have set up a further barrier between a serious novelist and the reading public. To be understood by the majority he would have to employ the clichés in which they are accustomed to think and feel, or rather, to having their thinking and feeling done for them.[140] The peculiar property of a good novel, as has already been observed, is the series of shocks it gives to the reader's preconceptions—preconceptions, usually unconscious, of how people behave and why, what is admirable and what reprehensible; it provides a configuration of special instances which serve as a test for our mental habits and show us the necessity for revising them. George Eliot, characteristically, seems to have been the first novelist to be conscious of this most important function of the novel; her comment on the crisis of *The Mill on the Floss* is extended into a general insistence that 'we have no master-key that will fit all cases . . . moral judgments must remain false and hollow, unless they are checked and enlightened by a perpetual reference to the special circumstances that mark the individual lot.' [141] The ordinary reader is now unable to brace himself to bear the impact of a serious novel (*vide* p. 62 and p. 74), a novel, that is, in which words are used with fresh meanings and for ends with which he is unfamiliar. And on the other hand, a twentieth-century novelist if he is intelligent and sensitive has necessarily to waste some of his energy in avoiding the stock responses, the popular associations of the current idiom, or at least to sacrifice the simplicity and directness which was observed (*vide* p. 125) to characterise Fielding's novels.

It is painful to compare the staple of eighteenth-century popular fiction and that exhibited by twentieth-century writers. But it is essential to see what has happened.

(i)   I cast myself at her feet.—Begone, Mr. Lovelace, said she, with a rejecting motion, her fan in her hand; for your own sake leave me! My soul is above thee, man! with both her hands pushing me from her! Urge me not to tell thee, how sincerely I think my soul above thee! Thou hast in mine, a proud, a too proud heart, to contend with! Leave me, and leave me for ever! Thou hast a proud heart to contend with!

.   .   .   .   .

And, as I hope to live, my nose tingled, as I once, when a boy, remember it did (and indeed once more very lately) just before some tears came into my eyes; and I durst hardly trust my face in view of hers.

What have I done to deserve this impatient exclamation?

O Mr. Lovelace, we have been long enough together,

to be tired of each other's humours and ways; ways and humours so different, that perhaps you ought to dislike me, as much as I do you.—I think, I think, that I cannot make an answerable return to the value you profess for me. My temper is utterly ruined. You have given me an ill opinion of all mankind; of yourself in particular: and withal so bad a one of myself, that I shall never be able to look up, having utterly and for ever lost all that self-complacency, and conscious pride, which are so necessary to carry a woman through this life with tolerable satisfaction to herself.

. . . I arose, and re-urged her for the day.

My day, sir, said she, is never. Be not surprised. A person of politeness judging between us, would not be surprised that I say so. But indeed, Mr. Lovelace (and wept through impatience) you either know not how to treat with a mind of the least degree of delicacy, notwithstanding your birth and education, or you are an ingrateful man; and (after a pause) a worse than ingrateful one. But I will retire. I will see you again tomorrow. I cannot before. I think I hate you—You may look—Indeed I think I hate you. And if, upon a re-examination of my own heart, I find I do, I would not for the world that matters should go on farther between us (a).

(j)   Love, the capacity for which she had so long denied, had become a force that, predominating everything, held her irresistibly. The accumulated affection that, for want of an outlet, had been stemmed within her, had burst all restraint, and the love that she gave to the man to whom she had surrendered her proud heart was immeasurable—a love of infinite tenderness and complete unselfishness, a love that made her strangely humble. . . . Her surrender had been no common one. The feminine weakness that she had despised and fought against had triumphed over her un-expectedly with humiliating thoroughness. Sex had super-vened to overthrow all her preconceived notions. The womanly instincts that under Aubrey's training had been

(a) Richardson, *Clarissa*.

suppressed and undeveloped had, in contact with the Sheik's vivid masculinity and compelling personality, risen to the surface with startling completeness (*a*).

(k) For to-night—could Erica but have known it—both heredities, her father's legacy of priggishness, of self-certainty, of religion beyond the law, and her mother's legacy (also beyond the law) of waywardness and passion and reckless self-abandonment to desire, were conspiring, even more surely than circumstances had conspired, against conscience and against self-knowledge and against all those inhibitions which are the soul's safeguard from Sin (*b*).

Richardson, an uneducated printer, can express himself with force and dignity yet quite simply. *The Sheik* and *Life—and Erica* will be found to consist almost wholly of such passages as (j) and (k), varied with dialogue of which specimens have been quoted earlier (*vide* Part I. Chapter III. and Part II. Chapter IV.). They appear to proceed from writers who attach no particular meaning to the language they use, they are at the mercy of words. Consequently most of what they write is nonsense. But it must convey something to its readers, for both (j) and (k) come from bestsellers. The careful reader will notice that these passages aim at psychological analysis, and it must be that at a certain level they impress as such. To the magazine and newspaper reader they would carry conviction and no doubt a vague meaning, because they employ words he has seen in similar connections in periodicals. The jargon of popular psychology and popular science is now at the writer's disposal; it saves him the trouble of dramatising a situation or visualising a scene, and apparently satisfies or flatters

(*a*) E. M. Hull, *The Sheik.*
(*b*) Gilbert Frankau, *Life—and Erica.*

his readers. A few extreme examples are worth quoting :

> At his words, the inhibitions went from her.
> . . . the ultimate inhibitions snapped in her brain. . . .
> The nurse, who had intuition but no psychology. . . .

and the novels of Gilbert Frankau are so thickly studded with mention of inhibitions and the subconscious that it is hardly possible to find a page without one or both.

As an illustration of the disabilities of the popular idiom I shall have to quote further passages from the novels (e) and (f) :

(l) ' Dear old Colet. There he goes. But I'll tell him again. I want to give the moths and rust a chance to corrupt something that belongs to me. I'll moth 'em, if they come near it.'

' I don't feel that way about it. But look here. If you do lift the lid off a hoard, watch me do the Highland fling with the accordant triumphant noises.'

' I know. You are like that. But it's not the right spirit. It's simply devilish. It's only your damned playful sympathy. You'd have been a nice Christian all complete with another touch of dreary misfortune. Colet, it makes me doubt you. You'll come to no good end. You really won't. I'm inclined to think that you might even fold your hands like a pale martyr, or a skinned rabbit, some day, and let the other fellow have the girl. It's wicked, you know. It's unfair to the poor darling. Don't you ever love your neighbour as yourself, unless you want him to know what a fool you are. . . .'

He waited a minute, and then picked up his gun again.

' I wouldn't have the nerve to look at the world unless I were sure of a cushioned corner in it. It would be a terror of a hole. There's no sense in it unless we put it there, so don't you try to find it. Just think of humanity messing up its planet with progress—shoving things about, piling 'em up, and especially getting cock-eyed with deep religious conviction when making its worst muck of its place. It's enough to bring down on us the Olympian sanitary inspector. I want a clear space in that jolly old riot. Then I shan't mind the Gadarene rush so much. It might be comic to watch it then, something to pass the time; but I've no fancy to be among the hooves.'

' Well, by God, Norrie, I never thought of it before. But you're afraid.'

' I am, when it comes down to it. You've given it a name. When I look at life in the eyes, in the hope of finding reason in it, my little inside turns pale. Cast your mind back to the Thames embankment at midnight, and get the horrors ' (a).

(m) ' Of course this death has been troubling me.'

' Aziz was so fond of her too.'

' But it has made me remember that we must all die: all these personal relations we try to live by are temporary. I used to feel death selected people, it is a notion one gets from novels, because some of the characters are usually left talking at the end. Now " death spares no one " begins to be real.'

' . . . I want to go on living a bit.'

' So do I.'

A friendliness, as of dwarfs shaking hands, was in the air. Both man and woman were at the height of their powers—sensible, honest, even subtle. They spoke the same language, and held the same opinions, and the variety of age and sex did not divide them. Yet they were dissatisfied. When they agreed, ' I want to go on living a bit,' or, ' I don't believe in God,' the words were followed by a curious backwash as though the universe had displaced itself to fill up a tiny void, or as though they had seen their own gestures from an immense height—dwarfs talking, shaking hands and assuring each other that they stood on the same footing of insight. They did not think they were wrong, because as soon as honest people think they are wrong instability sets up. Not for them was an infinite goal behind the stars, and they never

(a) *Gallions Reach.*

sought it. But wistfulness descended on them now, as on other occasions; the shadow of the shadow of a dream fell over their clear-cut interests, and objects never seen again seemed messages from another world (*a*).

The attempt to use the slang, the humour, and the catchwords of modern conversation as a medium for serious communication, for expressing, as in (l), the most private thoughts and feelings of human beings, is clearly a failure. A failure of such a kind that a sensitive reader winces. It is not merely that the author of (l) has a not very fine sensibility himself and not very profound sentiments to impart—that is in his favour in such an attempt. Had they been further removed from the level at which this idiom functions, the effect could not but have been yet more harrowing. It would be like *Lear* rewritten in the language of Sam Weller.

Yet to reject the rhythms of the contemporary idiom by returning to a language of the past is to sacrifice everything. That is why historical novels cannot be taken seriously by the critic, however seriously they may be taken by their authors; *Esmond* is a perfect *tour de force*, so is *The Brook Kerith*, and they are of great technical interest to those who are interested in technique for its own sake, and that is all that can be said for them. Even to use the English of Defoe and Richardson to treat contemporary life is no more satisfactory: *Lady into Fox* and its successors and imitators communicate nothing, they are merely graceful confessions of failure, of all gestures the most idle. What we see in (m) is the author using his privilege to express in his own terms what his personae are unable to express

(*a*) *Passage to India.*

in theirs. But to do this is to restrict the possible appeal of the novel to the topmost stratum of the reading public.

A novelist has now, therefore, to choose between these alternatives: either to deal in stereotyped humour (*Gentlemen Prefer Blondes* and the works of P. G. Wodehouse are examples of ingenious variations on a laugh in one place—cf. humour of the eighteenth and nineteenth centuries, which communicated a whole comic attitude), popular ideology (*The Constant Nymph* was a bestseller because of its moving treatment of the conventionally unconventional artist), popular prejudice (*vide* Part II. Chapter IV. for the bestseller as an exhibition of herd prejudice), at the level of seriousness permitted by an idiom in which neither particular states of feeling can be conveyed nor human relations treated with dignity and delicacy—in this way he can reach the bulk of the reading public; or, if he insists on offering the novel as a serious communication of organised experience, he must be willing to sacrifice a potential public and write only for the highbrow. (Of course, no such deliberate choice is ever made in practice, nature has taken the decision out of his hands; but such is the indirect *effect* of the state of the twentieth-century reading public). If he has made the latter choice there are these possibilities open to him:

(1) He may if he is peculiarly happily circumstanced find a stylisation in terms of a living traditional culture fine enough to permit him to do boldly and with economy what the author of (m) has to do tentatively and deviously (example, T. F. Powys).

or (2) He may compose a stylisation of contemporary cultivated life which—the best example is Henry James—will inevitably suffer from etiolation, besides having for obvious reasons to make paralysing sacrifices of scope. It has also to be a thoroughgoing stylisation with no hankering after verisimilitude : the fact that all the personae in any Henry James novel speak alike and none like life is too well known for comment (those interested will even find a telegram in Jacobean English in *The Great Good Place*).

or (3) If his interest lies in the comoedic he may make realistic conversation and the current idiom serve a satiric purpose, supplemented by a style of his own for explication. It is almost necessarily a style which extends the borders of the prose and exploits the possibilities of the language of the age. This seems to be the most fruitful field for the serious novelist of the twentieth century, and explains why the modern novel is said to be poetic or to exhibit poetic prose (examples—James Joyce, D. H. Lawrence, E. M. Forster, Virginia Woolf).

The important point, however, is that the general reader of our time is only getting his ' thought,' his explication of experience, at the level of (d) or at best of (e). Now the spectator of Elizabethan drama, though he might not be able to follow the ' thought ' minutely in the great tragedies, was getting his amusement from the mind and sensibility that produced those passages, from an artist and not from one of his own class (cf. p. 85). There was then no such complete separation as we have just seen to exist between the life of the cultivated and the life of the generality : the artist and the ordinary citizen felt and thought in the same idiom, there was a way of communication open between them. We have seen, too, that as late as George Eliot's day the serious novel could be, and actually was, read with interest and pleasure by the general reading public; since then such an occurrence has only taken place at rare intervals and has been something of an event in literary history. At the end of an earlier chapter (p. 169) Conrad and Hardy were named as the last great novelists known to the nation at large, and for different reasons. Conrad's popularity was of the kind that is liable to occur again—it actually has with the success of *Passage to India* in the year of publication as something of a bestseller at three levels. At the lowest it was ' a story that grips the imagination ' (*a*) (this kind of response means that the reader skips nearly everything but the dialogue), and heated discussions took place as to what really happened in the cave; at another, it was a revealing account of the Anglo-Indian situation (in this way it became popular in the United States); while the fact that the novel is a work of art concerned with the total human situation in the modern world of which India is taken as the particular concrete instance was probably realised by very few of those who read it.

Conrad, somewhat in the same way, became popular as ' the Kipling of the South Seas ' (when his first novel appeared he was so hailed in the *Times*), and the dust-jacket of the cheap edition of *Lord Jim* used to describe the contents as the story of a young man who after various failures finally made good. Conrad's best work—*The Secret Agent, Heart of Darkness*, and some

---

(*a*) ' In *Passage to India* he has told a story that grips the imagination.'— *A Study of the Modern Novel*, A. R. Marble.

others—is not popular: it allows no such romantic interpretation, the irony is too apparent and destructive. But on the strength of the earlier novels he was accepted as a classic without any dispute, if not by the man in the street at least by the readers of *John o' London's*; although his complicated technique made reading difficult it was evident that the author, like Marlowe, was a simple soul, that he subscribed unquestioningly to the romantic conventions, idealising woman and the strong silent man in the familiar magazine tradition and exhibiting in the person of his heroes an uplifting symbolism (it is a weakness of his early work that he is sometimes guilty of all this at moments. His power of recovery is amazing). All this made Conrad generally acceptable.

Hardy is popular for the right reasons. Compare his irony with Conrad's, and his technique for securing it. Hardy's novels are constructed in such a way that a certain type of critic is able to draw diagrams of them. The satisfaction Hardy obviously derived from arranging simple geometric designs was that of a simple mind which has succeeded in making a pattern out of the complexities of existence; what he has done is to sacrifice the complexity, so that in *The Mayor of Casterbridge*, an extreme case, not a sentence is uttered that does not serve to provide ironic contrast or to anticipate it. And this effect is found generally pleasing—it is always cheering to have an obvious (even if dismal) thread to follow. Hardy's irony is of the kind that most people can grasp—obvious, dramatic, and impressive. Conrad is engaged in expressing an infinitely more complex sense of the irony of human aspirations, and the at first sight unnecessarily tedious

unfolding of *Heart of Darkness* is essential to conduct
the reader in such a way that he is initiated into the
significance of vast backgrounds of emotional implication ; the full force of the situation of Mr. Kurtz
is thus gradually and overwhelmingly brought to bear
upon him. All that Hardy needs for his effect is a
mechanical concatenation of circumstances—coin-
cidences, factitious frustrations, conspiracies of the
elements, and so forth, play a major part in all his
novels. In Hardy's novels the words seem not to
matter, even at the crises, but it is impossible to read
satisfactorily *Heart of Darkness* without keeping in
touch emotionally with every cadence. Hence the
irony of Conrad, precipitated in the announcement
' " Mistah Kurtz—he dead," ' is not to be exhausted
as easily as Hardy's ' irony of Fate ' ; it is indeed
inexhaustible.

But Hardy, for reasons which may be deduced from
various sections of this essay, is the last of his order.
He was the kind of serious novelist whose popular
success inevitably arose from the nature of his achievement, and that ceased to be possible after the Victorian
era. The popular interest in such a novel as *Passage to
India* was a fluke which could not be expected to be
repeated with any other novel by the same author. The
importance of the Hardy type of artistic achievement
for purposes of this enquiry is that it lends itself to
self-education, it assists, that is, in the formation of
taste. Thus the reader of *The Return of the Native*
may quite well become in due time qualified to read
Lear, whereas the reader of *Lord Jim* at the level of
the publisher's blurb is not assisted to proceed to *The
Possessed* or even to *Nostromo*, any more than those

who go to *Lady Chatterley's Lover* or *Ulysses* in the belief that they are the latest successors of the tales of Paul de Kock are likely to obtain either benefit or satisfaction. Barring such accidents as are exemplified by the misapprehension of *Passage to India*, *Lord Jim*, and *Ulysses*, the serious novel can no longer percolate through successive strata of the reading publics; the machinery (*vide* Part III. Chapter II.) which cuts off each level from the one above steps in here to reinforce the effect of the recently formed reading habits discussed earlier. This probably explains the frequency of that purely modern phenomenon, the persistent reader, often well educated and not infrequently possessed of the best intentions, who sticks at a certain level—the level represented by, say, the drama of Shaw, the David Garnett school of fiction, Georgian poetry, and the criticism of Professor Lascelles Abercrombie. His reading habits will not admit him to the experience of great tragedy, serious novels, and genuine modern poetry, or to participation in a rigorous critical investigation, and he sees no necessity for revising his habits—habits formed and endorsed by environment.

At a lower level there is the question raised by this statement of Gene Stratton Porter's:

> I happen to know that thousands of young people form their ideas of what they consider a wonderful and a desirable life to live from the books of half-a-dozen popular authors, and they would be infinitely better off if the Government actually censored books and forbade publication of those containing sensual and illegitimate situations which intimately describe how social and national law is broken by people of wealth and unbridled passions. There is one great beauty in idealized romance: reading it can make no one

worse than he is. It may fire thousands to higher aspiration than they ever before have had.

In a previous paragraph the same authoress had written :

> Now what do I care for the newspaper or magazine critics yammering that there is not such a thing as a moral man, and that my pictures of life are sentimental and idealized. They are ! And I glory in them ! They form idealized pictures of life because they are copied from life where it touches religion, chastity, love, home and hope of Heaven ultimately.

This may be taken to be the description of his work which every great bestseller would be willing to endorse. If the reader will turn back a few pages he will find some reasons for supposing that such pictures of life are less healthy in their influence than Mrs. Porter imagined. Working from the findings of this essay a censorship of fiction would find it necessary to suppress most of the bestsellers of the last fifty years and some before them—Charles Kingsley, for instance, and the novel in which extract No. 429 of *The Oxford Book of English Prose* occurs ; while Joyce and Lawrence, the present objects of official and unofficial censorship, would receive recognition as the ' extremely serious and improving writers ' Mr. T. S. Eliot has recently described them as being. If this essay has given evidence only to this effect, it will in the writer's opinion have amply justified itself.

.   .   .   .

But perhaps something further may be thought necessary to justify a demonstration so depressing. And there is so much to offer under this head that it would be easier to write a chapter than a page. But such a chapter would be outside the plan of the present undertaking : a page must do.

In the introduction to this study I offered an account of my reasons for adopting the method of approach I call ' anthropological.' It is pertinent for the reader to enquire, after patiently following the exposition, To what end? I am able only to outline briefly the lines of the answer to that question. First, I have here isolated and shown the workings of a number of tendencies which, having assumed the form of commercial and economic machinery, are now so firmly established that they run on their own and whither they choose; they have assumed such a monstrous impersonality that individual effort towards controlling or checking them seems ridiculously futile. This is probably the most terrifying feature of our civilisation. If there is to be any hope, it must lie in conscious and directed effort. All that can be done, it must be realised, must take the form of resistance by an armed and conscious minority.

This minority has two main modes of usefulness, between which communication would have to be kept up. The first is in the field of research. It is of the utmost importance that as many as possible should be made aware of what is happening, and a fully documented presentment of the history of the reading public is an essential means to this end. It may be further argued that what we have here is a type case, a particular instance of a general process at work in the modern world. Many other studies of the same kind are needed in order to examine and document the cultural situation in as many relevant fields as possible, with a view to informing and equipping the active minority.

For example, the plight of the small countries—Scandinavian and English-speaking especially—in these days when mass-production conditions determine the supply of literature, ought to be investigated. And many kindred lines of enquiry open out (some are actually being pursued). Such research would more than justify postgraduate work under the head of the Humanities.

The profit would be not only a matter of books designed to foster general awareness. It would also mean the training of a picked few who would go out into the world equipped for the work of forming and organising a conscious minority. And this leads us to the second mode of usefulness of the minority, that of educational work in schools and universities. There is no reason why teaching, and the teaching of English in particular, should be a *pis aller* for the intelligent, as it so generally is. For though the fully-formed and -set when forced to face the findings of such a study as the present one are for the most part merely paralysed, or take refuge in anger or cynicism (or optimism), yet experience shows that when the young are made aware of these forces they readily see the necessity for resisting. They may even be fired with a missionary spirit. In fact, the possibilities of education specifically directed against such appeals as those made by the journalist, the middleman, the bestseller, the cinema, and advertising, and the other more general influences discussed in this study, are inexhaustible; some education of this kind is an essential part of the training of taste. Such a missionary spirit, however amusing to the psychologising observer, has played a considerable part in history. As a minor instance of what may be done by conscious resistance, the case of British

Honduras comes to hand. Here, I am informed, we have a community which in deliberately setting out to resist American influence is actually preserving a traditional way of life.

Research in Humanities and teaching might thus be closely correlated, to their mutual profit. There must be a considerable number of people at least potentially interested—all those concerned for the traditional culture—but at present rendered ineffective because isolated and out of touch. There might be enough such people, if rallied, to support a periodical and provide a sure public for a publisher. For to obtain the maximum efficiency for such a campaign as I have outlined two things would be necessary: an all-round critical organ and a non-commercial Press. One of the most depressing facts brought out by this study must be, for those aware of the importance of the critical intelligence, that the channels for disinterested criticism of any kind are rapidly being closed, if indeed any remain. One after another the serious politico-literary periodicals have disappeared or lowered their colours, and there is scarcely one left whose liberty of speech has not been sold to the advertiser or mortgaged to vested interests. They must pay their way, in a world in which the free exercise of the intelligence grows more and more unpopular. Similarly with publishing (*vide* Part II. Chapter III. § 3): if anything is to be done, it must be by way of pamphlets and publications by a private Press with a conscious critical policy. It is gratifying at this point to be able to name The Minority Press (*a*), and there is no reason

(*a*) Started in 1930 by Mr. Gordon Fraser, then an undergraduate, it began by publishing pamphlets which without any publicity have paid their way.

why the university public should not produce and support such a periodical as the *Calendar* (so soon defunct) but without being restricted like the *Calendar* to literary criticism.   The minority would look to such activities as these to register and sum up progress, to assist in creating awareness, and to provide organisation.

Such a hope may seem extravagant.   But if anything is done, it will be in this way.   If this way offers no hope, then there is none.

NOTES

[1] Whereas a German publisher only spends 3 per cent. to 4 per cent. of the *cost of production* on advertising, the English publisher spends about 6 per cent. of his *turnover* in advertisement, while the American publisher George H. Doran claims to spend 10 per cent. of his *gross income* on ' promotion.' This information, obtained from the article ' Publishing ' in the *Ency. Brit.* (14th ed.), of course proves nothing, but it does suggest the general proposition that the more cultured a country the less its publishers would have to spend in forcing books on the public attention.

[2] A really popular-at-all-levels novel like *The Constant Nymph*, which was the book of the year 1924-25, has only sold a million copies, and those largely in the 6d. Readers' Library edition.

[3] These figures are taken from the Report on Public Libraries (1927). It has been suggested to me by an eminent and experienced public librarian that the relative percentages of fiction and non-fiction would be even more disproportionate were it not that librarians, actuated presumably by local patriotism, endeavour to equalise matters by transferring such sections as ' Juvenile Fiction ' and ' Classical Novels ' over to the non-fiction classifications.

[4] The head of a big public library (and in a University town), when asked why there were no novels by D. H. Lawrence on the shelves, replied indignantly : ' I've always tried to keep this library *clean*.'

[5] Arthur Waugh, *A Hundred Years of Publishing* (1930), says there are 340 branches of Boots' Library, with a quarter of a million subscribers.

⁶ When these libraries sell off their out-of-date stock several times a year, the novels are generally worn and shabby, while the other books are ' good as new.'

⁷ A random instance from the *Times* (June 24th, 1930): ' In honour of the centenary of the French Romantic movement, the western façade of Notre Dame was brilliantly illuminated by flood-lighting on Sunday evening.' The English general public has never heard of the English Romantic movement, and the governing classes who possibly have would not in any case think of taking up a serious attitude to it. Cf. too the space given in any French newspaper to the death of a man of letters and a purely literary event with the absence of such an interest in England. Also the two main features of English journalism, the Sunday paper and the large-circulation newspaper, are both unknown in France. In contrast to the responsible interest in literature so evident in the French Press, the attention paid by the English journalist to the recent appointment of a Poet Laureate is significant. The announcement was made on a Saturday, and an inspection of the next day's newspapers showed that not one of the popular Sunday organs thought the news worth mentioning (one published a photograph of the new Laureate without comment), though the appointment was what might be called a popular one. This is what is meant by the assertion on p. 51 that poetry is no longer read.

⁸ Taken as common to a majority of the following : a flourishing shop in the centre of a market town, a back-street ' paper-shop,' the contents of the periodicals rack in a Boots' store, a W. H. Smith shop, a suburban newsagent's.

⁹ A foreigner's opinion of the English Press is illuminating. The intelligent and open-minded Dibelius (*England*, Cape, 1930) comments on the

superior appearance and good workmanship of English newspapers, and concludes: ' In this respect the English standard is very high indeed, certainly higher than the German. But a different picture is given by a comparison of the contents of the newspapers of the two countries. While, in this respect, the better-class English newspaper, like the *Morning Post*, *Manchester Guardian*, or *Daily Chronicle* [now defunct], certainly does not give its readers any more than the *Deutsche Allgemeine*, *Vossische*, the *Frankfurter Zeitung* or *Hamburger Fremdenblatt*, the great mass of English newspapers, even in the metropolis, are incredibly thin and empty. Most of them, in sharp contrast to the half-dozen or so papers with an international reputation, have practically no foreign news, little or no literary or general information, and no magazine page; they are made up of leaders, telegrams, local gossip, and a mass of sporting news. In the provinces, there is the *Scotsman* and *Glasgow Herald* in Scotland, and, in the industrial areas, the *Birmingham Daily Post*, *Liverpool Daily Post*, the *Yorkshire Post*, and the admirable *Manchester Guardian*; but outside this half-dozen there is an almost unbelievable dulness. No one who has not been condemned to read a local sheet of that sort regularly can understand the empty chatter that does duty as the average play or the popular novel. . . .'

[10] In the *Advertiser's ABC* it describes itself in these terms: ' JOHN o' LONDON'S WEEKLY has unique powers of appeal. It is not a paper only for women or only for men; it is a paper for both; for the whole family, and it is calculated to make a direct appeal to clear-thinking people of educated tastes and a discriminating standard of comfort.'

[11] The scope of these is best suggested by their own advertisements in the *Advertiser's ABC* (1929): ' It

exists to remind its readers that life is not all work and
worry; that there is a more leisurely, laughing side,
which contributes so much to make it worth living.
The Editorial policy of the TATLER embraces all the
lighter interests of the well-to-do Englishman—Sport,
Society, Motoring, Art, the Theatre. It is found in
every club and regimental mess, in every private house
of substance, in every doctor's waiting-room, hotel
lounge.' 'The SPHERE is representative of all that is
best in English life. The SPHERE is read by the very
rich, the moderately rich, and by the ordinary well-to-
do folk of intelligence and culture throughout the
Empire. It is the Empire's Illustrated Weekly Journal, and is to be found, not only in club-rooms, hotels
and libraries, but in the homes of the best people
throughout the English-speaking world.' 'The SKETCH
was the first expression of an entirely new idea in
British Illustrated Journalism. Before its appearance,
in 1893, illustrated newspapers devoted themselves
almost exclusively to the more serious of current hap-
penings. . . . It sets itself to provide cheery entertainment for the smoking-room and boudoir, and to
illustrate the subjects most commonly discussed when
men and women meet after the serious business of the
day is done. Its instant and signal success is a matter
of history. Inevitably it had many imitators,' etc.

[12] It may be useful to point out here that there is no
reason for supposing that novelettes are bought exclusively by the uneducated and the poor. A list kindly
made for me of the private reading-matter in a high-
class cramming establishment states that the young men
own all the varieties of film and detective-story magazine mentioned above, 3s. 6d. and 7s. 6d. novels by
Rider Haggard, Baroness Orczy, John Buchan, Edgar
Wallace, Freeman Wills Crofts, and also, 'There are
a great number of 9d. and 1s. paper novels circulating

among them, most of them by Edgar Wallace and Oppenheim.'

[13] The writer has vainly tried to buy the *Nation and Athenæum*, *New Statesman*, and *Times Literary Supplement* all over south-western England, and obtained them only (but not invariably) at the bookstalls at big railway junctions. The newsagents in many cases showed no knowledge of the names even. It is worth remembering that in France there are at least three serious literary weekly *newspapers* (*i.e.* literary journals in newspaper form which review intelligently all the notable poetry and criticism that appears as well as lighter works, and have leading articles on literary movements by distinguished writers), and they can all be bought in the ordinary way in the little provincial towns (and are usually sold out on the day of issue).

[14] For illustration see *Is Advertising To-Day a Burden or a Boon ?* (The New Advertiser's Press, 1930).

[15] On the contrary, for before the war Messrs. Nelson published pocket editions of the classics and good copyright novels (*e.g.* Jane Austen, George Eliot, Thackeray, the Brontës, in Nelson's Classics, the early Wells, and Henry James and Conrad, in Nelson's Library) at 6d. and 7d. each, that really were well printed and bound.

[16] The Manager of the Readers' Library Publishing Co. Ltd., when requested to put the writer into communication with the editor of the series, regretted that he was unable to do so or to furnish any information, so that not only the identity of the distinguished man of letters, but also the principle on which he chooses the volumes for publication, must remain a dark secret.

[17] ' Edgar Wallace, although so immensely successful in his own line of work, is too modest a man to claim that the mystery story necessarily belongs to the highest form of literature, although some of its examples

are assuredly among the best.'—From the introduction
to *The Melody of Death*, ' the first book by Edgar
Wallace that the READERS' LIBRARY has had the
honour to publish ' (1927).

[18] It is interesting to notice that Woolworth fiction
has revived 'best sellers' of the last generation with
considerable success : Garvice and Hocking appear to
sell nearly as well as P. C. Wren and Edgar Wallace.

[19] As opposed to the insecurity of the acknowledged ' highbrow ' organ in the twentieth century,
contrast the public of nine thousand genteel families
for the *Edinburgh Review* a century and a quarter ago :
' Of this work 9000 copies are printed quarterly, and
no genteel family *can* pretend to be without it, because,
independent of its politics, it gives the only valuable literary criticism which can be met with.'—Scott to Ellis,
November 2nd, 1808, six years after its first appearance.   And Mrs. Gore, who provided for the public
of a century ago the fiction of Ethel M. Dell at the
speed of Edgar Wallace, whose status was that of the
novelists in the advertisement on p. 8 (Horne, *A New
Spirit of the Age* (1844), says : ' Wherever you see a
board hung out at the door of a provincial or suburban
library, containing a list of the last batch of new books,
you may be quite certain of finding Mrs. Gore and
Mr. James prodigiously distinguished at the head of it
in Brobdingnagian letters '), describing the typical
night-scene in high-life for her readers : ' Scarcely has
the last " good-night " sounded in the last ante-room—
scarcely has the fair Viscountess, in her dressing-room,
abandoned her perfumed locks to the delicate fingers of
her French maid, and the worthy Viscount in the saloon
beneath ensconced himself in a Skelmersdale chair with
a copy of the last *Edinburgh Review* in his hands—
when,' etc. (*Mothers and Daughters*, 1831).   Again,
the mechanics' institutions and ' country associations,'

and even 'the smaller societies formed at different public-houses' mentioned by Mr. George Dawson in his evidence before the Select Committee on Public Libraries, 1849, are stated by him to take the *Edinburgh* and *Quarterly*. In 1817 the *Edinburgh* and the *Quarterly* were each selling 12,000 copies of each number.

The proportion of sales to total population is for the *Edinburgh* in 1810 c. one to every 1000, for the *Adelphi* one to every 10,000.

[20] For instance, to take a more obvious test case than a novel, a pseudo-philosophy published in the autumn of 1930 was noticed in two papers thus, by representatives of middlebrow and highbrow journalism :

'I would wish that this book might be read by thousands upon thousands of readers. It is a brave, honest philosophy, with no nonsense about it, coloured with generosity and poetry. It has helped me as no new book of the last twenty years. . . . The book should be called "*The Creed of a Modern Saint*." '— Hugh Walpole in a letter to *Everyman*.

'His book contains so much quackery and gush, such an enormous bulk of words for so small a kernel of matter, that it would be easy to make a great mistake and think the author must be posturing. . . . His book contains his "philosophy of life," and the matter which goes to it is so exiguous that he could have said all he really has to say in ten pages. The rest of the book is a flood of (perfectly sincere) gush and endless repetition. . . . Mr. —— has really written a really bad book. . . . He wraps it [the kernel of truth] up in voluminous swaddling clothes of sentimentalism, mysticism and honest quackery of the kind which is extremely fashionable nowadays.'—Leonard Woolf in the *Nation and Athenæum*.

The difference in taste and critical ability to be noticed

here is representative of the publics of the two kinds of
better literary periodical.

21 Cutting from the *Evening Standard*, 1928:
' " Vivandière." First Edition All Sold Out After
Mr. Arnold Bennett's Review.

' Mr. Arnold Bennett's reputation as a maker of
" best sellers " has been heightened by the addition of
one more to the list of other people's books which the
public has clamoured for on his word. Last week
" Vivandière " meant nothing to most people, and the
name of Miss Phoebe Fenwick Gaye conveyed no more.
Then Mr. Arnold Bennett, in his weekly article on
books in the " Evening Standard," mentioned that
" Vivandière " was this young woman's first novel,
and that it was very good. The demand for the book
which has suddenly arisen has cleared the first edition
right out of existence and still the clamour goes on.'

The only writer of the past who could do anything
like this was Andrew Lang in the '80's (*vide* Forrest
Reid in *The Eighteen Eighties*), and deplorable as his
taste and influence were, they did not interfere with
serious standards. He was a single case, and faded
into obscurity before he could do any real harm.

22 *E.g.* ' This book will be a classic.' ' Let there
be no mistake about it, this is a big book.' ' The best
novel I have read this week is *Iron Man*.' ' *Rogue
Herries* is a grand tale, a real full-time man's job in
fiction, and everybody should read it.' Taken at random from publishers' advertisements in the *Observer*.

23 While movie-magazines and women's periodicals
published in America are increasingly read here, there
is no give-and-take of exchange with English journalism. ' The American edition of that highly successful
British periodical, the *Strand Magazine*, however, had
only a small sale; and it has recently been discon-
tinued. The *Strand* prints a good many old-style

sentimental love-stories which strike the sophisticated American stenographer and shoe-clerk as amusing.' (Henry T. Baker, *The Contemporary Short Story*.) This kind of sophistication, which is revolutionising popular fiction in England, will be dealt with later.

[24] It must be noted here for future reference that 'worth-while' apparently indicates 'magazines that remunerate the author adequately' rather than 'magazines it is an honour to appear in.'

[25] From the booklet issued by K. MacNichol, where also 'The list of great writers to whom " Bob Davis " is literary godfather would certainly contain most of the big names in America, and many of our famous British authors who derive a large share of income from overseas.'

[26] For instance, Gilbert Frankau, a bestseller much read by the governing class, goes out of his way to satirise the *London Mercury* as the 'highbrow' organ (vide *Life—and Erica*).

[27] *Vide*, for instance, ' The Case of Mr. Hugh Walpole,' by J. M. Murry (*Athenæum*, July 16th, 1921); ' Wilder : Prophet of the Genteel Christ,' by Michael Gold (*New Republic*, October 22nd, 1930). See also *New Republic* (U.S.A.), October 29th to December 17th, 1930, for the public indignation raised by the latter article ; if such a critique were published in an English literary organ there is every reason to suppose that a similar storm of protesting correspondence would ensue.

[28] From word-of-mouth repute, since it is hardly possible that the *Sunday Dispatch* public possesses or is in a position to borrow an expensive book published in Paris, not pirated in England, and strictly banned. It is also worth noting, as evidence for the above conclusions, that in no case is the choice of *Ulysses* or *To the Lighthouse* accounted for, but merely listed.

[29] Of the sixty popular novelists circularised, about 80 per cent. write for the magazines; of the twenty-five that answered effectively, 60 per cent.

[30] B3 writes: ' Every publisher knows that there are certain figures—somewhere between 4 and 6000, then somewhere between 12 and 15,000—at which novels tend to stick, and possibly these represent roughly the extent of certain reading publics.' It was noticed on p. 20 that a highbrow literary organ sells at the outside about 4000, the *London Mercury* (which would be a B organ) 10,000, the lowbrow literary weeklies (class C) jointly sell about 200,000.

[31] ' George Bourne,' *Memoirs of a Surrey Labourer* (1907), *Change in the Village* (1912); George Sturt, *The Wheelwright's Shop* (1923).

In *Change in the Village* he describes the round of seasonal activities of two typical survivors of the older generation, and ends by summarising the texture of their lives thus: ' Not very spruce as to personal cleanliness, smelling of his cow-stall, saving money, wanting no holiday, independent of books and newspapers, indifferent to anything that happened further off than the neighbouring town, liking his pipe and glass of beer, and never knowing what it was to feel dull ' (p. 125). ' So his work varies, week after week. From one job to another up and down the valley he goes, not listlessly and fatigued, but taking a sober interest in all he does. You can see in him very well how his forefathers went about their affairs, for he is plainly a man after their pattern. His day's work is his day's pleasure. It is changeful enough, and calls for skill enough, to make it enjoyable to him. . . . He is a man who seems to enjoy his life with an undiminished zest from morning to night. It is doubtful if the working hours afford, to nine out of ten modern and even " educated " men, such a constant refreshment of acceptable incidents as Turner's bring to him. He is perhaps the best specimen of the old stock now left in the valley; but it must not be thought that he is singular. Others there are not very unlike him; and all that one hears of them goes to prove that the old cottage thrift, whatever its limitations may have been, did at least make the day's work interesting enough to a man, without his needing to care about leisure evenings' (p. 210). Cf. too D. H. Lawrence, 'Nottingham and the Mining Countryside' (*New Adelphi*, August 1930): ' So that the life was a curious cross between industrialism and the old agricultural England of Shakespeare and Milton and Fielding and George Eliot. The dialect was broad Derbyshire, and always " thee " and " thou." The people lived almost entirely by instinct, men of my father's age could not really read. And the pit did not mechanise men. On the contrary. Under the butty system, the miners worked underground as a sort of intimate community. . . . My father loved the pit. The great fallacy is, to pity the man. He was happy: or more than happy, he was fulfilled. . . . In my father's generation, with the old wild England behind them, and the lack of education, the man was not beaten down. But in my generation, the boys I went to school with, colliers now, have all been beaten down, what with the din-din-dinning of Board Schools, books, cinemas, clergymen, the whole national and human consciousness hammering on the fact of material prosperity above all things. . . . Even the farm-labourer to-day is psychologically a town-bird.'

[32] ' Though the normal hours were too long, the men were glad of overtime. In this connection it should be pointed out that in those days a man's work, though more laborious to his muscles, was not nearly so exhausting yet tedious as machinery and " speeding-up " have since made it for his mind and temper. " Eight

hours " to-day is less interesting and probably more toilsome than " twelve hours " then. . . . Already during the eighties and nineties of last century, work was growing less interesting to the workman, although far more sure in its results. . . . Of course wages are higher. But no higher wage, no income, will buy for men that satisfaction which of old—until machinery made drudges of them—streamed into their muscles all day long from close contact with iron, timber, clay, wind and wave, horse-strength. It tingled up in the niceties of touch, sight, scent. But these intimacies are over. Although they have so much more leisure men can now taste little solace in life, of the sort that skilled hand-work used to yield to them.'—George Sturt, *The Wheelwright's Shop*.

[33] Reprinted in *Books and Persons*, Arnold Bennett, ' Middle Class,' p. 67. For the state of the reading public before the war, see also 'The Book Buyer,' p. 25, and 'The Potential Public,' p. 76.

[34] *Vide* Scott's autobiography of his youth (Lockhart's *Life of Scott*): ' A respectable subscription library, a circulating library of ancient standing, and some private book-shelves were open to my random perusal. . . . I continued a long time reading what and how I pleased, and of course reading nothing but what afforded me immediate entertainment. The only thing which saved my mind from utter dissipation was that turn for historical pursuit, which never abandoned me even at the idlest period.' And he speaks for his age (and the next) when he sums up the case for and against the novel in his essay on Fielding in *Lives of the Novelists*: ' Excluding from consideration those infamous works, which address themselves directly to awakening the grosser passions of our nature, we are inclined to think, the worst evil to be apprehended from the perusal of novels is, that the habit is apt to

generate an indisposition to real history, and useful literature; and that the best which can be hoped is that they may sometimes instruct the youthful mind by real pictures of life, and sometimes awaken their better feelings and sympathies by strains of generous sentiments, and tales of fictitious woe.'

[35] The novelist B1 describes the plight of an intelligent writer in such conditions. ' By nature I am entirely a man of action and not of letters. I have no quarrel with life, and so I have to depend upon recaptured emotion. That is why my books which embody personal experience are always better. Fantasy is to me both tedious to read and tedious to write.' He adds that he makes ' scarcely any appeal to the unsophisticated public.' ' I have jumped about from style to style, and built up for myself a public unlike that of most other novelists of the day, because it is seldom the same public. There is the public which only cares for my writing when it is the lived thing written with the intensity of recaptured emotion; there is the public which dislikes me in that mood and which always wants me to be amusing. There *was* that public which only likes caviare. That of course did not survive long. The literary caviare of yesterday is so often the boiled mutton and caper sauce of to-day. There is a small public which likes my ecclesiastical work. So, to return to whether I have studied my public or not, what I have studied is how to keep my various publics entertained in turn.' [Of Scott and Dickens] ' Popular journalism had not been invented, and the writer on the whole preserved a dignity that added to his sense of responsibility, for his public was less fickle because there were fewer novelties. . . . It would be ridiculous for me to pretend that I could ever bring myself to find the superb aloofness to write a book like James Joyce's *Ulysses* or some of D. H. Lawrence's

books. I wish I could. But I should never have the courage to cut myself free. I am aware that my job as a novelist is to entertain the public, and the way I manage to entertain myself in the process is, as I have indicated above, by writing to entertain various publics.'

[36] 'Licenses increased steadily during 1930. During the summer period, normally regarded as an "off season," the average number of new licenses taken out each month, apart from renewals and after subtracting non-renewals, was in excess of 20,000. Statisticians will continue to argue about "saturation points." So far as the B.B.C. is concerned, there is no saturation point short of "wireless in every home." The number of licenses in force on September 30th, 1930, was 3,195,553, representing about 12,000,000 listeners, or roughly every second home in the country. . . . The possibility also of there still being a number of unlicensed listeners must not be forgotten.'—*The B.B.C. Year Book, 1931.*

[37] It is a commonplace that not only the younger but the older generation as well automatically turn on ' the Wireless ' as they enter the living-room. Midday and evening meals and evening parties are conducted with an undercurrent of sound from the loud speaker. The ordinary lower- and middle-class evening interior shows every member of the family with a library novel or a magazine and ' the Wireless ' ' on.'

[38] This does not mean that the novels of Scott, for instance, will not be abandoned by the public (as in fact they have been) in favour of such substitutes as this advertisement describes :

' An All Talking, Singing and Dancing Drama—
THE LOVES OF ROBERT BURNS
Britain's Great National Talkie—Bright with
Song and Dance.'

But the fantasy-novel is felt to yield more satisfaction in book form. Cf. the successful production of ' the book of the film ' in sixpenny editions discussed in Chapter II. Many of the D novelists stated that the sales of a novel rose suddenly after the film of it had appeared.

[39] Cf. the shrinking of social life in one generation caused by the changes that have replaced the axiom, ' No nice girl dances more than twice in one evening with the same man,' by the regular dancing-partner, evenings at home round the piano when friends dropped in to sing and dance, providing their own entertainment, by evenings at the dance-hall and the cinema, neighbourly informal visiting by whist-drives and bridge-parties and telephone calls, and the close contacts of religious interests by Sundays out in the car. The car has replaced the piano as the sign of social status.

[40] First published 1909, sold considerably more than 150,000 copies in the first nine months (Florence Barclay's first novel), a bestseller ever since, and in 1928 was running as a serial in *Woman's World* (' The Favourite Paper of a Million Homes '), 2d. weekly.

[41] *The Life of Florence L. Barclay*—By One of Her Daughters (1912); *Life and Letters of Gene Stratton Porter*, Jeannette Porter Meehan (1927); *Memoirs of Marie Corelli*, Bertha Vyver (1930).

[42] Florence Barclay's biographer states: ' My mother received a large number of letters . . . the quite intimate letters of lonely people seeking sympathy and understanding ; or of happy readers eager to tell from full hearts how much her books had meant to them, sometimes merely in simple enjoyment, sometimes spiritually, or in helping to solve life's problems.' For such readers Marie Corelli and Florence Barclay represent serious reading, as opposed to the novel or magazine that kills time. Cf. a sergeant-major during

the war trying to raise the conversation to the level of his educated companion by referring to Ella Wheeler Wilcox, Omar Khayyam, and Marie Corelli. Of the latter he said, ' It isn't the story you read her for, it's the thought.'

[43] Marie Corelli claimed ' literary honours ' and considered herself the prose Shakespeare; Gene Stratton Porter was bewildered by the critics who refused her ' a first-grade literary reputation '; Hall Caine also saw himself as the Shakespeare of the novel; Mrs. Barclay thought of her writings as religious and not literary at all. All these novelists were untroubled by doubt. If they attacked the critics, it was because they thought themselves deprived of recognition by jealousy.

[44] *E.g.* ' She " cut " church for it [packing] and felt (despite all her professed irreligion) more than a little guilty.'—Gilbert Frankau, *Life—and Erica.*

' For Sorrell's sufferings and struggles had not led him towards the illusion of socialism. He had seen too much of human nature. Labour, becoming sectionalised, would split into groups, and group would grab from group, massing for the struggle instead of fighting a lone fight. Only the indispensable and individual few would be able to rise above this scramble of the industrial masses. . . . Social service? Oh yes, ten thousand years hence—perhaps. But for the moment—arms—and not too much trust in your neighbour.'—Warwick Deeping, *Sorrell and Son.*

In the novels of Ethel M. Dell the Bohemian boyish heroines say ' damn ' and ' Hell,' shocking the company, the authoress, and presumably the reader.

[45] Cf. Jeannette Porter Meehan, *Life and Letters of Gene Stratton Porter*: ' Mother *knew* both sides of life, but she chose to write only about one side. She knew the stern realities, the immorality, and the seamy dis-

gusting sidelights of life. But why write about them?
Every one has his own trouble and heartache, so why
not give the world something happy to read, and make
them see visions of idealised life? Surely this does
more good than sordid tales of sex filth that only lead
to morbid and diseased thinking. . . . Mother's ideas
must have been right, for the few times she strayed
from the path and tried other themes, her audiences
were amazed and shocked. They did not like it ! '

And the literary agent : ' Comfortable sentiment is
absolutely necessary for popular success.'—George G.
Magnus, *How to Write Saleable Fiction* (14th edition
1926).

[46] Deloney in *The Gentle Craft* relates how Simon
Eyre's fellow prentices would answer his Northern Jigs
with their Southern Songs as they worked, and he
quotes approvingly the ' old proverbe They prove servants kind and good, That sing at their businesse like
birds in the wood.'

' Music spread upwards from the masses to the
classes.'—*Shakespeare's England*, Vol. ii. p. 21.

[47] Chappell, Vol. ii., ' The Reign of Charles ii.,'
adduces evidence to show that ' the cultivation of music
could not have declined to any extent, in spite of the
long reign and depressing influence of puritanism ; or
else the revival must have been singularly rapid.' And
he investigates *Pepys's Diary*, which shows that all
Pepys's household servants over a long period could at
least sing well and usually play various instruments
besides. The typical amusement of the Pepys household is represented by the entry under September 9th,
1664 : ' After dinner, my wife and Mercer [the ser-
vant-girl], Tom [his page] and I, sat till eleven at night,
singing and fiddling, and a great joy it is to see me
master of so much pleasure in my house.' And one
remembers the rather surprising part that music plays

in *Pilgrim's Progress*, Part II. (1684), especially the
rejoicing at Giant Despair's overthrow: ' Now Chris-
tiana, if need was, could play upon the viol, and her
daughter Mercy upon the lute ; so since they were so
merry disposed, she played them a lesson, and Ready-
to-halt would dance. So he took Despondency's
daughter, named Much-afraid, by the hand, and to
dancing they went in the road.'

    [48] Even Pepys at the comparatively degenerate date
of 1660 mentions (February 1st) how he ' met with
Mr. Lock(e) and Pursell, Master of Musique, and went
with them to the Coffee House. . . . Here we had
variety of brave Italian and Spanish songs, and a canon
for eight voices, which Mr. Lock had lately made.'

    [49] Vide *Annals of St. Paul's Cathedral*, Henry Hart
Milman (1869), p. 328. ' It is difficult for a Dean of
our rapid and restless days to imagine, when he surveys
the massy folios of Donne's sermons, a vast congregation in the Cathedral or at Paul's Cross, listening not
only with patience but with absorbed interest, with un-
flagging attention, even with delight and rapture, to
these interminable disquisitions, to us teeming with
laboured obscurity, false and misplaced wit, fatiguing
antitheses. However set off, as by all accounts they
were, by a most graceful and impressive delivery, it is
astonishing to us that he should hold a London congregation enthralled, unwearied, unsatiated. Yet there
can be no doubt that this was the case. And this
congregation consisted, both of the people down to the
lowest, and of the most noble, wise, accomplished of
that highly intellectual age.' (Quoted by Logan
Pearsall Smith, *Donne's Sermons*, p. xvii.) And *vide*
T. S. Eliot, *For Lancelot Andrewes*, on the nature of
the demand made by Andrewes' sermons. Sermon-
going was a regular pastime of the ordinary jolly
citizen (cf. Hollyband's conversation manual, *The*

French Schoolemaister (1573), reprinted in *The Eliza-bethan Home* (Cobden-Sanderson) as ' The Citizen at Home '; also John Manningham's Diary 1602-3, which, though he was not particularly religious, records at length forty odd sermons that he heard in the fifteen months).

50 Martin wrote his first tract, *The Epistle*, in reply to a treatise by John Bridges, Dean of Sarum, of which he complains : ' And learned Brother Bridges, a man might almost run himself out of breath before he could come to a full point in many places in your book ' (*The Epistle*, p. 36). Marginal note by Martin : ' Wo, wo ! Dean, take breath and then to it again ' (p. 37).

Nashe seems to have been aware of the demands he made : ' Be of good cheere, my weary Readers, for I have espied land, as *Diogenes* said to his weary Schollers when he had read to a waste leafe,' he observes cheer-fully at one point in *The Prayse of the Red Herring*—which nevertheless was written to make money when he was lying up at Yarmouth. No wonder the un-cultivated reader preferred his reading to offer him the guiding - lines of rime and metre. (*Vide* Webbe, Preface to his *Discourse of English Poetrie*.)

51 Pettie dedicates ' To the Gentle Gentlewomen Readers '—' Gentle Readers, whom by my will I would have only gentlewomen, and therefore to you I direct my words '; ' Euphues had rather lye shut in a Ladyes casket, then open in a Schollers studie '; it was ' the Countess of Pembroke's *Arcadia*.'

52 *Parismus, The Renouned Prince of Bohemia*, 1598-1599 (2 parts, the second being the history of Paris-menos). Esdaile records nearly three pages of sur-viving editions, up to 1730 *c.*

The Most Pleasant Historie of Ornatus and Artesia, referred to in *Palladis Tamia* (1598), ' The Eighth Impression ' 1683, and so till 1694.

The Famous Historie of Montelyon, Knight of the Oracle, and Sonne to the Renouned Persicles King of Assyria.

[53] Ornatus is described simply as ' of goodly stature, and commendable gifts,' Artesia as ' of exceeding comeliness, exteriorly beautified with abundance of gifts of nature, and inwardly adorned with abundance of divine perfections.'

[54] ' How popular his novels were may be judged from the long period in which they held the public estimation, often reprinted through the 17th century and surviving plentifully in chap-book form into the 18th (*e.g.* The B.M. and the Bodleian together contain seven 18th century chap-book versions of the *Gentle Craft*, I.).'—F. O. Mann, Introduction to Deloney's Works.

[55] *E.g. vide* Deloney's Works, ed. F. O. Mann, p. 24 : [' Welcome to mee Iack of Newberie (said the Queene) though a Clothier by trade, yet a Gentleman by condition ']; and p. 101 [particularly the Persian general's admission to his conqueror Crispianus the shoe-maker : ' I find it true, that Magnanimity and Knightly Prowesse is not alwayes tied within the compasse of Noble blood.' This is worth noticing to bring home another point, that the English ideal of a gentleman at this time had as focus the idea of the noble mind].

[56] Cf. the Greene King's wife (*The Gentle Craft*, II. Chap. x.) who made a success of her bankrupt hus-band's business, so that her neighbours began to offer her civilities. ' I neighbour (quoth she) I know your kindnesse and may speake thereof by experience : well may I compare you to him that would never bid any man to dinner, but at two of the clocke in the after noone, when he was assured they had fild their bellies before, and that they would not touch his meate, except for manners sake : wherefore for my part I will give you thankes, when I take benefit of your proffer.

'Why neighbour we speake for good will (quoth they):

'Tis true (quoth shee) and so say they that call for a fresh quart to bestow on a drunken man, when they know it would doe him as much good in his bootes as in his belly.' And Chapter vii. when Sir John Rainsford encounters the priest who will not bury the poor widow's husband without fee: 'Sir John Rainsford seeing him stand so peremptory on his points, swore a deep oath, that it were best for him to bury him or (quoth he) Ile bury thee;

'Bury me (said the Priest) a fig for you, and bury blind bayard when he is dead, or the dogs that your Hauks will not eate.

'The Knight at these words being marvelous angry commanded his men to take him up and cast him into the grave . . . at what time the Priest cried out, hold, hold, for God's sake, let me rise and I will bury him.

'Nay soft (quoth the Knight) thou art not like to rise, no rising heere before the generall resurrection, that thou shalt rise to iudgement.'

[57] It is now impossible to count on even an educated person's knowing his Bunyan.

[58] Far subtler in perception than that of many eighteenth and nineteenth-century professional novelists of repute. *Vide*, for instance, the account of Mr. Fearing (*Pilgrim's Progress*, Part II.), and Mr. By-ends of the town of Fair-speech (Part II.): '. . . " and to tell you the truth I am become a gentleman of good quality, yet my great-grandfather was but a waterman, looking one way and rowing another, and I got most of my estate by the same occupation. . . . My wife is a virtuous woman, the daughter of a virtuous woman; she was my Lady Feigning's daughter, therefore she came of a very honourable family, and is arrived to such a pitch of breeding, that she knows how to carry it to all, even

to prince and peasant." '   If one examines Fielding and
Smollett with Bunyan in mind, it becomes evident that
their principal characters are simply-perceived types
drawn from outside in the tradition of the Theo-
phrastian character-writing, and the minor rôles filled
up with variations on the conventional humorous and
eccentric characters of the contemporary drama.

[59] 'Wiseman: " Why, there was not any other
alteration in him than what was made by his disease
upon his body.   Sickness, you know, will alter the
body, also pains and stitches will make men groan ; but
for his mind he had no alteration there.   His mind was
the same, his heart was the same.   He was the self-
same Mr. Badman still.   Not only in name but conditions, and that to the very day of his death ; yea, so
far as could be gathered, to the very moment in which
he died."

' Attentive : " Pray, how was he in his death ? Was
death strong upon him ? Or did he die with ease,
quietly ? "

' Wiseman : " As quietly as a lamb.   There seemed
not to be in it, to standers by, so much as a strong
struggle of nature.   And as for his mind, it seemed to
be wholly at quiet." '

The deliberate sacrifice of an obvious ' lesson ' here
may be contrasted with Richardson in similar circumstances—for instance, the death of the bawd Mrs.
Sinclair in *Clarissa*.

[60] Similarly Roxana declares : ' Sir Robert and I
agreed exactly in our notions of a merchant.   Sir
Robert said, and I found it to be true, that a true-bred
merchant is the best gentleman in the nation ; that in
knowledge, in manners, in judgement of things, the
merchant outdid many of the nobility.'   This is an
interesting illustration of the point made below that
Defoe's position was more complicated than that of

the cynically conscious journalist of Part I. Chap. II.
The feeling that produced the passage ' a true-bred
merchant is the best gentleman in the nation ' was
obviously genuine, though the passage was put in for
strictly business reasons.   And the ideal of the true-
bred merchant is a dignified and respectable one.

[61] ' I must say he was a grave, sober, pious, and
most religious person ;   exact in his life, extensive in
his charity, and exemplary in almost everything he did.
What, then, can one say against my being very sensible
of the value of such a man notwithstanding his profession, though it may be my opinion, perhaps, as well as
the opinion of others who shall read this, that he was
mistaken? . . . he was not the first Catholic that I
had conversed with without falling into any incon-
veniences . . . as he was of a most obliging gentleman-
like behaviour, so he was, if I may be allowed to say
so, a man of good sense, and, as I believe, of great
learning.'—*Robinson Crusoe*, Part II.

[62] ' . . . our Spaniards, who were (to give them a
just character) men of the best behaviour, of the most
calm, sedate tempers, and perfect good humour, that
ever I met with. . . . Then the Englishmen asked the
Spaniards if they designed to take any of them? [the
women].   But every one answered, No : some of them
said they had wives in Spain ; and the others did not
like women that were not Christians ; and all together
declared, that they would not touch one of them ;
which was an instance of such virtue as I have not met
with in all my travels ' . . . ' the Spaniard governor,
who was the most gentleman-like, generous-minded
man, that ever I met with in my life.'—*Ibid*.

[63] Cf. Roxana : ' And let nobody conclude from the
strange success I met with in all my wicked doings, and
the vast estate which I had raised by it, that therefore
I either was happy or easy.   No, no, there was a dart

stuck into the liver; there was a secret hell within,' etc.
But it is not very convincing, and probably neither
author nor reader cared that it should be; all that
mattered was that the decencies were observed, and the
reader could continue to identify herself with the
heroine without any doubts as to the moral efficacy of
the book.

64 ' I have just been propounding to Forster if it is
not a wonderful testimony to the homely force of truth,
that one of the most popular books on earth has nothing
in it to make any one laugh or cry. Yet I think with
some confidence that you never did either over any
passage in *Robinson Crusoe*.'

65 That is to say, *Robinson Crusoe*, Cook's *Voyages*,
Anson's *Voyage Round the World*—among the most
popular books of the age.

66 The civilising influence of Methodism in the
eighteenth century can hardly be exaggerated. Besides
doing the work of the Salvation Army kind at the
lowest level—turning brutes into decent citizens—it
was directly a cultural force, the equivalent of the Scot's
Calvinism described by the Ettrick Shepherd when he
protested against the proposed measures for ' educating ' the rural population (*Noctes Ambrosianæ*, April
1826), asserting that ' kintra folk in Scotland hae a', or
maistly a', gude education already. What will you
think, when I tell you that in Ettrick there are three
debatin' societies? . . . they're a' young chiels, and
they debate about doctrinal points o' religion and
morals, and subjects interesting to men as members and
heads o' families. They are a' Calvinistic, and no
sceptical—but on the contrar, they haud to the Scrip-
tures. They are a' gude kirk-goers, and keep a sharp
ee on the minister in the pulpit.' Cf. Lackington on
the influence of Methodism : ' It was by their preaching that I was taught to call upon God for his grace

to enable me to turn from my vicious course of life, and through which I became a real Christian. It was by their means also that I was excited to improve a little my intellectual faculties . . . and it is well known that many, very many, instances of the same kind might be adduced ' (*Sequel to the Life of James Lackington*).

⁶⁷ *Vide* the violently Tory Matthias : ' We are no longer in an age of ignorance ; and information is not partially distributed according to the ranks, and orders, and functions, and dignities of social life. I am scarcely able to name any man whom I consider as wholly ignorant. Our peasantry now read the *Rights of Man* on mountains, and moors, and by the way side.' —*Preface to the Fourth and Last Dialogue of the Pursuits of Literature* (1797).

⁶⁸ The degree of self-education incidental to a specific interest in theology appears to account for the remarkable civilisation of the Scottish poor in the last century. A vivid account of the social life of the poorest quarter of Edinburgh in 1815 is given by William Chambers in his *Memoir of William and Robert Chambers*, Chap. iv. : ' In the evenings, when mason and carpenter lads dropped in, the conversation turned chiefly on sermons. Each visitor brought with him experiences as to how texts had been handled on the preceding Sunday ; on which there ensued discussions singularly characteristic of a well-known phase in the Scotch mind,' etc. The well-known and century-old ambition of every poor Scotch family to have a son in the Church led to a general dissemination of culture that is perhaps the most pleasing result of the Puritan conscience. To take one instance out of a host—Eliza Fletcher's account of her summer in the Highlands in 1820, with its ' pleasant intercourse with Farmer Buchanan, whose character had more of the Lowland than of the Highland type. He was a very fine speci-

men of human nature, and we used to enjoy a talk with
him much when he was binding up his sheaves, or
when the labours of the day were over he returned to
his cottage and the enjoyment of his books. His knowledge of what was passing in the literary world was
kept up by his five sons, who had all been distinguished
students at Glasgow College. The only one who had
not shewn any thirst for knowledge assisted him in his
farm. The others had all been sent off with their
winter supply of potatoes and meal to Glasgow, where,
after the first year, they never cost their parents anything, being able to save by summer private tuition
what defrayed their expenses in winter. Farmer
Buchanan's eldest son afterwards became Professor of
Logic at Glasgow College. . . . One of the old man's
chief pleasures we found to be reading Milton, and so
great a master was he of Gaelic lore that he had translated several books of *Paradise Lost* into Gaelic verse.'

[69] Addison's list of Leonora's library in *Spectator 37*
(1711) includes only these novels: *Cassandra, Cleopatra* (Calprenède); *Astræa* (d'Urfé); Sydney's
Arcadia; *The Grand Cyrus* and *Clelia* (Mlle. de
Scudéry); Mrs. Manley's *New Atlantis*; and one
of the numerous collections of novels of the day.

[70] Agnes de Castro in the novel so called is described
simply as ' beautiful to excess, wise, discreet, witty,'
Don Sebastian in *The Nun* as ' of a sweet conversation,'
Miranda in *The Fair Jilt* as ' tall and admirably shaped ;
she had bright hair and hazel eyes, all full of love and
sweetness. She had an air, though gay as so much
youth could inspire, yet so modest, so nobly reserved,
without formality, or stiffness, that one who looked on
her would have imagined her soul the twin-angel of her
body. To this she had a great deal of wit, read much,
and retained all that served her purpose. She sang
delicately, and danced well, and played on her lute to a

miracle. She spoke several languages naturally; for being co-heiress to so great a fortune, she was bred with the nicest care, in all the finest manners of education; and was now arrived to her eighteenth year.'

[71] Vide *Tatler 204*: 'We writers of diurnals are nearer in our styles to that of common talk than any other writers'; and in *Tatler 5* Isaac Bickerstaff explains that 'the nature of my miscellaneous work' demands that he be given a licence for 'writing in an air of common speech.'

[72] Considering that it was taken by all the coffee-houses, and so passed through scores of hands in each. The coffee-houses were the channels by which culture was disseminated, and by 1715 there were nearly two thousand in London alone, ' and by them, and in them, every class, profession, trade, calling, occupation, and shade of political opinion was fully represented' (Sydney, *England and the English in the Eighteenth Century*, Vol. 1. p. 816). As late as 1754 the writer of the first number of *The Connoisseur*, giving ' a view of The Town,' confines himself to the coffee-houses.

[73] Typical names of her novels: *The Fatal Secret; or, Constancy in Distress, Persecuted Virtue, Constancy Rewarded, The Agreeable Caledonian, The Unequal Conflict; or, Nature Triumphant, The Capricious Lover; or, No Trifling with a Woman*. These may be set off against the type-titles of twentieth-century popular fiction quoted on p. 54. The appeal made by Mrs. Haywood's titles is not infrequently to a frank interest in the amorous, but she never exploits a sensual response, and is extremely practical and matter-of-fact (like Richardson and Defoe) even in her earlier manner. There is, in fact, a sort of unromantic directness about such titles as *Love in Excess*, and *The Power of Love in Seven Novels* (Mrs. Manley); they completely lack the suggestiveness of the typical film-title—e.g. *Man, Woman*

and Sin, The Call of the Flesh—and so are free from the
nastiness that comes from invoking the Puritan sense
of sin to spice a surreptitious taste for the erotic, visible
in the modern bestseller and film.

[74] More explicit references are to be found scattered
through Jane Austen's novels than anywhere else,
except in Addison's essays, e.g. *Emma*, Chap. xx.:
' Living constantly with right-minded and well-
informed people, her heart and understanding had
received every advantage of discipline and culture.'
It is essentially a social ideal in which conversation
played an important part.   One cannot read any novel
of Jane Austen's without constantly meeting references
to the rôle of conversation as a recognised social pastime
and therefore an accomplishment. ' " My idea of good
company is the company of clever, well-informed
people, who have a great deal of conversation " '
(*Persuasion*, Chap. xvi.). ' Their powers of conversation were considerable ' (*Pride and Prejudice*) is high
praise, and ' He has no conversation ' damning.   In
1853 ' conversation ' still held its place—a high one—
in the approved methods of using leisure : Philip in
The Heir of Redclyffe says solemnly of an undesirable
relative, ' " I am convinced that he does not know what
conversation is." '   William Hutton (one of the self-
educated writers discussed in the previous chapter)
writes in his *History of Derby* (1791) of the recreations
of the town, that for ' the more refined ranks ' recreation ' consists in conversation, which is much cultivated
here by small clubs or societies in nocturnal meetings.
In these well regulated associations are united entertainment and improvement.   To converse with the dead
is the next pleasure to that of conversing with the
living ; both form the man.   This pleasure is well
known in Derby.   Men of reading not alone abound,
but there are many book societies who keep pace with

the press.' The positive ideal of self-discipline and austerity implied in the phrase ' a well-regulated mind ' survived through the last century, as witness casual phrases in the novels—*e.g.* ' the misery of ill-regulated feelings and of incapacity for mental exercise ' (*Modern Accomplishments ; or, the March of Intellect*, by Catherine Sinclair, dedicated to Queen Victoria).

[75] Coleridge noticed the change of taste as he noticed nearly everything. ' Walter Scott's poems and novels supply both instance and solution of the present conditions and components of popularity, viz. to amuse without requiring any effort of thought, and without exciting any deep emotion. . . . Compare *Waverley, Guy Mannering, and Co.*, with works that had an *immediate run* in the last generation, *Tristram Shandy, Roderick Random, Sir Charles Grandison, Clarissa Harlowe*, and *Tom Jones* (all which became popular as soon as published, and therefore instances fairly in point), and you will be convinced that the difference of taste is real, and not any fancy or croaking of my own ' (January 1821. *Allsop's Letters, Conversations and Recollections of S. T. Coleridge*).

[76] There is no room to support this statement, but any one who thinks of the weary expanses of Scott's historical scenes, especially the dialogue, and compares their effect on him with the pleasingly (though rather stilted) eighteenth-century conversation in *Udolpho*, will no doubt agree. If not, let him consider the family history of the historical novel, not merely the Westward Hos and Richards Yea-and-Nay but the Jeffery Farnols and Baroness Orczys, and finally such indisputable offspring as the following advertisement :

' *Where Shakespeare told his love*

' Shakespeare was a poet who got in some good lines, but he wasn't writing poetry all the time. He fell

in love with Anne Hathaway, and used to sit in the
chimney corner with her. Wouldn't it be great to
know what Shakespeare said to her, what was the tale
that Shakespeare told his love. Go to Stratford and
sit in the corner where Shakespeare sat and feel your
spirit lift at the touch of an Immortal.' [L.M.S.R.]

77 This illuminating anecdote is related in Lockhart's shorter *Life*, Chap. XII. The old lady concluded : ' But is it not a very odd thing that I, an old
woman of eighty and upwards, sitting alone, feel myself ashamed to read a book which sixty years ago I
have read aloud for the amusement of large circles,
consisting of the first and most creditable society in
London?' So *Clarissa* was read aloud, and abandoned
in its turn. In 1863 Charles Knight, writing of a
project of his early publishing days, forty years or so
earlier, for reprinting ' Great Writers in a Volume,'
says : ' It was well for me that this project was not
matured into a costly series, for it would not have commanded a remunerative sale. There are some works of
imagination that are almost unknown to the present
race of readers. Who can avoid lamenting that *Tom
Jones*, and *Roderick Random*, and *Tristram Shandy* are
utterly gone out of the popular view?'

78 ' Now, had the same young lady been engaged
with a volume of *The Spectator*, instead of such a work,
how proudly would she have produced the book, and
told its name! though the chances must be against her
being occupied by any part of that voluminous publication of which either the matter or manner would not
disgust a young person of taste . . . and their
language, too, frequently so coarse as to give no
very favourable idea of the age that could endure
it.'—*Northanger Abbey*.

79 *Vide* the Everyman Edition (1931) of *The Mysteries of Udolpho*, for which a detective novelist was

L

selected to write an introduction. It maintains an apologetic note. To compare the degree of effectiveness of Mrs. Radcliffe's novel and R. Austin Freeman's is a useful exercise.

⁸⁰ *E.g.* ' " Betsy has just lost as good an offer as any girl could desire, young Wilson, an honest substantial grazier as any in the country. He not only knows everything proper for his station, but is pleasing in his behaviour, and a pretty scholar into the bargain ; he reads history books and voyages of a winter's evening to his infirm father, instead of going to the card assembly in our town. . . . Well, for all this, Betty despised him and laughed at him ; but as he is both handsome and rich, I thought she might come round at last. . . . But it would not do. He scorned to talk that palavering stuff which she had been used to in the marble covered [circulating library] books I told you of. He told her, indeed, that it would be the happiness of his heart to live with her, which I own I thought was as much as could be expected of any man. But Miss had no notion of marrying one who was only desirous of living with her. No, no, forsooth, her lover must declare himself ready to die for her, which honest Wilson was not such a fool as to offer to do." '—*The Two Wealthy Farmers*.

⁸¹ For the next twenty or thirty years the Cheap Repository was ' the principal part of many an English cottager's library ' (*Life of Hannah More*, Henry Thompson, 1838, p. 50), and ' the staple light literature in such orthodox village lending libraries as existed ' (*Hannah More*, Charlotte Yonge, p. 122).

⁸² I am aware that this is a highly controversial subject, and that some historians maintain that the loss of the commons meant little to the peasant. Statistics on this point are of little value, but the more sensitive kind of evidence offered by such a detailed study as George

Bourne's *Change in the Village* shows conclusively that in some districts at any rate a whole popular culture was destroyed by the enclosure of the commons. Whether the peasant was better off or not as a farm-labourer from a material point of view does not matter (and actually he was not in most cases).

[83] *Vivian Grey*, Disraeli (1826); *Granby*, Henry Lister (1826); *Sayings and Doings*, Theodore Hook (1826-29); *Tremaine, or, The Man of Refinement*, Robert Plumer Ward (1825); *Pelham*, Lytton (1827); *Mothers and Daughters*, Mrs. Gore (1831). All these bestsellers were necessarily confined to the well-to-do, until Routledge's Railway Library issued *Pelham* at 1s. 6d. in 1853.

[84] 'In 1866 and '67 *The Last Chronicles of Barset* was brought out by George Smith in sixpenny monthly numbers. I do not know that this mode of publication had been tried before, or that it answered very well on this occasion. Indeed, the shilling magazines had interfered greatly with the success of novels published in numbers without other accompanying matter. The public, finding that so much might be had for a shilling, in which a portion of one or more novels was always included, were unwilling to spend their money on the novel alone. Feeling that this certainly had become the case in reference to novels published in shilling numbers, Mr. Smith and I determined to make the experiment with sixpenny parts. If I remember right, the enterprise was not wholly successful.'—Trollope's *Autobiography*, Chap. xv.

[85] Matthias, writing in 1797 (*The Pursuits of Literature*), pillories the popular novel as 'Travels for the Heart, and not the head,' and appends a footnote to 'Travels for the Heart': 'All such works as abound in what is called in modern jargon, the sublime instinct of sentiment.'

[86] The sales of Lytton's *Pelham* are suggestive. It was first issued in 1828 in 3 vols. at 31s. 6d. by Colburn. Routledge's published their 1s. 6d. Railway Edition in 1853, and in five years it sold 46,000 copies; the 2s. Railway Library Edition of 1859 sold 35,750 in thirty-four years, the 2s. 6d. Standard Edition sold 4000 from 1861 to 1874, a 3s. 6d. edition in 1873 sold 21,250 in twenty years, another 1s. Railway Edition in 1878 sold 4000, a 7s. 6d. Library Edition in 1877 sold 2260 in eleven years, the Shilling Pocket Edition in 1886 sold 20,000 in one year, the Sixpenny Edition from 1879 to 1890 sold 66,000. That is to say, of a not very popular novel and after the circulating libraries and immediate demand were supplied, nearly 200,000 copies were sold at 3s. 6d. or less twenty-five to sixty-five years after it had been published.

[87] From mid-nineteenth century onwards an arrangement existed ' between certain publishers and the libraries by which the latter bought at least a fixed number of every novel issued by them. This sale nearly covered the cost of production, and generally relieved the publisher from any possibility of loss. The publisher being thus largely secured, was more ready to speculate in the work of a new author than he is to-day. By the present form in which a novel is issued the publisher must sell nearly ten times more to recoup his outlay than was necessary in the old three-volume days ' (' The Issue of Fiction,' by Joseph Shaylor, *Publishers' Circular*, October 15th, 1910). And in 1930 the outlay is very much greater than it was in 1910.

[88] *Adam Bede* ' put her at once and permanently beyond the reach of any pecuniary pressure ' (Leslie Stephen). *Middlemarch* brought her £12,000.

[89] Mr. E. H. Lacon Watson, who as a journalist and novelist speaks with some authority, writes of the con-

tinuation of this process whereby cheap re-issues of popular fiction destroy the livelihood of the novelist of the few : ' The fact is, that in recent years every change that has been made in the world of publishing and bookselling has been in favour of the few big sellers and against the author with a small, if select, audience. The cheap sixpenny and sevenpenny editions that we had before the war were all to the good of the popular writer : they gave his novels another lease of life, and himself another set of royalties. More than this, they assisted in spreading his name and fame among a class of readers whom he had perhaps not reached before. But these cheap novels, excellently produced as they were, and eagerly welcomed by the railway traveller and the lover of fiction who could not afford to buy crown octavo volumes at 6s. apiece, got sadly in the way of the less successful novelist who was accustomed to receive his fifty or a hundred pounds down in advance on account of royalties. Now that prices of novels are beginning to rise again, it is possible that his lot may become easier, but I doubt it. The cost of production has increased also, to such a degree that publishers look askance at any author who can only claim a small following. I have often wondered how some of our great novelists of the past would have fared if they had been born in the present age of cheap books. Meredith himself, for example. He had the fortune to produce most of his early fiction under the old system of the three-volume novel—a system that ensured some monetary return for good though not necessarily popular work. If a new Meredith were to arise to-day it is not impossible that publishers would get tired of producing his books at a loss before he had succeeded in educating a sufficient section of the reading public into a proper and profitable appreciation of his genius.'—*Lectures on Dead Authors.*

[90] ' In my boyhood I was brought up among plenty of people of the poorer sort, whose childhood dated from before the Act of 1870. Some were illiterate; but the number who could read was not very much less than it is to-day. But, anyhow, the older England was not illiterate. Of the dependants about my relatives all read the Bible; many the *Pilgrim's Progress*. The difference between the old England and the newer England is that people have by now fallen into a habit of *perpetual* reading, which in the better days the great mass of English men and women did not.'—Hilaire Belloc, *New Statesman*, March 29th, 1930.

[91] A selection from the coinages made by one contemporary bestseller: sex-instinct, sex-essence, sex-distrust, sex-awareness, sex-thrill, sex-duty, anti-sex resolutions, sex-thrilled, sex-foolish, sex-fool, sex-desire, sex-abyss, sex-craving, sex-issue, sex-outlook, sex-lesson, passion-hot moment, passion-cold. Most of these are used more than once in the pages of *Life— and Erica*, *Gerald Cranston's Lady*, and *Masterson : A Story of an English Gentleman*. But over against them ought perhaps to be set this sentence from the first-named novel : ' Sexless as a schoolboy, she looked into the future.'

[92] Consider the history of John Passmore Edwards (b. 1823), son of a carpenter, who eventually made a fortune by buying the *Echo*, and founded 26 public libraries, 9 hospitals, 3 art galleries, and many charitable institutions. In his reminiscences, *A Few Footprints* (1906), he published his credo :

' I BELIEVE

' I believe, with Shakespeare, that a divinity is shaping our ends, rough hew them how we will, and that " Heaven hath a hand in all "; with Schiller, that " Justice is the keystone of the world's wide arch, sustaining and sustained by all " ; with Elizabeth Barrett Browning, that "no lily-muffled hum of summer bee but finds· some coupling with the spinning stars " ; with Herbert Spencer, that . . .; with Mazzini, that "the word Progress, unknown to antiquity, is destined henceforth to be a sacred word to Humanity, as in it is indicated an entire social, political and religious transformation " ; with Thomas Carlyle, " that modern majesty consists in work " ; with Victor Hugo . . .; with Frederic Harrison . . .; with J. S. Mill . . .; with Emerson, that " there will be a new Church founded . . . that will have heaven and earth for its beams and rafters, and service for symbol and illustration " ; with Humboldt . . .; with Longfellow . . .; with Spinoza . . .; with Ruskin . . .; and with Tennyson, who " doubts not through the ages one increasing purpose runs, and the thoughts of men are widened with the process of the suns " ; and that " the face of Death is turned towards the Sun of Life." '

[93] Appended to a memoir of Marie Corelli by her companion Bertha Vyver is ' A Personal Tribute ' by J. Cuming Walters, in which the following occurs : ' It was only an advocate of purity and of the higher life, a believer in the divinity of the overruling purpose and in the uplift of the race, who could have set herself the mission of preaching against desecration and debasement.' An Oxford undergraduate wrote to her : ' Your immense popularity is the result, as it seems to me, of your originality and sincerity, your passionate appeals to the people's feelings (which, often unlike their opinions, have always truth in them) combined with dramatic power, are directed on the points which at present most nearly touch the hearts, as, for instance, the vague impression that science is overthrowing religion and the best hopes of man.'

[94] *Vide*, for instance, the first of the ' Letters to the Industrious Classes ' (*Reynolds' Miscellany*, Vol. 1., No. 12), in which, pending his address on the slogan ' the discontent which is based on reason and justice,' Reynolds urges that ' the millions have a right to *something which they have not got*, and which is sure to be unfolded to them by the book of education. . . . You are intelligent and enlightened by *self*-education (no thanks to the State !) ; whereas, fifty years ago, not one of your class was able to read, where now a hundred can not only read and write fluently, but are also possessed of much useful information and miscellaneous knowledge. Is it not, then, a sin to withhold from you, or to attempt to withhold, any means of intellectual improvement which it may be in the power of the wealthy and great to afford ? ' etc. Compulsory elementary education set going our neat system of examinations and ' subjects ' which replaced the old vague ideal of a liberal education. The new ideal can be studied in *Love and Mr. Lewisham*, or less directly in any other of the works of Mr. H. G. Wells.

[95] How primitive and amateur his technique was may be gathered from the following (pitying) quotation from a modern journalist and advertising expert : ' The headlines were often picturesquely worded, though the type was modest. Even the greatest stroke of his career, " The Maiden Tribute of Modern Babylon," was not heralded with bold captions. The first of a series of articles that produced an unparalleled sensation in the country was begun a few lines from the foot of a column. Imagine an editor of to-day, even of the most conservative paper, tucking away his biggest feature in the bottom corner of a page ! ' (Harold Herd, *The Making of Modern Journalism*, p. 26). When Northcliffe took over the *Times* in 1908 he found it necessary to make such elementary alterations in the

make-up as fixed places for the regular features and proper sequence, according to the same authority.

[96] Soon after *Tit-Bits* had established itself, he is reported to have said to Max Pemberton : ' The Board Schools are turning out hundreds of thousands of boys and girls annually who are anxious to read. They do not care for the ordinary newspaper. The man who has produced this *Tit-Bits* has got hold of a bigger thing than he imagines. He is only at the very beginning of a development which is going to change the whole face of journalism.'

[97] ' One of the many fallacies associated with Fleet Street in the mind of the outside world is that journalism requires a high standard of education and ability.'—Michael Joseph, *Journalism for Profit.*

[98] He is, of course, his own advertising agent as well ; journalism has learnt a good deal from the art of advertising, but advertising had first to catch up with journalism, which had consciously been practising the principles of copywriting since Northcliffe broke into Fleet Street. *Vide*, for instance, his—or his brother's—insistence on ' human stories only,' the definition of a human story being, ' If there is a fire in the City and £5000 worth of merchandise is burnt, that's a news item worth three lines. But if at the same fire a fireman risks his life to rescue a black kitten from the top story—that's a human touch worth half a column.'

[99] I am indebted for my acquaintance with the business side of the process to Vol. ii. of the Labour Research Department Studies in Labour and Capital— *The Press* (1922). The influence of the modern Press on society, though chiefly in its political bearing, is admirably discussed by Norman Angell in *The Press and the Organisation of Society* (1922). A naïvely uncritical and therefore peculiarly valuable account of the

new Press is to be found in Harold Herd's *The Making of Modern Journalism* ['The romantic story of the re-making of British Journalism readably told'] (1926), the author being the Principal of the Regent Institute (which teaches journalism and short-story writing) and author of text-books on advertising. An equally naïve biography of Northcliffe by one of his staff, to which frequent reference has been made in this chapter, is of great anthropological interest, and Tom Clarke's *My Northcliffe Diary* (1931) is another illuminating document.

[100] Northcliffe, being the Napoleon of the Press, naturally disliked having to play second fiddle to the advertiser, but Hamilton Fyfe notes the effect on his papers of the growing power of the Advertising Director, against which he was helpless.

[101] 'He [Northcliffe] discovers how easy it is to work up public interest. He notes that the mass of people have no tastes of their own ; they will adopt any that fall in their way. Give them a great deal to read about any topic within their comprehension : they will think they are getting what they want, will ask for more. . . . What he and K. J. have discovered, what they are exploiting, is the docility of the public : its lack of ideas. They can compel it to be interested in this or in that. Football, for example. That has been an interest for a small number, for those who could go to see matches played, for staunch supporters of the various teams. The newspaper can make football interest an enormous number. Not only by printing a great deal of news and gossip about the game, but by competitions for money prizes.'—Hamilton Fyfe, *op. cit.*, p. 65.

[102] When Northcliffe edited the New York *World* for one day, 'the style which he asked the staff to follow was that of what he called "tabloid journalism." No

piece of news was to be given at greater length than
250 words. No pictures were admitted, which showed
that for once his instinct was faulty : he did not foresee
that tabloid treatment of newspaper topics would cause
a desire to grow for " something to look at " in place
of " something to read." '—Hamilton Fyfe, *op. cit.*,
p. 156.

[103] *Vide* Fremantle's account of the level of intelligence in the early nineteenth century (*England in
the Nineteenth Century*, 1801-05, pp. 96-98): ' No
country in the world had so well-informed a middle
class. Higher in the scale, the quintessence of
intelligence was fully developed. It was a society
which worshipped wit . . . a standard was set up. . . .
The leading public men of the day, Pitt, Fox, Wynd-
ham, Wilberforce, and above all Sheridan, were noted
for the good things they said.' ' When and how the
governing classes received their high intellectual equipment it is not easy to see,' Fremantle confesses. And
he goes on to say that at schools and universities they
seemed to do nothing, though ' the precocity of the
youth of that age was, indeed, remarkable.' The
explanation perhaps is that a real intellectual life
animated the educated classes. There was, for instance,
a cultivated Parliament. And the upper class showed
their interest in letters by surrounding themselves with
the literary figures of their time. Lytton in *Eugene
Aram* pays the governing class a lengthy compliment
on their intellectual attainments which nowadays would
be ludicrous, but a sounder witness is Moore, who in
his diary records (April 28th, 1831) his opinion that
' in high life one met the best (*i.e.* most intelligent)
society,' and gives a list of above a dozen peers who
are striking testimony to his argument.

' The recognised defect of the Public Schools in the
reign of George III. was a moral rather than an intel-

lectual one ; Arnold's intense earnestness of character and fidelity to principles became great agencies in transforming the life, not only of Rugby, but of the Public School group. The Clarendon Commission of 1861-64 noted the moral change that had passed over these schools within the preceding generation ; it affected the proprietary schools which were being founded in the latter part of Arnold's life, and subsequently it passed through Rugby boys to Oxford and Cambridge and so to English education as a whole.' (J. W. Adamson, *English Education 1789-1902*, p. 67.)

One of the B novelists replying to the questionnaire (*vide* Part I. Chap. III.), wrote : ' I once asked D. H. Lawrence if he realised how grateful he should be for not being hampered by the impedimenta of a public school and University education.'

[104] No better anemometer than the new (Fourteenth) edition of the *Encyclopædia Britannica* could be found. Part of the advertising matter announces, under the heading ' Anticipates Better Salesmanship,' that ' The New Edition of the *Britannica* is a business man's Encyclopædia.'

[105] Cf. advice to copy-writers by English advertising agents and journalists, *e.g.* ' When writing think of the masses. Practise Mass Psychology ' (*An Outline of Advertising*, Elwyn O. Hughes). ' Advertisement Copy is rooted in human nature. It ought to be plain even to the inexperienced that successful copywriting depends upon insight into people's minds ; not into individual minds, mark, but into the way average people think and act and the way they react to suggestions of various kinds ' (*Advertisement Writing*, Gilbert Russell). The close connection between fiction and copy-writing is brought out in Sir Wm. Crawford's (of Crawford's Advertising Agency) injunction to read the Bible, Kipling, and Stevenson, because ' they know

how to touch the human heart,' and Gilbert Russell who for the same reason recommends for ' A Copywriter's Bookshelf ' Shakespeare, C. E. Montague, the Bible, Macaulay's *Essays*, *The Art of Writing*, and dictionaries of quotations and similes, and adds : ' What you have to remember is that, for the most part, your public is the great middle class. What kind of reading does the great middle class prefer? It buys " bestsellers " in enormous quantities. You must not write such slipshod stuff. But what you write must be not so very far removed from it.'

The copywriter employs ' mass psychology ' when he announces that the Right People or the Best People smoke—cigarettes, wear—linings to their coats, etc., or that ' Everyone is reading—.' A somewhat more subtle case is an advertisement that appeared recently :

' A Book for the Few,
120th thousand.'

[106] About five thousand churches now exhibit Wayside Pulpit posters. *Vide* the *Advertising World*, December 1925, for an article by the Church Publicity Secretary on ' How the Wayside Pulpit Scheme was Organised ': ' At the Church Advertising Section of the great World's Advertising Convention at Wembley, I had met leading Americans who ran big Church advertising movements in the States. Their enthusiasm was infectious, and their charts, diagrams and statistics, inspiring,' etc. *Vide* booklets published by the Church Publicity Section of the National Free Church Council, especially ' The Wayside Pulpit at Work,' for evidence of the success of ' this result-bringing enterprise.' The same organisation issues a ' *Free Churchman* inset ' which helps to make ' a bright, homely and thoroughly alive Church Magazine,' for ' however well edited the local pages of a Church Magazine may be, if an inset

is commonplace, narrow in outlook and lacking the bright journalistic touch that the public is accustomed to in modern popular journals, the Magazine will fail to " grip " ' (from the Publication Department Report presented to the Annual Assembly of the National Free Church Council, 1930). It also circulates ' " Worth While " Leaflets.' The activities of the Church Publicity Department form a record of the influence of journalism on the modern Church. Apart from the idiom, which may equally well derive from the Press, I can find no particular trace of transatlantic influence beyond the initial impulse referred to. The significance of the form the movement has taken lies in the fact that it might equally well have been home-grown. It is a beautiful instance of the workings of the herd instinct. The success of Rotary in England was made possible only by the breakdown of a social and religious tradition.

[107] Cf. the change of national character which modern business methods are rapidly effecting. The 1929 Interim Report of the Committee on Education for Salesmanship devotes a chapter to ' The Salesman '; its implications may be gathered from the following extract : ' The importance, in a modern phrase, of being " a good mixer " is emphasised by a large number of witnesses from very different countries, both new and old. . . . This remark is supported by an interesting article in a recent issue of the *River Plate Review* which lays stress on the importance of " the combined virtues of personality and appearance, the height of merit [being] a certain affability—even effusiveness— . . . and a consistent habit of looking at the bright side of life in general." ' The virtues of being ' a good mixer ' and ' voting the good-fellow ticket ' have acquired value in other worlds than that of business— for instance, in academic circles.

[108] ' *Punch's* attitude seldom caused much surprise, for his opinions and views could generally be foretold. It was the manner in which they were put forth that carried weight and influence ' (M. H. Spielman, *The History of ' Punch.'*). ' The fault here, as always, lies in regarding *Punch* as a comic journal ; it has lived and thrived and prospered where others have wilted and decayed by making itself first and foremost a picture news-book. . . . Said a friend once to me—and he had lived for many years in India—with whom I was discussing the question : " You would hardly credit the number of times when in India I was referred by my people at home to some joke in *Punch* as typical of the spirit in which they were carrying on during a crisis." ' (Kennedy Jones, *Fleet Street and Downing Street.*)

[109] For instance, when the values of the minority were prevalent there was a sanction behind self-cultivation. Round about 1840 working-men all over the country themselves formed and named Mutual Improvement Societies, shopkeepers and skilled artisans enthusiastically joined Athenæums, and Philosophical Institutions flourished even in such an unlikely place as Mile End. [These continued in many cases till the 'eighties and 'nineties and even later, when they degenerated into amusement-halls for billiards, dancing, and whist drives. The history of this movement and its end has yet to be written.] There was apparently no self-consciousness about the somewhat pathetic nomenclature. Cf. too the titles of the ordinary successful magazines of the late eighteenth century, *e.g. Westminster Magazine, or Pantheon of Taste, Town and Country Magazine, or Universal Repository of Knowledge, Instruction and Entertainment.* It was this sanction, the sympathetic atmosphere, that made possible the histories of Lackington, Samuel Drew, and others mentioned in Part II. Chap. II. The influence of the con-

temporary environment is in the opposite direction ; a complaint made by a young man in an educational office is typical : ' If you try to improve yourself or read books that you think will be educational, they say, " Well, thank God, *I'm* a damn good Philistine ! " '

[110] *Vide* the burst of hostility that greets an exhibition of Epstein's work, which to the rational mind would seem quite uncalled for, since no one need see it unless he chooses. But see the vindictive correspondence on the subject in the *New Statesman and Nation* during April and May 1931. The anti-highbrow attitude to criticism can be studied in the article ' Criticism ' by an eminent belletrist in Vol. III. No. 18, of *Life and Letters.*

[111] Kipling is actually mentioned by Gilbert Russell (*Advertisement Writing*) as having the natural gifts required in a copywriter, above all ' the ability to introduce into his writing a note of authority and " knowledgeableness." ' ' Of two suggestions, that which the more perfectly embodies the voice of the herd is the more acceptable. The chances an affirmation has of being accepted could therefore be most satisfactorily expressed in terms of the bulk of the herd by which it is backed. It follows from the foregoing that anything which dissociates a suggestion from the herd will tend to ensure such a suggestion being rejected. For example, an imperious command from an individual known to be without authority is necessarily disregarded, whereas the same person making the same suggestion in an indirect way so as to link it up with the voice of the herd will meet with success.' (W. Trotter, *Instincts of the Herd in Peace and War*, p. 33.)

[112] Appropriately value for money. The recent popularity of extremely long novels published at half a guinea (*The Forsyte Saga, A Modern Comedy, The Good*

Companions, Angel Pavement, Rogue Herries, Imperial Palace, Broome Stages, etc.) is only to be explained thus.

[113] Cf. the following advertisement taken at random from one of the luxurious women's magazines:

'FOR THOSE WHO LIVE GRACIOUSLY'

'Those who golf at St. Andrews . . . grouse hunt on the Scotch moors . . . shop in the Rue de la Paix . . . sun themselves on the shores of the Mediterranean . . . those who live graciously, are fastidious in their choice of ships. They are in that discriminating coterie of travellers who invariably sail on the Majestic (world's largest ship).'

It is in this way that the standard and aims of living of the majority are changed.

[114] Cf. note 74; and *vide* the eighteenth-century inscriptions in Westminster Abbey, which testify to the strength of a mode of thinking and living now extinct. A characteristic ending: ' In him strong natural parts and the love of justice and humanity improved by education formed the valuable character of a good man.'—Epitaph on William Wragge.

[115] That the public knows what it wants is made evident from the titles and advertisements of novels seeking bestseller success. A sedate or unromantic title is likely to damn a novel or film which might otherwise have had a large public, *e.g.* : ' It was unfortunate that Griffith should have chosen so essentially abstract a word as " Intolerance " for the title of his most ambitious film. It was unfortunate from the commercial standpoint, that is ; for if we disregard the box office, we shall find that the word " Intolerance " constitutes a very good title indeed ' (R. P. Messel, *This Film Business,* p. 96). Whereas novels in the early nineteenth century would be called *Patronage* or *Per-*

suasion, and even in Mrs. Gore's more commercial age, *Female Domination* or *A Terrible Temptation*, unless they followed the more usual rule of being named after hero or heroine or place, in the twentieth century they must promise romance or fail. *Vide* p. 54, for variations on the type-title, *The House of Dreams-Come-True*. It is not only the great public that is thus suggestible. A kind of cultured fantasy is extremely popular with the middle-brow public—of late there has been a string of successes of this type at this level. David Garnett, to take a striking instance, may be said to owe his success to his style (*vide* pp. 36-7) and his flair for this kind of theme and title.

[116] It may be urged that in the twentietn century the machinery of advertising and publicity is employed to make the public demand what Big Business chooses to provide. And this is so of most things : the women's magazines serve to force up the standard of living (with consequent economic trouble), the Northcliffe Press created an interest in professional football (*vide* note 101), and such matters. But in fiction and films no advertiser could force a non-existent interest; what the producers do is, having discovered a latent need, to make it an active one and the satisfaction of it habitual. In this sense they do control taste, by keeping it down at the lowest level of awareness. The process at work on the film is described thus by Mr. Paul Rotha in *The Film Till Now* (1930), (*q.v.* also for the merging of gramophone-, cinema-, and film-owning companies, so that the supply of popular amusement is now practically in the hands of one organisation): ' After some consideration, I have ultimately decided (with a few notable exceptions) to regard Hollywood much as I would a factory, managed and owned by a few capable business men, who seek only large financial returns from the goods that they manufacture. . . .

Now the vagaries of public taste are well known, and it has been the constant occupation of the film producer to gauge that taste and to keep abreast with its fluctuations. But, not content with pandering to the public taste, the film producer has also set out to create public likes and dislikes by clever advertising and world-wide distribution of certain classes of films. In a business-like way the film men of Hollywood have experimented with the appetite of the public, and they are not to be blamed from a commercial point of view for having turned out stereotyped productions when the masses have shown their acceptance of such forms. When any new type of film comes from Hollywood and is successful, there quickly follows a swarm of similar but inferior pictures, trading on the reputation of the first. To the shrewd observer of the cinema, the difficulty lies in differentiating between films demanded by public taste and movies deliberately foisted upon the masses. The public does not by any means choose its own players. . . . Actually, it is simply the basic principle of advertising.'

[117] Cf. too jazz-lyrics. Useful collections of these are sold by Messrs. Woolworth as Talkie Song Books and Record Song Books.

[118] The wide use by advertisers, in order to attract, impress, and coerce, of the words ' personality,' ' creative,' ' inspiration,' is suggestive.

[119] Vide *Tristram Shandy*, Book II. Chap. xi.: ' Writing, when properly managed (as you may be sure I think mine is), is but a different name for conversation. As no one, who knows what he is about in good company, would venture to talk all :—so no author, who understands the just boundaries of decorum and good-breeding, would presume to think all : The truest respect which you can pay to the reader's understanding, is to halve this matter amicably, and leave him

x

something to imagine, in his turn, as well as yourself,' etc.

[120] A parallel example is the imposition of an ideal of photographic art on the public by means of the periodical. Any one who consults *The Pictorial Press : its Origins and Progress*, by Mason Jackson, will be agreeably impressed by the examples of woodcuts which illustrated early publications and equally distressed by the final illustrations (reproduced in all good faith). Arthur Waugh in *A Hundred Years of Publishing* (p. 190), has a useful note on an unsuccessful editor : ' When he started *Black and White*, the first plank in the programme was the restoration, in a popular illustrated weekly, of the finely executed wood-engraving ; and that in the very hour when the general public's taste had been debauched already by the spate of half-tone blocks, and by the popular doctrine that photographs must be the best pictures, since " the camera can never lie." ' As a result, the affair of the Haig memorial, for which see the correspondence that appeared in the *Times* and the comments of the popular Press.

[121] As witness the survival of the old romances as the light reading of the lower orders (Richardson makes the fire in *Clarissa* due to ' the carelessness of Mrs. Sinclair's cook-maid who, having sat up to read the simple *History of Dorastus and Faunia*,' etc.). The equally fearsome light reading of the eighteenth century survived for the lower orders of the nineteenth. *Pamela* was peddled by the number-man, Jane Eyre's nursemaid Bessy told her ' passages of love and adventure taken from old fairy tales and other ballads ; or (as at a later period I discovered) from the pages of *Pamela* and *Henry, Earl of Moreland*,' etc.

[122] In an article on advertising in *Posters and Publicity 1929* there is a discussion of what is called the

' shock value ' of the poster and how it may most successfully be used, which unconsciously suggests the
tempo of twentieth-century life. ' The shock value of
a poster,' the writer states, ' is such a very important
asset to an advertiser, that when the same shock has
been used widely, it becomes a very small shock indeed.'

[123] It is an increasing temptation, now that amusements are organised by Big Business: *e.g.* an article in
the *Film Weekly*, September 20th, 1930:

' ALL-DAY CINEMAS, PLEASE !

WHY don't cinemas open earlier?

In few districts outside the West End of London do
film programmes commence before the afternoon. In
some towns it is impossible to visit the pictures until
the evening.

Morning and afternoon picture-going is proving
increasingly popular. . . . We are glad to hear that a
movement in favour of all-day cinemas has been started
in the provinces. The custom should become universal.'

The extent to which the next generation will be
affected by these conditions may be suggested by
stating the results of an informal enquiry conducted by
the writer : elementary school teachers from industrial
areas and cities were asked whether any or what proportion of their pupils visited the cinema regularly, and
the answers were always, ' Oh, all of them, two or three
times a week,' or, ' As often as they can afford.' The
larger cinemas in some parts of England have special
1d. seats for children in the afternoon.

[124] Writers who furnish weekly essays for newspapers and periodicals develop a ' personal ' style
compounded of archaisms, whimsical phraseology, and
echoes from Lamb, Hazlitt, etc. The letters of

privates in the last war revealed this influence—' ere '
instead of ' before,' and so on.

125 ' The literary quality of advertising copy must be
kept at the high level it has reached. Authorities admit
that the best examples of modern, vigorous English are
to be found in the advertising pages of newspapers and
magazines.'—*Advertising and Selling, 1924,* p. 248.

126 The writer is inclined to suggest tentatively that
here may be an explanation of the interesting fact that
the twentieth-century public is less easily moved than
any of its predecessors. The eighteenth century, which
did not have to train itself to hold out against intensive
and scientific shock appeal, wept at *Sidney Biddulph* (*vide*
Dr. Johnson) and shuddered at Mrs. Radcliffe, stimuli
too delicate to affect the modern nervous system. It
now takes a greater stimulus than they provide to
produce any effect at all. *Mary Rose* and the fiction
recommended by the Crime Club have to work much
harder to achieve the same end. Layers of the public
from time to time become hardened to certain effects—
this is known as sophistication—and it then becomes
necessary to disguise the particular appeal by finding a
new formula for it (*e.g.* Hemingway's *A Farewell to
Arms, vide* the concluding pages). It is then described
as ' piquant.' The ironic cheers, or amusement otherwise expressed, of sophisticated cinema audiences at the
old-fashioned type of film are instructive. Cf. note 23.

127 This is not to say that we do not—and rightly—
require the author to preserve internal consistency (as
in *Wuthering Heights*), so that Masson was perfectly
justified in complaining in his *British Novelists and
their Styles* (1859): ' The very element in which the
novelist works is human nature ; yet what sort of
Psychology have we in the ordinary run of novels ? A
Psychology, if the truth must be spoken, such as would
not hold good in a world of imaginary cats.'

128 See, for instance, the account of Lord Gayton and Nancy Blow (*Mrs. Dalloway*, pp. 266-7), which the reader is regretfully obliged to conclude was not intended to be ironical. (If it is objected that they are seen through the medium of Mrs. Dalloway, a comparison with the accent which conveys her impression of Hugh Whitbread ought to decide the point.) This represents a pervasive element in *Mrs. Dalloway*, a remarkable and dazzling novel rather than a great one. But this is not to say that even the early novels of this author are not in another class altogether from those of the novelists classified as B in Part I. Chap. III.— These last will not stand consideration at all.

On the other hand, Virginia Woolf is able to bring off a far more subtle irony than Jane Austen's because of her command of a more complex technique; the presentation of Mr. Ramsay (*To the Lighthouse*, pp. 56-61) is an achievement of which Jane Austen could have no conception.

129 The immense technical progress of fiction, in the sense that means for achieving ends with the utmost economy are now taught by any school of journalism (the slickness of the magazine story and the post-war circulating library novel reveal the novel of Fielding and Dickens to be a patched-up, cumbersome, and wasteful affair), enable any one desirous of being an author to achieve his ambition by studying his predecessors.

130 Charlotte Brontë in this is in the same camp as Ethel M. Dell, and such of the novels of the immensely popular Rhoda Broughton (*Cometh Up as a Flower* (1867), 3rd ed. same year, etc.) as the writer has found time to examine are all repetitions of one another. Moreover, they have had innumerable avatars (the success of *Precious Bane* is easily explained), particularly the classic Victorian bestseller *Comin' Thro' the Rye*

(1875), but these later authors need not have read their predecessors to produce their versions, which obviously come straight from the heart.

[131] (a) and (b) are mere tissues of clichés. It would be a valuable piece of research that would trace the clichés of the Victorian and Georgian bestsellers to their sources. Where, for instance, did Florence Barclay's ' He was sobbing as only a strong man can sob ' come from originally (variant, ' He wept like a little child ')? and ' He swore softly to himself '?

[132] For example, the right way for a fascinating woman to behave, from Arnold Bennett and the magazines; the emotions proper to a manly man, from Kipling, Masefield, and Gilbert Frankau.

[133] A mild instance of the process from Florence Barclay, in which an ideal that directly conflicts with experience is none the less quite gratuitously given moral support : ' The doctor's face was grave. For a moment he looked silently into the fire. He was a man of many ideals, and foremost among them was his ideal of the relation which should be between parents and children ; of the loyalty to a mother, which, even if forced to admit faults and failings, should tenderly shield them from the knowledge or criticism of outsiders. It hurt him, as a sacrilege, to hear a daughter speak thus of her mother ; yet he knew well, from facts which were common knowledge, how little cause the sweet, lovable woman at his side had to consider the tie either a sacred or a tender one ' (*The Mistress of Shenstone*). A whole line of novels, from *The Way of All Flesh* (begun 1873) to *Death of a Hero* (1929), have been provoked as a reaction against this sort of thing, and though no doubt healthier than the bestsellers have no more relation to art than they.

[134] The enormous sales of the writings of Marie Stopes show conclusively that a considerable part of the

community requires elementary advice (and takes it without flinching at the level and in the idiom of the C novelist—I am not thinking of the medical or moral problem) on the most elementary and essential matters of emotional conduct. I could find no more convincing proof of the incapacity of the twentieth century to manage its emotional life for itself.

[135] A note on *Gallions Reach* seems called for. Though the 'thoughts' are lame enough taken in this way, they are found impressive in their context by suitable readers. In some ways the author is a distinguished writer—at that level; at any rate he is not a literary novelist. The direct transcript of jungle experience is much more satisfactory, but it occupies a very small proportion of the novel, which otherwise contains anti-highbrow sentiment, such evidences of getting laughs cheaply as 'a quiet chuckle'—humour at the *Strand Magazine* level—and plenty of traces of the characteristic middlebrow attitude of disavowing seriousness after enjoying the unaccustomed sensation of profundity and 'mysticism.'

[136] 'In the English novel, more than in any other, there is a traditional difference between that which people know and that which they agree to admit that they know, that which they see and that which they speak of, that which they feel to be a part of life and that which they allow to enter into literature. There is the great difference, in short, between what they talk of in conversation and what they talk of in print. The essence of moral energy is to survey the whole field, and I should directly reverse Mr. Besant's remark and say not that the English novel has a purpose, but that it has a diffidence.'—*The Art of Fiction* (1884).

[137] These are extracts from two letters received by popular novelists from their readers: 'I love your work, and delight in its appearing now, when ideals in

life and fiction are dim, too often.' ' I must send you a message of intense gratitude for the uplift and stimulant God has sent me through your pen.' Jeanette Porter Meehan in her Life of her mother writes : ' The boy Freckles [in the bestseller of that name] is a composite of high ideals merged with field experiences of an oil man who helped her.'

[138] ' It is not merely phrases, slogans and speeches that are demanded of advertising men ; rather is it truth, philosophy, and vision ' (*Advertising and Selling* (1924)). This book is itself a useful document of what is happening to the language. It consists of ' Digests of the Leading Addresses of the Nineteenth International Convention of the Associated Advertising Clubs of the World ; Held in Atlantic City, N.J., 1923.' On p. 250 W. S. Crawford declares : ' This meeting of American and British advertising agents is one of those quiet unassuming events, not uncommon in history, which give no outward sign of their real significance.' One outward sign is that it is impossible to distinguish on internal evidence the speeches made by English business men and advertisers from those made by Americans. The speeches were not only on such subjects as ' Literature and Art in Advertising ' and ' The New Vision in Community Advertising,' but also on ' Making Advertising Appeal to Emotions,' ' Making the Lay-Out Dynamic,' ' Class Appeal in Mass Media,' and a whole section which can only be described as ' Advertising God '—lectures on ' Business Principles Applied to Church Advertising,' ' Advertising the Bible,' ' Spirituality in Church Advertising,' etc. In 1930 English religious societies have taken to calling their periodicals by such titles as ' The Brotherhood Uplift.' It is, of course, impossible to separate words from current modes of thinking and feeling associated with them. Cf. the use of ' virile.'

[139] *E.g.* ' " We females don't really change," re-
torted that woman. " We only pretend to " ' ; ' that
sub-conscious judgment which sways the heart of
womanhood ' ; ' the suspicion, which comes at times
to all of us who think deeply, that life without love is
unworth the living.'—All taken at random from *Life—
and Erica*.

[140] Cf. the journalist in *Life—and Erica* : ' When
I've got anything important to tell the public, I always
tell it to them in clichés—because that's the way they
understand it best.' But this is not all the truth ; those
who write at that level are unable to express themselves
except in clichés—cf. passage (b).

[141] Cf. D. H. Lawrence : ' For even satire is a form
of sympathy. It is the way our sympathy flows and
recoils that really determines our lives. And here lies
the vast importance of the novel, properly handled. It
can inform and lead into new places the flow of our
sympathetic consciousness, and it can lead our sympathy away in recoil from things gone dead. Therefore
the novel, properly handled, can reveal the most secret
places of life. . . . But the novel, like gossip, can also
excite spurious sympathies and recoils, mechanical
and deadening to the psyche. The novel can glorify
the most corrupt feelings, so long as they are *conventionally* "pure." Then the novel, like gossip, becomes
at last vicious, and, like gossip, all the more vicious
because it is always ostensibly on the side of the
angels.'—*Lady Chatterley's Lover*.

THE OUTLINE OF POPULAR FICTION

No attempt is made here to record *all* popular successes or even all popular novelists. Each novel is chosen as representative of the popular fiction of its time, and if a gap in years is left it may be assumed that the same kind of fiction was being read in the interval. In general the first successful novel only of a steady bestseller is recorded. Translations that affected popular fiction and taste are enclosed in square brackets.

1578 *Euphues: The Anatomy of Wit*—John Lyly.

1580 *Euphues and his England*—Lyly (reprinted together, and only stopped 1636).

1590 *Arcadia*—Sidney (6th Ed. 1622).

1594 *The Unfortunate Traveller*—Nashe.

1597 *Jack of Newbury*—Deloney.

Before 1598 *Ornatus and Artesia*—Emanuel Forde (8th Impression 1683).

1598 *The Gentle Craft*, I.—Deloney (till 18th C.).

Parismus—Emanuel Forde (7th Ed. 1724).

Before 1600 *Thomas of Reading*—Deloney.

[1612 Shelton's translation of *Don Quixote*, Part I.] (immensely popular, and other translations).

[1637 Cervantes' *Exemplary Novels*] (very popular).

[1652 *Cassandra* and *Cleopatra* of Calprenède] (many editions, and several translations).

1655 *Parthenissa. A Romance. In Six Tomes*—Roger Boyle (continued to be issued in parts, reissue of whole 1676).

[1655 and onwards, translations of Mlle. de Scudéry.]

1660 *Bentivolio and Urania*—Nathaniel Ingelo (4th Ed. 1682).

[1660 c., Scarron translated.]

1665 *The English Rogue*—Richard Head (7th Ed. 1723).

[1677 Brémond's *Happy Slave*] (5 editions by 1729).

1678 *Pilgrim's Progress*, I.—Bunyan (25th Ed. 1738.)

1680 *Life and Death of Mr. Badman*—Bunyan (5 editions by 1724).

1682 *The Holy War*—Bunyan (9 editions by 1738).

1683 *The Travels of True Godliness*—Benjamin Keach (9th Ed. 1726).

1683 *The London Jilt*—Alexander Oldys (2nd Ed. 1684).

1684 *Pilgrim's Progress*, II.—Bunyan (15th Ed. 1732).

The Progress of Sin . . . in an apt and Pleasant Allegory—B. Keach (4th Ed. 1707).

The Adventures of the Black Lady—Aphra Behn.

Before 1685 *The Unfortunate Lady : a True History*—Aphra Behn.

1687 *Cynthia* (8th Ed. 1726).

1688 *Oroonoko, The Fair Jilt*, etc.—Aphra Behn.

1692 *Incognita : or, Love and Duty Reconcil'd*—Congreve (3rd Ed. 1713).

[1692 Marie Catherine La Mothe's *Ingenious and Diverting Letters of the Lady ——*] (10th Ed. 1735).

1696 Collected novels of Aphra Behn (6th Ed. 1718, 8th Ed. 1735).

[1708 *Arabian Nights*] (innumerable editions).

1709 *The New Atlantis*, I. and II.—Mrs. Manley.

1710 *The New Atlantis*, III. and IV.—Mrs. Manley.

1719 *Robinson Crusoe*—Defoe (7th Ed. 1726).

Love in Excess, I. and II.—Mrs. Haywood.

1720 *Love in Excess*, III., and reprinted entire (6th Ed. 1725).

Captain Singleton—Defoe (2nd Ed. 1722).

The Power of Love in Seven Novels—Mrs. Manley.

1721 *Moll Flanders*—Defoe (3rd Ed. 1722).

1722 *Secret History of Cleomira*—Mrs. Haywood (5th Ed. 1732).

1726 *Gulliver's Travels*—Swift (10 separate editions by 1727).

1740 *Pamela*—Richardson (5 editions this year).

1742 *Joseph Andrews*—Fielding.
1748 *Clarissa*—Richardson.
  Roderick Random—Smollett.
1749 *Tom Jones*—Fielding.
1751 *Peregrine Pickle*—Smollett.
  History of Miss Betsy Thoughtless—Mrs. Haywood (4th Ed. 1768).
1754 *Sir Charles Grandison : A Good Man*—Richardson.
1759 *Tristram Shandy*, I.—Sterne (and so on).
1761 *Memoirs of Miss Sidney Biddulph*—Frances Sheridan.
1765 *The Castle of Otranto*—Walpole.
1766 *The Vicar of Wakefield*—Goldsmith.
  The Fool of Quality—Richard Cumberland.
1771 *The Man of Feeling*—Henry Mackenzie (and so till 1810+).
[1773 Baculard d'Arnaud's *Tears of Sensibility*.]
1775 *The Correspondents* (Minerva Press, reprinted 1775, 1776, 1784).
1777 *The Old English Baron*—Clara Reeve.
1778 *Evelina*—Fanny Burney (4 editions by 1778).
1789 *A Sicilian Romance*—Ann Radcliffe (4th Ed. 1809).
1790 *Ethelinda*—Charlotte Smith.
1791 *The Romance of the Forest*—Ann Radcliffe (4th Ed. 1795).
  A Simple Story—Mrs. Inchbald.
1795 *The Monk*—Gregory Lewis (4th Ed. 1798).
  Henry—Richard Cumberland (3rd Ed. 1798).
1798 *The Children of the Abbey*—Regina Maria Roche (10th Ed. 1825).
1803 *Thaddeus of Warsaw*—Jane Porter (passed through several editions straightway).
  Belinda—Maria Edgeworth.
1806 *The Wild Irish Girl*—Lady Morgan (7 editions in less than 2 years).
  A Winter in London ; or, Sketches of Fashion—T. S. Surr.

1814 *Waverley*—Scott (sold 12,000 copies rapidly, considered remarkable).

1821 *Life in London, or the Adventures of Tom and Jerry*—Pierce Egan.

1823 *Theresa Marchmont, or the Maid of Honour*—Mrs. Gore.

1825 *Tremaine, or The Man of Refinement*—Robert Plumer Ward.

1826-29 *Sayings and Doings*—Theodore Hook.

1828 *Pelham*—Lytton.

1829 *Richelieu*—G. P. R. James.

1831 *Mothers and Daughters*—Mrs. Gore.

1832 *Eugene Aram*—Lytton.

1834 *Last Days of Pompeii*—Lytton.

1837 *Pickwick Papers*—Dickens.

1838 *Oliver Twist*—Dickens.

1841 *Ten Thousand a Year*—Samuel Warren.
Charles O'Malley, the Irish Dragoon—Charles Lever.

1844 *Coningsby*—Disraeli.

1847 *Jane Eyre*—Charlotte Brontë.

1848 *Vanity Fair*—Thackeray.

1852 *Uncle Tom's Cabin*—Harriet Beecher Stowe (1 million sold in England this year).

1853 *The Heir of Redclyffe*—Charlotte Yonge.

1854 *Westward Ho!*—Charles Kingsley.

1855 *Paul Ferroll*—Mrs. Archer Clive.

1856 *John Halifax, Gentleman*—Mrs. Craik.
'*It is never too late to mend*'—Charles Reade.

1857 *Guy Livingstone, or Thorough*—George A. Lawrence.
Tom Brown's Schooldays—Thomas Hughes.

1858 *Adam Bede*—George Eliot (7th Ed. 1859, 10th Ed. 1862).

1860 *The Woman in White*—Wilkie Collins.

1861 *East Lynne*—Mrs. Henry Wood.
The Cloister and the Hearth—Reade.
Framley Parsonage—Trollope.

1862 *Lady Audley's Secret*—M. E. Braddon (3 editions of 500 copies each sold out in ten days).

1863 *Held in Bondage*—Ouida.

1864 *Lost Sir Massingberd*—James Payn.

1867 '*Cometh up as a Flower*'—Rhoda Broughton (enormous sales till the end of the century).

1869 *Lorna Doone*—R. D. Blackmore.

1871 *A Daughter of Heth*—Wm. Black.

1874 *Far from the Madding Crowd*—Hardy.

1875 '*Comin' Thro' the Rye*'—Helen Mathers.

1876 *The Golden Butterfly*—Besant and Rice.

1880 *John Inglesant*—Shorthouse (9 editions in twelve months).

(Silas Hocking from now till 1900+ sells an average of 1000 copies a week to his Methodist public).

1886 Rider Haggard, Hall Caine, and Marie Corelli begin.

1888 *Robert Elsmere*—Mrs. Humphry Ward.
      Plain Tales from the Hills—Kipling.

1889 *Three Men in a Boat*—Jerome K. Jerome.
      The Master of Ballantrae—R. L. Stevenson (4 editions in 1889).

1891 *The Little Minister*—J. M. Barrie.

1893 *Ships that Pass in the Night*—Beatrice Harraden.
      A Gentleman of France—Stanley Weyman.

1894 *Prisoner of Zenda*—A. Hope.

1895 *Trilby*—George du Maurier.

1900 *The Life and Death of Richard Yea-and-Nay*—Maurice Hewlett.

1905 *The Scarlet Pimpernel*—Baroness Orczy.
      The Morals of Marcus Ordeyne—W. J. Locke.
      The Hill—H. A. Vachell.
      The Garden of Allah—Robert Hichens.

1908 *The Blue Lagoon*—H. de Vere Stacpoole.

1909 Wells becomes popular as a propagandist in fiction.
      The Rosary—Florence Barclay.

1910 *The Broad Highway*—Jeffery Farnol.

1912 *The Way of an Eagle*—Ethel M. Dell.

1914 *Tarzan of the Apes*—Edgar Rice Burroughs.

1919 *Peter Jackson, Cigar Merchant*—Gilbert Frankau.
1921 *If Winter Comes*—A. S. M. Hutchinson.
1922 *The Forsyte Saga*—Galsworthy (3 reprints in 1922).
1923 *The Middle of the Road*—Philip Gibbs.
1924 *The Green Hat*—Michael Arlen.
       Beau Geste—P. C. Wren.
1925 *The Constant Nymph*—Margaret Kennedy.
       Sorrell and Son—Warwick Deeping.
1926 *Gentlemen Prefer Blondes*—Anita Loos.
[1927 *Jew Süss*—Feuchtwanger.]
1928 *The Bridge of San Luis Rey*—Thornton Wilder.
1930 *The Good Companions*—J. B. Priestley.
       Vile Bodies—Evelyn Waugh.

SELECT BIBLIOGRAPHY

1. History of the Reading Public.

   Self-Education:

   Memoirs of Thomas Holcroft—Hazlitt.

   *Memoirs of the first forty-five years of the Life of James Lackington. Written by Himself (1791—further editions with additions 1792, etc.).

   *The Life, Character and Literary Labours of Samuel Drew, A.M. By his Eldest Son (1834).

   Advice to Young Men (1830); *Life and Adventures of Peter Porcupine* (1796)—Wm. Cobbett.

   *The Life of Francis Place—Graham Wallas.

   *Memoirs from Childhood—William Hone (reprinted in *Wm. Hone : his life and times*—F. W. Hackwood).

   *Early Days (1848); *Passages in the Life of a Radical* (1842)—Samuel Bamford.

   Life and Character of Henry Hetherington (1849)—G. T. Holyoake.

   James Watson, a Memoir (1879)—W. J. Linton.

   *The Life and Struggles of William Lovett, in his pursuit of Bread, Knowledge and Freedom (1876)—Wm. Lovett.

   *Memoir of William and Robert Chambers (1872)—Wm. Chambers.

   *The Life of Thomas Cooper. Written by Himself (1872).

   The Autobiography of a Working Man, by ' One who has whistled at the plough ' (1848)—Alexander Somerville.

   A Few Footprints (1905)—J. Passmore Edwards.

   The Life of William Hutton, F.A.S.S. Written by Himself (1798).

Autobiography of an Artisan (1847)—Christopher Thomson.

[For purposes of contrast, *Edward Bok. An Autobiography* (1921), with introduction by Northcliffe, and the Lives of twentieth-century journalists and newspaper proprietors generally.]

THE BACKGROUND:

Shakespeare's England (1917, Oxford).

Rural Rides (1830)—Wm. Cobbett.

The Whistler at the Plough; containing Travels, Statistics, and Descriptions of Scenery and Agricultural Customs in most parts of England (1842-47, 1852)—Alexander Somerville.

Autobiography of Mrs. Fletcher (1875).

The Rural Life of England (1838)—Wm. Howitt.

The Age of the Chartists (1930)—J. L. and Barbara Hammond.

English Literature and Society in the Eighteenth Century —Leslie Stephen.

Education and Social Movements (1919)—A. E. Dobbs.

English Education, 1789-1902 (1930)—J. W. Adamson.

Some Habits and Customs of the Working Classes. By a Journeyman Engineer (1867).

Change in the Village (1912); *Memoirs of a Surrey Labourer* (1907); *William Smith, Potter and Farmer, 1790-1858; The Wheelwright's Shop* (1923)— ' George Bourne ' (George Sturt).

The Agricultural Labourer; A short summary of his position (1887 and 1893)—T. E. Kebbel.

The Village Labourer, 1760-1832—J. L. and Barbara Hammond.

' *England's Green and Pleasant Land* ' (1925, Cape).

Passages of a Working Life (1864)—Charles Knight.

*' Nottingham and the Mining Countryside '—D. H. Lawrence (*New Adelphi*, August 1930).

Some of the English (1930)—Oliver Madox Hueffer.

HISTORY OF THE PRESS:

Some Forerunners of the Newspaper, 1476-1622—Matthias A. Shaaber.

The Fourth Estate : contributions towards A History of Newspapers, and of the Liberty of the Press (1850)—F. Knight Hunt.

The Literary Profession in the Age of Elizabeth—Phoebe Sheavyn.

English Newspapers (1887)—H. R. Fox Bourne.

The History of 'Punch' (1895)—M. H. Spielmann.

The Pictorial Press : its origins and progress (1885)—Mason Jackson.

The Making of Modern Journalism (1927)—Harold Herd.

Lord Northcliffe, A Memoir (1922)—Max Pemberton.

*Northcliffe : An Intimate Biography (1930)—Hamilton Fyfe.

*My Northcliffe Diary (1931)—Tom Clarke.

The Life of Sir George Newnes, Bart. (1911)—Hulda Friederichs.

Fleet Street and Downing Street (1920)—Kennedy Jones.

*The Press—Labour Research Dept. (Labour Publishing Co., 1922).

THE TRADE:

A History of Booksellers (1873)—H. Curwen.

Annals of a Publishing House (1897)—Mrs. Oliphant.

The Profession of Letters, 1780-1832 ; Authorship in the Days of Johnson—A. S. Collins.

Le publique et les hommes de lettres au dix-huitième siècle (1881)—A. Beljame.

The Truth about Publishing (1926)—Stanley Unwin.

A Hundred Years of Publishing (1930)—Arthur Waugh.

The Story of W. H. Smith and Son (1921)—G. R. Pocklington.

Illustrations of the Literary History of the Eighteenth Century (1817)—John Nichols.

' Publishing '—*Ency. Brit.* (11th Ed.).

The Publishers' Circular.
The History of the Catnach Press (1886)—Charles Hindley.
Autobiography (1883)—Anthony Trollope.
Daniel Defoe—P. Dottin.

LITERARY DOCUMENTS:

Autobiography (1834)—Sir Egerton Brydges.
*Culture and Anarchy (1869)—Matthew Arnold.
Passages of a Working Life (1864)—Charles Knight.
' Signs of the Times,' *Edinburgh Review* (June 1829).
The Progress of Romance (1785)—Clara Reeve.
Polly Honeycombe, a dramatick novel of one act (1760)—George Colman.
The Two Wealthy Farmers (1795?)—Hannah More.
*Cakes and Ale (1930)—W. Somerset Maugham.
The *Tatler, Spectator, Rambler, Idler, Monthly Review, Literary Gazette, Edinburgh Review, Quarterly Review, Fraser's, Blackwood's, The Yellow Book, Punch* (1841-).

2. THE CONTEMPORARY READING PUBLIC.

USE OF LEISURE:

B.B.C. Book (1931 and 1932).
*' Motion Pictures '—*Ency. Brit.* (14th Ed.).
Panoramique du Cinéma (1929)—Léon Moussinac.
*Star-Dust in Hollywood (1930)—Jan and Cora Gordon.
The Film Till Now (1930)—Paul Rotha.
[For comparative purposes, *Middletown* (1929)—Helen M. and Robert S. Lynd, and *Babbitt* (1922)—Sinclair Lewis.]

' ROTARY INTERNATIONAL ':

The Meaning of Rotary: By a Rotarian; with an Introduction by John Galsworthy (1927); *The Rotary Wheel; a Magazine of Vocation, Fellowship and Service; Synopsis of Rotary.*

Leaflets, booklets, etc., issued by Church Publicity Section of the National Free Church Council.

The Book Society News, The Book Guild Bulletin.

*_Journalism for Profit_ (1924); _Short Story Writing for Profit_ (1926); _The Commercial Side of Literature_ (1925)—Michael Joseph.

The Contemporary Short Story—Harry T. Baker.

How to Write Saleable Fiction—George G. Magnus.

*_Advertising and Selling_ (1924)—ed. Noble T. Praigg.

Outline of Advertising (1929)—Elwyn O. Hughes.

Nuntius : Advertising and its Future (1926); *Advertisement Writing* (1927)—Gilbert Russell.

Advertising : its Problems and Methods (1926)—John H. Cover.

Bigger Results from Advertising (1926); *Effective Sales Letters* (1925)—Harold Herd.

Commercial Advertising (1919)—Thomas Russell.

Fame and Fiction (1901); *How to Become an Author* (1903)—Arnold Bennett.

*_The Books You Read_ (published by the Book Society); *The Bookworm's Turn* (published by the Book Guild); weekly articles in the *Evening Standard*, by Arnold Bennett.

Advertisement pages of *Punch*, the *Observer* and *Times Literary Supplement*, *New Statesman and Nation*, *Good Housekeeping*, etc., *Tatler*, etc.

CRITICISM:

*_The Press and the Organisation of Society_ (1922)—Norman Angell.

*_Mass Civilisation and Minority Culture_ (1930); *D. H. Lawrence* (1930)—F. R. Leavis.

The Dance of the Machines (1929)—E. J. O'Brien.

Hunting the Highbrow (1927)—Leonard Woolf.

Books and Persons (1908-11)—Arnold Bennett.

' The Decay of the Book '—(*The Nation*, August 30th, 1913).

' The Peril to Letters '—*New Statesman* (December 7th, 1929); ' The Commercialisation of Books ' (*New Statesman*, March 29th, 1930)—Hilaire Belloc.
Books and the Public [a symposium]—(Hogarth Press, 1927).

EVIDENCE OF PERIODICALS:

Punch, *Week-End Review*, Life and Letters, Daily Mail, John o' London's, *The Listener*.

3. THE NOVEL.

CRITICISM:

Principles of Literary Criticism (1925)—I. A. Richards.
Notes on Novelists (1914)—Henry James.
The Craft of Fiction (1921)—Percy Lubbock.
The Common Reader (1925); *Mr. Bennett and Mrs. Brown* (1924)—Virginia Woolf.
Prefaces to the novels of Henry James.
*Review of *The Modern Novel*, by Elizabeth Drew (*The Calendar*, July 1926); ' A Note on Fiction ' (*The Calendar*, October 1926)—C. H. Rickword.
The Handling of Words (1923)—Vernon Lee.
Axel's Castle (1931)—Edmund Wilson [on Joyce and Proust].

POPULAR FICTION:

' Sensation Novels '—*Quarterly Review* (1863).
Novelists on Novels [an anthology], ed. R. Brimley Johnson.
*' A Novelist's Feelings on Publication Day '—Gilbert Frankau (*Publishers' Circular*, January 30th, 1926).
' The Musical Novel '—H. E. Wortham (*Nineteenth Century*, February 1927).
Lectures on Dead Authors (1927)—E. H. Lacon Watson.
' Three Famous Men '—*Adelphi*, August 1926 [on Gilbert Frankau].

'Sentiment and Sensibility in the Eighteenth-Century Novel'—Edith Birkhead (*Essays and Studies of the English Association*, Vol. XI.).

'The Tosh Horse' (*The Strange Necessity*, 1928)—Rebecca West.

Dickens, Reade and Collins (1919)—W. C. Phillips.

Life and Romances of Mrs. Eliza Haywood (1915)—G. F. Whicher.

Lives of the Novelists (1821-24)—Walter Scott.

Richardson (1928)—Brian W. Downs.

'The Lesser Novel, 1770-1800'—H. W. Husbands (M.A. thesis, 1922, in London University Library).

The French Revolution and the English Novel (1915)—Allene Gregory.

The Oriental Tale in England in the Eighteenth Century (1908)—M. Pike Conant.

My First Book (1894)—ed. Jerome K. Jerome [contributed by Walter Besant, James Payn, W. Clark Russell, Grant Allen, Hall Caine, George R. Sims, Conan Doyle, Kipling, M. E. Braddon, Rider Haggard, Ballantyne, Israel Zangwill, Morley Roberts, Marie Corelli, 'Q', R. L. Stevenson, Jerome K. Jerome, David Christie Murray, etc.]

*'Tarzan and Literature'—E. H. Lacon Watson (*Fortnightly Review*, June 1st, 1923).

Marie Corelli, The Writer and Woman (1903)—T. F. G. Coates and R. S. Warren-Bell.

Memoirs of Marie Corelli (1930)—Bertha Vyver.

Mrs. Humphry Ward (1912)—J. Stuart Walters.

The Life of Mrs. Humphry Ward (1923)—Mrs. G. M. Trevelyan.

*'The Case of Mr. Hugh Walpole'—J. M. Murry (*Nation and Athenæum*, July 16th, 1921).

*'Wilder: Prophet of the Genteel Christ'—Michael Gold (*New Republic*, October 22nd, 1930).

*Review of *Go She Must*, by David Garnett (*The Calendar*, July 1927).

*'Defoe's Novels'; 'Richardson's Novels'—Leslie Stephen (*Hours in a Library*, I., 1877).

Life and Letters of Gene Stratton Porter (1927)—
Jeannette Porter Meehan.

Review of *A Modern Comedy*, by P. Q. (*Life and Letters*,
Vol. III. No. 17).

[*Dictionary of National Biography.*

A List of English Tales and Romances published before
1740—Arundell J. K. Esdaile.]

[Parodies of bestsellers are useful, e.g. *Sensation Novels
Condensed* and *Lothaw*—Bret Harte; *Novels by Eminent Hands*—Thackeray.]

INDEX